Cultures of Commemoration

Pacific Islands Monograph Series 25

Cultures of Commemoration

The Politics of War, Memory, and History in the Mariana Islands

Keith L Camacho

CENTER FOR PACIFIC ISLANDS STUDIES

School of Pacific and Asian Studies

University of Hawai'i, Mānoa

UNIVERSITY OF HAWAI'I PRESS • Honolulu

Printed in the United States of America

Paperback edition 2012

17 16 15 14 13 12   6 5 4 3 2 1

Library of Congress Cataloging-in-Publication Data
Camacho, Keith L.
  Cultures of commemoration : the politics of war, memory, and history in the
Mariana Islands / Keith L. Camacho.
      p. cm. — (Pacific islands monograph series ; 25)
  Includes bibliographical references and index.
  ISBN-13: 978-0-8248-3546-0 (hardcover : alk. paper)
  ISBN-13: 978-0-8248-3670-2 (pbk. : alk. paper)
  1. World War, 1939–1945—Social aspects—Mariana Islands.   2. War and soci-
ety—Mariana Islands.   3. Collective memory—Mariana Islands.   4. Chamorro
(Micronesian people)—History—20th century.   5. Mariana Islands—Colonial
influence.   I. Title.   II. Series: Pacific islands monograph series ; no. 25.
  D744.7.M37C36 2011
  940.54'609967—dc22

                              2010043048

Maps by Manoa Mapworks, Inc.

University of Hawai'i Press books are printed on acid-free paper and meet the
guidelines for permanence and durability of the Council on Library Resources.

Design by University of Hawai'i Press Design & Production Department
Printed by Edwards Brothers, Inc.

for my grandparents

Editor's Note

Conventional war histories have focused on the major combatants, with special attention to celebrating or otherwise promoting national identity through a narrative strategy that extols triumphal participation in a just cause. Social historians such as John Keegan and Paul Fussell, however, have written of the complex, profoundly human, and deeply traumatic experience of battle. More recent work by feminist and gender-sensitive historians reveals the patriarchal dimensions that characterize the promotion, justification, conduct, and study of war, and the more general ways in which patriarchy informs imperial and militaristic projects. What remains neglected are the histories of indigenous peoples caught in the crossfire of a conflict not of their making, but fought on their lands and surrounding seas. *Cultures of Commemoration* is a remarkable contribution toward filling this void. Keith Camacho has produced a unique interdisciplinary work that examines the social construction of World War II memories in the Mariana Islands, and the degree to which they are informed by the politics of colonialism, indigenous cultural agency, and commemoration. Building on the extant ethnographies of war in the Pacific region, Camacho foregrounds Chamorro experiences of war, and their mediation and articulation through memory and commemorations.

Camacho argues convincingly that the complexity of contemporary intra-island relationships across the Marianas cannot be fully grasped without an appreciation of the varied and conflicting ways in which different groups of Chamorros experienced World War II. While Guam passed from Spanish to American colonial rule in 1898, the rest of the Mariana Islands fell under first German and then, in 1914, Japanese control. The outbreak of war in 1941 would further intensify, and violently, the differences created by life under separate and now hostile colonial regimes. These distinctive colonial and wartime experiences exacerbated long-standing tensions among Chamorros that persist to this day, and are reflected in the ways the war and its principal combatants are remembered.

As noted in his introduction (1), and following John R Gillis (1994, 5), Camacho treats commemorative activity as a social and political process that entails "the coordination of individual and group memories, whose results may appear consensual when they are in fact the product of processes of intense contest, struggle, and, in some instances, annihilation." Camacho sees in the study of multiple and varied commemorations an opportunity to explore the politics of remembrance among indigenous Chamorros on the one hand and Americans and Japanese on the other.

There is much at stake in these commemorations; nation-states, groups of people, and individuals all contest over what is remembered and how. A close attention to the politics of war commemorations offers critical insight into the process of remembering and into the construction of competing histories that inform public memory. At the same time, Camacho reminds us that some memories, such as those involving the experiences of the Chamorro women who served as "comfort women" for Japanese colonial and military personnel in the Marianas, are hidden away because of the pain, shame, and embarrassment they recall. Camacho also examines the colonial politics, local nostalgia, and internal tensions around the imaging of the "loyal Chamorro subject" on Guam, grateful for the liberation from oppressive Japanese wartime rule delivered by returning US forces. Camacho shows how a sentimental longing for the peace of the prewar period actually elides the violence of earlier American and Japanese colonial rule in the Marianas. In its emphasis on indigenous agency, the book argues for recognition of the flows of power in the relationship between colonizer and colonized, and of the inadequacy of the term "victim" in understanding all that Chamorro survival required.

There is certainly nothing provincial or narrow about *Cultures of Commemoration*. Camacho's work draws inspiration from a larger global literature that examines the complex, entangled linkage between memory and history, and the determining role that power differentials and variable social factors play in what is remembered, recorded, and forgotten. This study reaches beyond the Marianas to address broader issues involving contrasting and conflicting colonial regimes, native and national identities, local and imperial histories, and group and individual memories. There are also the three larger goals that underpin the book. Camacho seeks (1) to demonstrate that culture functions as a process of local and global identification and differentiation; (2) to emphasize the ambivalent and mutable nature of colonialism as a process of control; and (3) to underscore how people engage in interpretations and representations of their past in ways that are culturally determined and socially significant.

The Pacific Islands Monograph Series is delighted to publish as its twenty-fifth volume this first extended study of the marginalized and underappreciated histories of war in the Mariana Islands by a Chamorro author.

The work rests on a solid review of the archival record, complemented effectively by interviews with Chamorro war survivors, their descendants, and contemporary community leaders that rightfully privilege local understandings of the war. In so doing, this timely, most welcome study underscores the need for more comparative, indigenous-oriented, and interdisciplinary approaches to the study of war and the larger past.

DAVID HANLON

Contents

Illustrations

Acknowledgments

Many people helped me to complete this book on war, memory, and history. Throughout the entire research and writing process, they identified archives, located photos, organized interviews, provided travel funds, and translated documents. I thank Carl Alerta, Baltazar Aguon, Antonio Babauta, Ed and Jill Benavente, Omaira Brunal-Perry, Jennings Bunn, Dr Debra Cabrera, Hope Cristobal, Dr Jose Q Cruz, Dr Lawrence Cunningham, Herbert Del Rosario, Greg Dvorak, Fr Eric Forbes, Lynette Furuhashi, Joe Garrido, Mary Gushiken, Dr Anne Perez Hattori, William Hernandez, Dr Wakako Higuchi, Robert Hunter, Dr Kerri Inglis, Emilie G Johnston, Jessica Jordan, Cinta Kaipat, Gus Kaipat, Dr Kimberlee Kihleng, Kayoko Kushima, Samuel McPhetres, Tanya Champaco Mendiola, Dore Minatodani, Shannon Murphy, Andrea Nakamura, Lou Nededog, Jean Olopai, Lino Olopai, Mark Ombrello, Peter Onedera, Perry Pangelinan, Dr Karen Peacock, Cecilia Perez, Lahela Perry, Carmen Quintanilla, Tony Ramirez, Sister Remedio, Scott Russell, Rita Santos, Chuck Sayon, Carrie Ann Shirota, Dr Donald Shuster, Fata Simanu-Klutz, Sa'ili Steffany, Monique Storie, Dr Beret Strong, Masami Tsujita, Dr Robert Underwood, and Dr Faye Untalan. *Un dangkolo na si yu'us ma'ase para todus hamyo.*

I also thank the sponsors for my archival and ethnographic research trips to Guam, Hawai'i, Saipan, and Washington, DC. They include the Dai Ho Chun Graduate Fellowship, the John F Kennedy Fellowship, the Tanahashi Peace Scholarship, the University of Guam Doctoral Fellowship, and the Young Men's League of Guam Scholarship. Members of my dissertation committee—Jerry Bentley, David Chappell, David Hanlon, Margot Henriksen, and Geoffrey White—similarly assisted me in more ways than one. David Hanlon and Geoffrey White particularly deserve recognition for patiently reading countless drafts. Their influence is evident in the ways in which I understand history and memory. And while Vicente Diaz was not a formal member of my committee, his advice and expertise nevertheless enriched my work. Doug Fuqua, Ty Kāwika Tengan, and Kathryn Wellen also critiqued earlier versions of my study, as did the participants of a symposium on "US Wars in Asia" organized by Yen Le Espiritu and Lisa Yoneyama at the University of California, San Diego, in 2004. I thank them, too.

The Macmillan Brown Centre for Pacific Studies at the University of Canterbury, Aotearoa/New Zealand, awarded me a research scholarship to revise my manuscript for publication. I thank Centre Director Karen Nero, Senior Lecturer David Gegeo, and Administrative Assistant Moana Matthes for offering me this privileged opportunity. Jo Diamond, Brett Graham, Helen Hayward, Simon Lambert, Trish Shaw, and Alice Te Punga Somer-ville merit a special *kia ora* for sharing their *kai* and friendship with me and Juliann. Others welcomed us into their homes as well, frequently feeding us with their warmth, humor, and generosity. In Wellington, I extend a *fa'afetai lava* to George and Natalie Churchward, including the entire Anesi and Carter *aiga*, for opening their doors and their lives to us.

At the University of Canterbury, the "Subject to Change" writing group met frequently to review and revise our written contributions. They often read parts of my manuscript, providing direction for the ways in which I might frame my arguments. I thank Sofia Daly, Jamon Halvaksz, Bruce Harding, Peter Hempenstall, Liz Keneti, Malakai Koloamatangi, Danielle O'Halloran, Kaitiaki Paerua, Phillipa Pehi, Sailau Su'aalii, Patricia Te Arapo Wallace, Fa'amanu Telea, Eric Waddell, and Steven Winduo. *Vinaka vaka levu* to Robert Nicole and Katerina Teaiwa for coordinating many of these gatherings and for forging new anticolonial trajectories.

Based on my research findings in this book, I also prepared seminars on the topics of colonial rule, wartime conflict, and postwar reconciliation in the Mariana Islands. In Saipan, I lectured for a teachers' workshop and presented a paper for the public at the American Memorial Park Theater, Garapan, in 2006. Members of my extended family, *familian Pakito yan Potu,* attended this talk, as did the wider public. Elders and youth alike engaged in fruitful discussions about the war, bridging the gaps between academic learning and public participation. I thank the Northern Mariana Islands Humanities Council for sponsoring my visit, notably Board of Directors Chair Herman T Guerrero and Vice-Chair Felicidad Ogumoro. I also thank Executive Director Paz Younis, Assistant Executive Director Scott Russell, and Administrative Assistant Honora Tenorio, all of whom make commu-nity workshops like these possible on a daily basis.

Elsewhere, various versions of my manuscript have been presented at conferences sponsored by the Association for Asian American Studies, the Chamorro Studies Association, Famoksaiyan, Stanford University, the University of California (UC), the University of Guam, the University of Hawai'i, and the University of Tokyo. I thank the organizers for inviting me to these sessions, particularly Miget Bevacqua, Martha Dueñas, Peter Hof-fenberg, Florine Hofschneider, Tiffany Lacsado, Victoria Leon Guerrero, Laurel Monnig, Masako Notoji, Jocelyn Pacleb, Sabina Perez, Marilyn Salas, Johnny Sablan, Sharleen Santos-Bamba, Setsu Shigematsu, Theresa Suarez, Tritia Toyota, Migetu Tuncap, and Yujin Yaguchi. As I prepared my book for publication, moreover, Takashi Fujitani of UC San Diego, Pat Hilden of UC

Berkeley, and Lin Poyer of the University of Wyoming provided insightful criticisms. Their comments and questions greatly shaped the content and form of the final manuscript. Former editor Linley Chapman and Managing Editor Jan Rensel of the University of Hawai'i Center for Pacific Islands Studies have been particularly valuable in this regard. Their editorial assistance, knowledge, and patience are most appreciated, as is the fine work of indexer Elizabeth Tsukahara.

I also acknowledge the support of the faculty, staff, and student body of the Department of Asian American Studies and the Center for Asian American Studies at the University of California, Los Angeles. Former Department Chair C Cindy Fan and Vice-Chair Jinqi Ling granted me leave to pursue my research and writing fellowship in Aotearoa. Further, Center Director Don T Nakanishi and Assistant Director Melany Dela Cruz Viesca provided me with funds to conduct follow-up research in the Marianas. Iosefa Aina, Amanda Aquino, Jay Aromin, Victor Bascara, Keith Castro, Jolie Chea, Elizabeth DeLoughrey, Joe Fa'avae, Alfred Flores, Gil Gee, Jean-Paul deGuzman, Kristopher Kaupalolo, Kare'l Lokeni, Fuifuilupe Niumeitolu, Nefara Reisch, DeAnna Rivera, Lola Sablan Santos, Joe Santos, Christine Santos, Christen Sasaki, Elenasina Smolinski, Amy Sueyoshi, Meg Thornton, Kehaulani Vaughn, Pua Warren, and Erin Wright similarly supported my outreach, research, and teaching.

Finally, I thank Rick Castro, Michael and Francine Clement, Vince Diaz and Tina DeLisle, Manny and Emma Dueñas, Betty and Warren Ickes, Kim, Simeon, and Emelie Kihleng, Julie and Scott Kroeker, Lola and Juancho Quan-Bautista, Setsu Shigematsu and Dylan Rodriguez, and Dominica Tolentino for sharing food, shelter, and companionship over the years. The Anesi families of Carson, Compton, and Orange County, the Camacho families of Garapan and Harmon, the Blas and De Leon Guerrero families of San Vicente, and the Lujan families of Barrigada, Dededo, and Waipahu also deserve a shout-out. Mom, Dad, and Jacob, and Grandpa and Annie likewise deserve my deep gratitude. *Fa'afetai lava* to Juliann Anesi for being a partner whose patience, humor, and love keep things real.

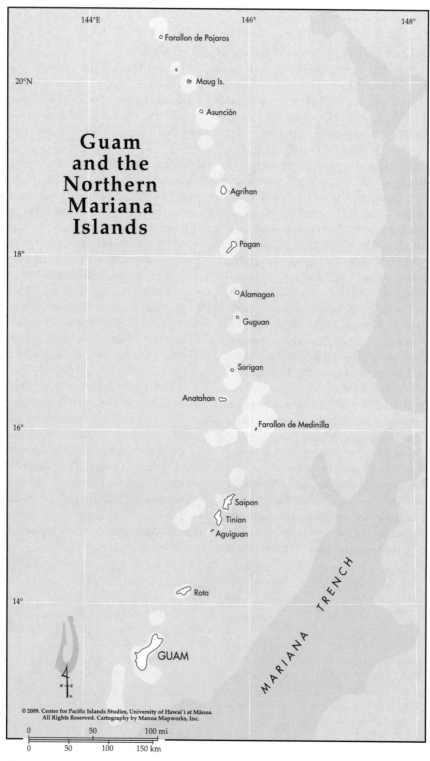

Guam
and the
Northern
Mariana
Islands

144°E · 146° · 148°

Farallon de Pajaros

20°N

Maug Is.

Asunción

Agrihan

Pagan

18°

Alamagan

Guguan

Sarigan

Anatahan

Farallon de Medinilla

16°

Saipan

Tinian

Aguiguan

MARIANA TRENCH

Rota

14°

GUAM

© 2009. Center for Pacific Islands Studies, University of Hawaiʻi at Mānoa.
All Rights Reserved. Cartography by Manoa Mapworks, Inc.

0 · 50 · 100 mi

0 · 50 · 100 · 150 km

Map 1.

Introduction
War, Memory, History

The relationship between war, memory, and history resonates deeply and profoundly in what Naoto Sudo called the first "postcolonial" literary history of the western Pacific region (2004, 2).[1] Referring to the 1986 publication of Chris Perez Howard's *Mariquita: A Tragedy of Guam,* Sudo observed that this biographical novel highlights both American and Japanese colonialisms in Guam (2004, 2). Unlike most postcolonial writings that target Euro-American colonialism in the Pacific, Howard's novel offers a radical postcolonial intervention in its critique of what might be understood as "Asian" and "Western" forms of colonialism (Sudo 2004, 2). The book focuses on a family tragedy in Guam, the southernmost island in the Mariana archipelago invaded and occupied by the Japanese military during World War II (map 1). In particular, it portrays the life of an indigenous Chamorro woman, Mariquita Perez, who rises in social status in prewar Guam, then ruled by the United States Navy, only to perish for unknown reasons in the subsequent war between Japan and the United States.

In Howard's account, Mariquita's ascendancy to the upper political and social spheres of prewar Guam stems from her fierce sense of independence—an independence fostered by her curiosity about and passion for imitating the "modern" American woman of the early twentieth century (Howard 1986, 10). In her attempt to stand apart from her more "traditional" peers, she maintains close ties to the island's indigenous and military elite, dresses in the latest American fashions and eventually marries a US Navy sailor, Eddie Howard. They have two children, Chris and Helen. The family forms a relationship that is tolerated and contemplated by their friends and families, Americans and Chamorros alike, in local gossip and print media.

On 7 December 1941, the Japanese military bombs Pearl Harbor (Pu'uloa), O'ahu, and invades various countries in the Pacific and Southeast Asia. The Japanese military attacks Guam on this same day, which is 8 December in Guam. The Japanese invasion of Guam abruptly interrupts and transforms the novel's nostalgic portrait of an intercultural marriage among the island's prewar cultures of the "colonizer" and the "colonized." Mariquita's modern world suddenly faces, however reluctantly, another vision of modernity as inscribed in Japan's call for "Asia for Asians" and an Asia without Western colonial tyranny. The Japanese militarization of the

1

island and its indigenous people soon leads to a series of conflicts, radically altering the setting from a peaceful prewar past to a violent wartime present. In the novel, the conscription of indigenous interpreters and police assistants, the physical and psychological abuse of civilians, and the institutionalized rape of Asian and indigenous "comfort women" all surface as conflicts of varying degrees and with varying consequences among the indigenous and colonial communities of Guam.

Furthermore, at the demand of the Japanese military, the couple is forced to separate, signaling the gradual, and at times rapid, escalation of tragedies to come. Like some of his American and Allied counterparts in the European and Pacific theaters of the war, Eddie becomes a prisoner of war of Japan. The dictates of Japanese colonial policy and racial prejudice dehumanize Eddie and emasculate him, given the loss of his honored position as a "fighting man in the service of his country" (Howard 1986, 52). Mariquita, on the other hand, lives with her extended family in preparation for what would be nearly three years of Japanese wartime rule. Another separation occurs when the Japanese military enlists Mariquita, now twenty-three years old, as one of the female domestic "aides" to a Japanese agricultural officer in the village of Tå'i. The final separation, indeed the novel's dramatic climax, occurs when she mysteriously disappears in the jungles of Guam, under the muffling reverberation of American aerial bombardment and rapid gunfire in the summer of 1944.

In this book, I examine memories of World War II in the Mariana Islands, and the degree to which they are informed by the politics of colonialism, indigenous cultural agency, and, finally, commemoration. I argue that Chamorro public memories of the war have developed in distinct and often divergent ways because of a complex past premised on American and Japanese colonial histories of the archipelago. Invoking T Fujitani, Geoffrey White, and Lisa Yoneyama's notion of "perilous memories," I view public memories as "precarious or endangered memories in need of recuperation and as memories that continue to generate a sense of danger for various peoples throughout the Asia-Pacific region" (2001, 3). In their groundbreaking anthology, *Perilous Memories: The Asia-Pacific War(s)*, Fujitani, White, and Yoneyama astutely observed that much is at stake politically in the erasure or remembrance of war memories, for nation-states and citizens alike, as well as for everyday peoples caught in between or excluded from the various categories of nationhood and citizenship. Like the novel *Mariquita*, my project focuses on the Chamorro people of the Mariana Islands, their experiences under American and Japanese colonial rule, and the ways in which they remember World War II. Of all the historical events during the twentieth century, World War II remains the pivotal subject of conversation, celebration, and contestation among Chamorros of various genders and generations (Guerrero 1994, 91). The war is very real and relevant today, as are the contested memories of it, long after the last guns were fired. As Chamorro scholar Laura Torres Souder once argued, "the war has not ended" (1991, 123).

But rather than simply present a history of the war that seeks closure to a violent past, my intent is to foster further discussion about some of the understudied and long marginalized histories of the war in the Mariana Islands. Toward this effort, this book is the first sustained attempt by a Chamorro author to narrate a history of the Mariana Islands that considers Chamorro cross-cultural and intracultural relations throughout the archipelago. To date, most studies of the Mariana Islands have focused on its two current political entities: the US Unincorporated Territory of Guam, and the Commonwealth of the Northern Mariana Islands (CNMI). What results is an increasing historiographical tendency to view histories of Guam and the Northern Marianas as seemingly separate and unrelated areas of study when, in fact, much contact and exchange occurs between the colonial, indigenous, and settler populations of these island groups. In focusing comparatively on Guam and the Northern Marianas, I urge readers to acknowledge, address, and examine the divided histories of this archipelago. My aim is to explore the roots of these divisions as products of competing colonial histories, and to create, instead, inclusive venues for representing Chamorro cultural and political narratives of the past.

This study also advances a heretofore rarely acknowledged understanding that the histories of American and Japanese colonialisms in the Pacific have been profoundly shaped and made possible by the existence of lesser-known actors and narrators of the past—lesser-known, that is, to peoples in and beyond Japan and the continental United States. Comparative attention to colonial and indigenous relations across the Americas, Asia, and the Pacific is severely lacking in studies of these regions (Okihiro 2006, 326). Conversely, histories of American and Japanese colonialisms have compellingly influenced the ways in which colonial subjects at the periphery of these empires came to view themselves and others, as well as their wider participation in and memories of World War II.

Given the understudied histories of American and Japanese colonialisms in postcolonial studies of empire, then, the urgency to foreground colonial and indigenous relations in comparative frameworks becomes readily apparent. As Amy Kaplan observed, the "absence of the United States in the postcolonial study of culture and imperialism curiously reproduces American exceptionalism from without" (1993, 17). The United States is either "absorbed into a general notion of 'the West,' represented by Europe, or it stands for a monolithic West" (Kaplan 1993, 17). American colonialism, if considered at all by scholars of US history, is often construed as an aberration of US constitutionalism, a misnomer for American democracy and governance, or a recent phenomena of the post-9/11 era (Johnson 2004, 4).[2] Even histories of American colonialism that employ a transnational lens tend to analyze border crossings in the continental United States and the economic, political, and social relations of Latin America without fuller consideration of American colonialism beyond the Americas (Stoler 2007, 30). The limitations of these historical interests and methodologies are sometimes compounded, if not made increasingly exceptional and parochial, by the invocation of postcolonial theories. As Ann Stoler argued, students of US history aptly borrow from the work of Edward Said and Gayatri Spivak, among other postcolonial theorists, but they "seem to consider less relevant the specific colonial *histories* in which colonial relationships and their gendered dynamics were produced" (2007, 31; emphasis in original). Rarely do these studies of US history look to Asia and the Pacific Islands, let alone the colonial and indigenous histories within which relations of power have been engendered, transformed, or extinguished. In light of these considerations of American colonialism in postcolonial studies of empire, Kaplan asserted that scholars should "have the obligation to study and critique the meanings of America in their multiple dimensions, to understand the enormous power wielded in its name, its ideological and affective force, as well as its sources for resistance to empire" (2004, 10).

How scholars might respond to Kaplan's call for studying American colonialism is a question of relevance for historians of Japan, many of whom seldom converse with specialists beyond their field (Miyoshi 1991, 12). Adding to this general lack of interdisciplinary engagement, the "remarkable indifference about Japan's prewar and wartime legacy of colonialism, military aggression, and other imperial practices" has contributed to a view of Japan as being outside scholarly discussions of colonialism (Yoneyama 1999, 5). As Leo Ching noted, a "conspicuously missing element in the burgeoning critique of colonialism is the lack of any concerted reference to Japan, the only non-Western colonial power that, even in the postcolonial era, still situates itself ambivalently in the West/non-West divide" (2001, 29–30). Therefore, the relative absence of Japan in recent studies of colonialism and postcolonialism partly stems from academic disciplinary understandings of colonialism as "perceived categorically—each distinct and unique— and not relationally or associatively, with regard to the way their differences are interconnected and unequally organized" (Ching 2001, 30). Following these lines of inquiry, in this book I foster a conversation about how scholars might study colonialisms in Japan, the Mariana Islands, and the United States. Addressing the associative and relational links within colonialism that are shaped by colonial and indigenous peoples, I examine the case of the Mariana Islands to suggest that "the power and authority wielded by macropolities are not lodged in abstract institutions but in their management of meanings, their construction of social categories, and their microsites of rule" (Stoler 2007, 42).

Archival materials used in this book are drawn from the University of Guam's Micronesian Area Research Center, the University of Hawai'i's Pacific Collection, the Northern Marianas College's Pacific Collection, the

United States Library of Congress, the United States Navy Historical Center, and the United States National Archives and Records Administration. Autobiographical manuscripts, commemorative brochures, government policies, correspondence, military studies, oral histories, and newspaper articles written by American, Chamorro, and Japanese authors constitute some of the archival materials under study. Supplementing such written documents is a series of interviews that I conducted from 2002 to 2004 with cultural activists, educators, priests, scholars, and war survivors and their descendants. Like the archival materials, the interview sessions foreground Chamorro cultural and political understandings of war, memory, and history.

Wherever possible, the Chamorro labels of deference, Tun and Tan, are used in identifying elder Chamorro men and women, respectively. Although some of the *manamko*, or elders, have passed on, I have chosen to treat their names, words, and ideas as living, breathing examples of Chamorro productions of memory and history. Given that some of the Chamorro elders in this book are related to me, they are cited as academic and cultural texts of authority, subject to scrutiny in ways I have deemed appropriate and sensitive. In doing so, I have tried humbly but critically to impart a sense of *inafa'maolek*, or respectful relations, in the writing of the past; this is my modest attempt to use the written word to heal the violence of the past, to understand the politics of the present, and to generate reciprocal relations for the future (see L Smith 1999, 15). For example, the mentioning of Chamorro individual and family surnames in this book is not meant to bring ridicule and shame—what Chamorros call *mamahlao*—to anybody; nor does it imply an uncritical attention to people's attitudes and behaviors. My intention is to generate a compassionate and contextual understanding of the various colonial and indigenous peoples who are the agents of knowledge production in the Mariana Islands. The span of time considered here is 1898 to 1994, an era that began with the Spanish-American War of 1898 and concluded with the fiftieth anniversary of the end of World War II in 1994.

A Historiography of War

Far from positing interdisciplinary approaches, the study of the writing of war has largely been the concern of military historians in the United States.[3] Since the turn of the twentieth century, American military historians have gained prominence in the field of military history, rivaling their peers in Britain, Germany, and France. The voluminous works produced by American military historians on the two world wars often focus on "biography, fiction, battle narratives, memoirs, theoretical treaties, scientific discourses, philosophy [and] economic studies" (Votaw 1979, 41). The content and scope of such works fall into two general overlapping categories, with sol-diers seeking the utilitarian value of military history on the one hand, and with scholars observing its educational value on the other. Soldierly con-cerns with strategy, combat, and morale do not differ much from schol-arly analyses of war. Historical specialists and soldiers often read similar documents and sources, engage common problems, and arrive at their own conclusions.

Feminist scholars and civil rights activists, however, have challenged the intentions of military historians, military policy makers, and military institu-tions in ways that focus needed attention on the understudied social and gendered aspects of war. Although military historians have long shown interest in the relationships between war and society, activist, feminist, and gender scholars have argued that such studies generally associate war with "activity, heroism and masculinity," and view its antithesis, peace, as "quiet, mundane, feminine" (Kelly 2000, 48). Feminist scholars reveal more clearly the "patriarchal" and "feminine" dimensions of war, and especially, the lan-guages and discourses of war. As Karen Warren and Duane Cady noted, "much of feminist critique regarding war and violence focuses on language, particularly the symbolic connections between sexist-naturist-warist lan-guage, that is, language which inferiorizes women and nonhuman nature by naturalizing women and feminizing nature" (1994, 12). These feminist, semiotic analyses have urged others to understand war "as a *gendering* activ-ity, one that ritually marks the gender of all members of a society, whether or not they are combatants" (Higonnet, Jenson, Michel, and Weitz 1987, 4; emphasis in original).

In times of war, for example, women who "consort with the enemy are stigmatized, humiliated, even executed, while soldiers' romantic inter-ludes in enemy territory are idealized" (Higonnet and Higonnet 1987, 37). National wartime propaganda provides an abundant variety of instances when the friendly and the hostile are gendered feminine or masculine. In World War II, the governments, militaries, and popular media of Japan and the United States produced racist and gendered images of each opposing society (eg, the "Japanese ape" and the "American barbarian"). For both countries, the purpose of generating these images was to justify the defeat of a feminine or masculine-worthy opponent, yet an ultimately weak and nonhuman enemy (Dower 1986, 9–10). Such gendered images serve a vari-ety of purposes during war, and are often employed to glorify violence or to dehumanize people.

Cynthia Enloe and bell hooks have separately argued that criticisms lev-eled against colonial militaries and industries, as well as wars and conflicts, can be framed within the larger study of "militarism." They believed that by focusing on militarism one is better able to examine the intersecting relationships and processes linking the military, society, and war. For exam-ple, in listing some of the strengths of a feminist study of militarism, Enloe noted that the concept of militarism avoids being subjected "to patriarchal historiography in the same way as the concept of war" and encouraged cross-cultural dialogue and the analysis of ideological change (1987, 540).[4] hooks, on the other hand, added that although feminists view militarism as a gendered process in certain ways, they must first understand that "imperialism and not patriarchy is the core foundation of militarism" (1995, 61).

By engaging in discourse analyses of imperialism, militarism, and patriarchy, activist, feminist, and gendered studies present new approaches for the study of war. For example, more women pursue the study of war, a field once dominated by men, in ways that draw from a variety of disciplinary and theoretical approaches on race, class, and gender (Shy 1993, 23). As diverse approaches to the study of war increase in scope, it becomes clear that the study of war in the American context is no longer the exclusive preserve of soldiers and military historians. Yet, despite recent innovative efforts to reshape and rethink war studies, few studies focus on the cultural dimensions, political implications, and theoretical concerns of wars as they specifically pertain to indigenous people.

The impact and influence of World War II in the Pacific Islands region is a case in point.[5] For example, military historians commonly interpret World War II as "essentially an American-Japanese war" (Sandler 2001, viii). Conventional military historiography reads the war as "the result of a clash of political goals: the Japanese calling for 'Asia for the Asiatics' . . . and the Americans demanding an 'open door' policy in China" (Sandler 2001, vii). Even studies by economic and social historians frame the war as grounds to discuss exclusively American international diplomacy, the Japanese mandate of Micronesia, and Japanese-American social relations in general.[6] What results is a historiographical perception that the war affected only Japan and the United States (Fujitani, White, and Yoneyama 2001, 3).

It is no surprise that histories of World War II rarely mention the roles of Pacific Islanders, presuming that they do not fit nicely into the schemes of colonial history and historiography. As anthropologists Lamont Lindstrom and Geoffrey White noted, "Military historians writing about the Pacific war, for their part, have ignored wholesale the people living on the islands over which the armies were 'hopping.' . . . We can augment and enrich reinterpretations of the war by listening to the stories, songs, and personal recollections of some of the thousands of Pacific Islanders who took part in the events of the 1940s. Their stories, too, compose a valuable historical archive" (1989, 6). As if to emphasize the point, the recent publication of *The Typhoon of War* (2001) and *Memories of War* (2008) by Lin Poyer, Suzanne Falgout, and Laurence M Carucci draw from Micronesian oral histories of the war, relying heavily on indigenous experiences and memories as valuable sources of data.[7] Given that Micronesia is poorly represented in almost all spheres of academic inquiry, these books on Micronesian oral narratives of the war are welcome additions.

Indigenous agency in all contexts

The archive Lindstrom and White mentioned continues to grow, also producing studies on nationalism, oral history, and race.[8] These contributions to the study of World War II underscore the significance of Pacific Islanders as coast-watchers, community leaders, couriers, laborers, mediators, soldiers, and translators. As Solomon Islander scholar David Welchman Gegeo explained, "One thing Pacific Islanders can teach historians . . . is about the roles Islanders took in the war, the activities and events they witnessed and participated in, and the changes the war brought about in their understandings about the world" (1988, 7). An awareness of and sensitivity to Pacific Islander involvement in and perceptions of World War II, along with the perspectives of the colonial nations, can help scholars to appreciate more fully the complexity of the war in local and global terms. Above all, Pacific Islanders constitute a vibrant diversity of indigenous women and men, elders and youth, whose long histories of colonialism and resistance in the region, as well as in the diaspora, merit academic recognition and representation.

Although the present political and social usage of the term "Pacific Islander" connotes both indigenous-settled and indigenous-migratory sensibilities, it is a term that can be temporarily, though strategically, used to describe the indigenous collectivities of Melanesia, Micronesia, and Polynesia and their migrant counterparts in the diaspora (Spickard, Rondilla, and Wright 2002). Here, the term "Pacific Islander" is used not only to call attention to these social groups or to the discursive nature of things "native" or "non-native" (T Teaiwa 2005, 31), but also as a term whose changing ideals emanate from nationalist and solidarity movements from the 1960s to the present, invoking a wide spectrum of ethnic, political, and religious aspirations and conditions for greater sovereignty. Comparable to terms like "indigenous," "Kanak," "Native," or "Wantok," the label "Pacific Islander" represents an almost universal aspiration for indigenous autonomy in the Pacific despite, and perhaps because of, the colonial and racist histories associated with these terms (T Teaiwa 2005, 17; see also Macpherson 1996). The use of "Native" by some Hawaiian scholars, for example, illustrates what Hawaiian scholar Lilikalā Kameʻeleihiwa called a concerted attempt "to communicate to non-Native readers our position as the first people of this Land, and to restore dignity to the term, so degraded over the past two hundred years by white racism" (1992, 342). Efforts to participate in the discourses of political authority and representation occur elsewhere as well. With respect to the notion of a "Melanesian voice," itself an important category of identification, Bernard Narokobi described this sense of indigenous agency as "conceived deliberately as a positive, creative and a constructive force. It is aimed at the good, the beautiful and the just" (1983, 4).

These various labels of self and collective identification indicate that cultural, political, and social significance resonates in terms about and especially by indigenous peoples of the Pacific. Given its wide usage, the category "Pacific Islander" perhaps represents the most accepted appellation for indigenous peoples from the region (Diaz 2004, 186). Until most of the indigenous aspirations for sovereignty are met, or until another term of regional import and solidarity emerges, the label "Pacific Islander" will continue to permeate academic and public discourses. Its use is a matter of rigorously examining the agency of indigenous peoples, in their words and in their terms, and in ways that compel scholars to value Pacific Islanders as participants in the shaping of their lives and futures, of which the writing of the past is one aspect (Diaz and Kauanui 2001, 324).

How, then, can scholars incorporate indigenous perspectives into the study of war? What methodological and theoretical concerns should be considered?[9] What can Pacific Islander experiences and memories of the war tell about the power of colonialism and indigenous cultural agency? How can these studies of war rethink not only historiography, but also, more broadly, the nature of humanistic inquiry in the Pacific and elsewhere around the world?

Memory and History

Such questions of Pacific Islander representation in the historical record of World War II are the focus of this work. An interdisciplinary approach informed by "memory studies" has given shape to the methodological scope of this project.[10] Increasingly, anthropologists, historians, literary critics, and sociologists are turning to memory studies in their analyses of traumatic events, such as conflicts, genocide campaigns, and natural disasters. Memory studies differ from the conventional historiography of war in a concern with collective remembrances of the past; in general this field of study focuses on questions of cultural, religious, and national remembrances of traumatic pasts. "The historical study of memory opens exciting opportunities to ask fresh questions of our conventional sources and topics and to create points for fresh synthesis since the study of memory can link topics we have come to regard as specialized and distinct" (Thelen 1989, 1117). Fundamental, then, to memory studies is the relationship between "memory" and "history."

However, it would be erroneous on my part to suggest that memory and history are two uncontested categories of analysis. Different traditions of history and memory exist in the fields of psychology and history.[11] In the field of history, for example, the identification of truth requires documentable recollection. However, "psychologists generally confine themselves to aspects of memory testable or replicable in the laboratory; historians study the past by scrutinizing accounts of what has happened in the real world" (Lowenthal 1997, 212). Some writers have also cautioned that history and memory should not be conflated, as they sometimes signify different meanings altogether. "Memory and history, far from being synonymous, appear now to be in fundamental opposition" (Nora 1989, 8). That opposition rests on the notion that "history," by which Pierre Nora meant the academically distanced study of the past, bears no sustainable comparison to "memory," an ephemeral and emotional remembrance of the past. Nora suggested that history and memory are not only antithetical to each other, but that "history is perpetually suspicious of memory, and its true mission is to suppress and destroy it" (1989, 9). Nora's stark observations rightly attest to conventional historians' views of memory. For a traditionally trained historian, memory endangers the historian's fact-finding mission to interpret and to portray the past objectively. Emotional and personal feelings taint the historian's narrative, and distort the objective interpretation of the past.

The task of memory studies, however, entails an understanding of the determinative role that social factors play in the processes of remembering and forgetting. As Marita Sturken observed, there is "so much traffic across the borders of cultural memory and history that in many cases it may be futile to maintain a distinction between them. Yet there are times when those distinctions are important in understanding political intent, when memories are asserted specifically outside of or in response to historical narratives" (1997, 5). Following Sturken, I posit "memory and history as *entangled* rather than oppositional" (1997, 5; emphasis in original). Moreover, in this project I recognize that the production of knowledge about the past "is always enmeshed in the exercise of power and is always accompanied by elements of repression" (Yoneyama 1999, 27). Whether analyzing the traumatic events of World War II, the Vietnam War, or 9/11, the analysis of collective and individual memory now stands at the forefront of memory studies, tracing its origins to historical, psychological, and sociological understandings of memory and history (Sturken 2007, 4).

In the study of Pacific Islanders' involvement in the war, as well as their remembrances of it, one must consider that memory and history also function as processes that exert power in shaping *how* the past is constructed, represented, and interpreted. "Power differences within a culture, and those between different cultures, affect the significance attributed to events of the past" (Falgout, Poyer, and Carucci 2008, 26). Pacific Islander experiences and remembrances of the war thus present much in terms of trying to understand the politics of historical remembrance and erasure, especially since many of the societies draw from oral traditions rather than written ones. "It is societies whose social memory is primarily oral or which are in the process of establishing a written collective memory that offer us the best chance of understanding this struggle for domination over remembrance and tradition, this manipulation of memory" (Le Goff 1992, 98). The rise of World War II commemorations in the Mariana Islands, the general subject of this book, provides an opportunity to explore the politics of remembrance among one oral and two written societies: indigenous Chamorros on the one hand, and Americans and Japanese on the other.

Cultures of Commemoration

The power and reach of local and national identity, collective and individual memory, and colonial and indigenous history is revealed in the study of commemorations. In this respect, commemorations can be read as "mnemonic technique[s] for localizing collective memory" and can be studied as a means to revisit and rethink current theoretical notions of war, memory, and history (Hutton 1988, 315). In this work I have specifically employed John Gillis's definition of commemorative activity as a social and political process, entailing "the coordination of individual and group memories, whose results may appear consensual when they are in fact the product of processes of intense contest, struggle, and, in some instances, annihilation" (1994, 5). This concept of commemorative activity, Gillis reminded scholars, derives from twentieth-century understandings of commemorations. But commemorations are by no means unique to one society, geographical locale, or time period.

Commemorations are as varied as the memories and histories they represent. In nineteenth-century Europe, for example, commemorations served the interests of "fallen kings and martyred revolutionary leaders" of monarchial societies such as France (Gillis 1994, 9). The commemorations focused on men of the clergy and aristocracy, tributes to the elite members of a society. "National commemorations were largely the preserve of elite males, the designated carriers of progress" (Gillis 1994, 10). Since that time, military cemeteries, pilgrimages, monuments, and other kinds of commemorative activities and structures have emerged throughout America and Europe. The gendered and social dynamics of these commemorative activities emphasized the place of elite men in the formation or disintegration of nations, as well as inscribed histories for the people premised on the lives of these various leaders. Women therefore occupied marginal spaces in the commemoration of events and individuals. The role of women "was largely allegorical. . . . The figure of Liberty [for example] came to stand in both France and the United States as a symbol of national identity, but the history of real women was systematically forgotten" (Gillis 1994, 10). "It was not until after the Second World War that national commemoration began to alter" (Gillis 1994, 12). The widespread destruction that had occurred and the tremendous political and economic changes that took place throughout the world greatly affected the content and style of commemorative activities.

In terms of style, parades rapidly replaced pilgrimages as the primary memorial activity. Aspects of mourning that first transpired in World War I lingered into World War II, again suppressing the rank and class of the fallen in favor of acts of collective bereavement (Winter 1995, 227). Veterans, the survivors of war, were also glorified more than common soldiers of past wars. Further, as Gillis suggested, the construction of "living memorials," such as parks and sports stadiums, proliferated in honor of civilians lost in the war (1994, 13). These social forms of celebrating and mourning, as well as architectural innovations in monument development, again transformed the meaning of commemorative activities. Gradually, the commemorations shifted, though did not lose entirely, their focus from the memories of "elite" individuals to the memories of cultural, national, and religious groups.

Some did not even commemorate World War II, or at least did not do so in ways comparable to commemorations of it in Europe. For example, Wang Gungwu asserted that some people in Southeast Asia did not "seem to be keen to remember the war. Compared with the range of writings by the Europeans about the war in Europe, it is obvious that the people in this region either do not wish to remember, or do not feel as intensely about their experiences" (2000, 14). Some indigenous peoples of this region did not possess dominant memories of their wartime occupiers, the Japanese, as antagonists of war. Consequently, they did not collectively resent the Japanese. As Wang explained, this "was partly because the Japanese had been skillful in the discriminatory policy they had devised to support the claim that they had launched the war to rescue the local peoples from Western colonialism" (2000, 19).

The perceived sense of liberation from Western colonialism shared by some people in Southeast Asia gave rise to "prospects of nationhood to which they could look forward" (Gungwu 2000, 20). Indonesian cooperation with the Japanese, for example, was "the highest form of patriotism because it advanced Indonesian nationalism" and opposed further Dutch colonization of Southeast Asia (Steinberg 1967, 15). The general absence of national commemorations of World War II in Southeast Asia further demonstrates the degree to which memories of the war are influenced by the politics of the past and the present. Still, the proliferation of war commemorations is now a global phenomenon.

Four features best describe the recent internationalization of these commemorations (Ashplant, Dawson, and Roper 2000, 1–5). First, the debates encircling the commemoration of the Shoah, otherwise known as the Holocaust, constitute the most apparent transnational manifestation of war remembrance and commemoration.[12] The "recent past has been marked by the proliferation of museums, monuments, and memorials dedicated to the Holocaust" (LaCapra 1998, 10). Commemorations of the Shoah and the Holocaust have varied over time, as have their focus on religious rites and nationalist aspirations in Israel and in the Jewish diaspora (Friedländer 1998, 346–348). The three other indications of the increase in global commemorative activities include the rise in anniversary commemorations of various wars, legal demands for redressing wartime injustices and injuries, and civil strife in former Soviet territories. With regard to the last, the very continuation of wars—ethnic, nationalist, or religious—creates the conditions for future forms of remembrance and erasure, legal debate, and reparation.

At stake in the study of these commemorative activities of war are rituals of national identification, collective and individual mourning, and familial life-stories of war. These studies reveal that the nation-state, as much as the individual or group, controls and shapes the means by which peoples and institutions remember wars. As I aim to demonstrate here, a close attention to the politics of institutional and personal memories of war enables one to better understand the competing histories on which public memories are built. The increasing variety of political, national, and personal expressions from which to commemorate or contest war, and the growing international-ization of these activities, certainly indicate an urgency for the study of war memory and commemoration. This situation applies as well to the Pacific region, where various war commemorations have emerged since the end of World War II.

In the Pacific, war commemorative activities have been influenced by narratives of defeat and triumph, death and survival. Pilgrimages of mourn-ing, the construction of war and peace memorials, ceremonial speeches, and a whole host of commemorative activities have taken place in this region (Turner and Falgout 2002, 119). The most internationally visible commemorations of the war in the Pacific include the remembrance of its "beginning" and its "end": America's Pearl Harbor of 1941 and Japan's Hiroshima of 1945. These studies criticize both Japan and the United States for commemorating the war in terms of victory and victimization, which often disregard competing and lesser-known memories of the war (Rosen-berg 2003, 6; Dower 1996, 66).[13] By calling into question the dominant nar-ratives of Pearl Harbor and Hiroshima, respectively, these scholars tend to publicize marginalized remembrances of the war.[14] In doing so, as in the case of the Smithsonian Institution's 1995 exhibition of the *Enola Gay,* they find that challenging dominant views of the war often leads to politically and morally charged discussions over interpreting the past.[15] Although the Smithsonian Institution eventually commemorated an American celebra-tory view of the airplane and the atom bomb, the debates surrounding the *Enola Gay* demonstrate that the exhibit drew its meaning from cross-cul-tural notions of war, memory, and history.

Elsewhere, in areas like Micronesia, "most islands quickly instituted com-memorative holidays marking the local end of the war" (Poyer, Falgout, and Carucci 2001, 338). "Liberation Day" celebrations emerged, for instance, in such areas as the Marshall Islands and Pohnpei to commemorate the arrival of US military forces and the surrender of the Japanese military in 1944. Interestingly, neither island society used commemorations to encourage active remembrances of the war. In the Marshall Islands, religious prayer, feasting, and field games characterized Liberation Day, but did not recreate the war "as a part of national or local history" (Poyer 1997, 67). For those in Pohnpei, Liberation Day's "primary focus was on shore and field athletic competitions," and not on indigenous attempts to recall the war (Turner and Falgout 2002, 119). Although commemorative activities usually mediated notions of memory and history, the commemoration of the war in the Marshall Islands and Pohnpei showed that such mediations were not as significant for the people of these areas.

On Kosrae, commemorative activities were "deliberately scripted so as to teach" a war history of survival (Poyer, Falgout, and Carucci 2001, 338). World War II commemorations in the Solomon Islands have increasingly become associated with narratives of heroism, loyalty, and valor due to the efforts of returning foreign veterans (White 1995, 531). And in the Mariana Islands, Chamorros "on Guam, and to a lesser extent on Saipan, have long made something of a memory industry of the war" (Poyer, Falgout, and Carucci 2001, 337). The mere presence of commemorative activities, therefore, does not suggest that all island societies participated in collective acts of war remembrance, nor do such commemorative activities imply that island societies conformed to only one method of remembering the war.

In large part, indigenous memories of the war are not limited to national or transnational commemorations of the war. The principal mediums for conveying indigenous experiences and memories of the war include storytelling, legends, songs, art, and chants. For example, songs, like all of these mediums, are often appreciated for their "historical weight" by Pacific Islanders and scholars alike (Lindstrom and White 1993, 193). These traditionally regarded modes of retaining indigenous memories of the war are also supplemented by such "nontraditional" mediums as radio broadcasts, video and audio recordings, and government policies (Turner and Falgout 2002, 119). Through such mediums, Pacific Islanders recall their memories as survivors of the war. These memories are then shared, across generations, with friends and family.

However, not all memories are conveyed to different generations, let alone in public spaces of commemorative activities. Some memories are suppressed because of their disrespectful, shameful, or violent content. For example, memories of indigenous women who served as "comfort women" for the Japanese colonial and military administrations are not easily disseminated across generations or among outsiders.[16] Memories regarding "comfort women" in the Pacific are largely repressed for cultural reasons. For some island societies, the general subject of sex is guarded from public exposure, ridicule, and scrutiny. On the other hand, sexuality can be openly discussed by Pacific Islanders as gossip, humor, and social critique (Hereniko 1995; Erai 2004).

Nevertheless, it can be challenging to discuss such emotionally charged topics as abortion, prostitution, and rape—English terms that partly reflect the meanings, conditions, and consequences of colonial and indigenous constructions of gender and sexuality (Marsh 1998, 673). The endeavor to understand wartime female agency is further compounded by a patriarchal historiography of war that privileges the exploration of military policy and strategy rather than the examination of the human and social dimensions. Under certain circumstances, these memories of Asian and Pacific Islander women may be shared and understood, but in ways viewed as respectful, sensitive, and relevant by the women themselves and their families.[17] Overall, many Pacific Islanders recall a period of conflict prompted by foreign agendas and politics, as well as a time for reflecting on the impact of colonial rule and race relations in the region (White 1991, vi).

Structure of the Book

In this work I examine three conceptual themes. My first objective is to explore the ways in which "culture" functions as a process of local and global identification and differentiation. This is an important consideration, given that group cultural labels sometimes homogenize generational and intracultural variations and divisions, or even serve the competing interests of colonial, indigenous, and settler peoples (Kauanui 2007, 151). In the context of indigenous peoples, the notions of "Indian" or "Hawaiian" that are "utilized to describe collective identities take for granted categories invented by colonizers and imposed upon the colonized in remapping and redefining diverse peoples" (Dirlik 1999, 77). However, the reification of cultural categories does not result from colonization alone. Notions of cultural identity, solidarity, and difference are also shaped by anthropological concepts of culture, race, and tradition (see, eg, Hobsbawm 1997). With regard to the Pacific, Jocelyn Linnekin argued that conventional concepts of culture "have in common an essentialist project: they . . . rely on and advance the proposition that a core or essence of customs and values is handed down from one generation to another, and that this core defines a group's distinctive cultural identity" (1992, 251). What results is the objectification of culture, whereby notions of Pacific Islander cultural identity remain fixed and resistant to adaptation and change (Linnekin 1990, 162–163).

As an alternative to reductive notions of cultural change and continuity, I here posit a constructionist view of culture, which implies that culture is a "selective representation of the past, fashioned in the present, responsive to contemporary priorities and agendas, and politically instrumental" (Linnekin 1992, 251). In the following chapters I explore colonial and indigenous constructions of culture in the twentieth century, with a focus on how colonial loyalties affect intra- and cross-cultural relationships and memories of the war in the Mariana Islands. Geoffrey White's thesis that competing memories of World War II in the Solomon Islands have shaped historical narratives of "loyalty" and "liberation" (1995, 531) applies especially to my own study of war, memory, and history. Exploring the fiftieth anniversary of the war, White argued that concepts of loyalty and liberation have produced idealized images of the "national subject" in memories and histories of the war (1995, 552). Moreover, these concepts have helped to develop dominant paradigms in the remembrance of the war in places like the Solomon Islands, where triumphal narratives of American and Allied victory sometimes subsume dissonant indigenous memories of the war (White 1995, 552). Here, I invoke White's thesis, examining the "internal tensions among contending memories or the flow of images and image-making practices across national boundaries" (White 1995, 531).

In chapter 1, I draw from White's argument in my discussion of the politics of American and Japanese colonialisms and indigenous cultural agency in the Mariana Islands. I analyze colonial and indigenous efforts to produce the "loyal Chamorro subject"—that is, one who is simultaneously embraced and renounced as a member of the American and Japanese nation-states. The setting is the era that Chamorros call *antes gi tiempon guerra* (the time before the war). Many Chamorros, especially the older wartime generations, remember this era—1898 to 1941—in terms of peace and peaceful social relations. "Life was pleasantly simple," recalled the late Chamorro educator Pedro C Sanchez (1979, 4). Chamorros often romanticize rural life and idealize the American, German, and Japanese colonial administrations of the early twentieth century. Some island societies affected by the war share this perception, and many of them divide time into two categories: before the war and after the war (Lindstrom and White 1989, 22). In this chapter I show that prewar memories of peace actually work to conceal what was, in reality, a violent era of American and Japanese colonialisms in the Mariana Islands. This prewar nostalgia suppresses histories of "Asian" and "Western" wartime expansion and colonial rule in the Mariana Islands, most notably histories of the Spanish-American War in 1898 and World War I in 1914.

Chapter 1 partly fulfills the second goal of this book, which is to examine how "colonialism" operates in ways attentive to the needs of both the colonizer and the colonized. This position on colonialism recognizes the forceful and violent histories of political conquest, religious conversion, and economic subjugation that have come to define, in part, the historiography of colonialism and resistance. Chapter 1 and the chapters that follow also understand colonialism as an ambivalent process of control and resistance, adaptation and mutation on the part of the colonized and the colonizer.[18] As Vicente Diaz argued, the sometimes ambivalent character of colonialism in the Mariana Islands can be described as a "two-way flow of power that constrains but also furnishes possible modes (and often competing levels) of indigenous expression and survival only insofar as the layered expressions are themselves constituted in a two-way process of historical and political action and reaction between the colonizer and the colonized" (1992, 35).

In this book I adopt Diaz's theoretical premise on the various "flows" of power in the relationships among the colonized and the colonizer. My goal is to examine some of the parallels and differences among American and Japanese forms of colonialism, as well as the various adaptations to and resistance of these colonialisms on the part of different and divergent Chamorro political identities. I also foreground the ways in which an older past of Spanish Catholicism in the Mariana Islands informs these Chamorro political identities in mediating American and Japanese colonialisms of the twentieth century.

In chapter 2, I broaden this discussion on the politics of colonialism and indigenous cultural agency with an examination of World War II in the Mariana Islands. I survey the history of this war in the archipelago, paying attention to the motives and consequences of wartime colonial policies and indigenous cultural politics. In my exploration of American and Japanese wartime invasion and occupational policies, I here consider the agent/victim dichotomy as "not mutually exclusive categories but contextually signified roles" (Chappell 1995, 316). As Pacific historian David Chappell noted, "Everyone is acted upon every day, no matter how independent they may pretend to be. Victims need not be passive, nor the passive weak, nor actors free agents, for history to happen" (1995, 315). In this chapter I treat indigenous agency in terms of everyday survival in the Mariana Islands, set against the grain of American and Japanese wartime colonialisms. Further, as a matter of clarification, the terms "colonialism," "empire," and "imperialism" are used interchangeably, not to conflate the etymological roots and distinct historical developments of each term, but to emphasize how processes of colonial expansion and ideology, as well as indigenous agency and resistance, are very much intertwined.[19]

The aftermath of the war in the Mariana Islands is my focus in chapter 3. I ask, if loyalty and liberation functioned as key concepts in the narrating of colonial histories in the time before the war, how would these concepts function in its aftermath? I address this question alongside the issue of the American "rehabilitation" project in the Mariana Islands in the context of the emerging Cold War. I examine American postwar expansionist policies in the Pacific, the displacement of village populations in Guam, and the establishment of an American internment compound for civilians in Camp Susupe, Saipan, among other examples of American rehabilitation efforts. My intent is to show that the American rehabilitation project, like the war itself, profoundly affected Chamorro perceptions of themselves and of their colonial "Others." Both the war itself, and the postwar era, created the conceptual foundation, indeed a contested collective memory of the past, through which future remembrances of the war would draw direction, value, and purpose.

In this respect, my third goal in this book is to argue that people actively engage in the remembrance and commemoration of the past; that is, everyday people "make history," as much as they are made by it. In chapters 4 and 5, I show that Americans, Chamorros, and Japanese of varying generations continue to remember the war and to interpret it in ways they find appropriate and meaningful. Here I examine the development of World War II commemorations in Guam and the Northern Mariana Islands, respectively, placing particular emphasis on the emergence of the commemoration called Liberation Day. Both Guam and the Northern Marianas celebrate Liberation Day, though on different days and for different reasons.

In the Northern Mariana Islands, as formerly mandated islands of Japan, Liberation Day commemorates 4 July 1946 to mark the time when American military forces released Chamorros and Refaluwasch from Camp Susupe, an internment compound not only for the indigenous population, but also for Japanese, Korean, and Okinawan civilian and military populations.[20] The Refaluwasch, also known as Carolinians, are descendants of the indigenous peoples of Woleai, Lamotrek, Elato, and Satawal atolls in the Caroline Islands, which are located south of the Mariana Islands. Long-time trading partners with the Chamorros, the Refaluwasch settled in the Mariana Islands in the early 1800s and, since that time, have experienced similar histories of colonialism with the Chamorros. Occasional reference is made to Refaluwasch memories and histories of the war, but the main focus is on Chamorros. I sincerely hope that future scholars will address the roles of the Refaluwasch, many of whom have created familial and political relations with Chamorros and others in the Mariana Islands.

Unlike the Northern Marianas, which has a history of wartime internment, Guam witnessed no large-scale internment of the indigenous population and, as a result, celebrates Liberation Day differently. Whereas the Northern Marianas commemorates the release of Chamorros and Refaluwasch from wartime internment, the Chamorros of Guam commemorate Liberation Day to recall the re-invasion of American forces in Guam on 21 July 1944. Couched in the language of "liberation," the Chamorros of Guam celebrate their freedom from Japanese wartime rule and the return of American colonialism. In chapters 4 and 5 I demonstrate that the colonial and indigenous memories that inform these commemorations of the war are premised on the politics of the past and the present (Trouillot 1995, 23).

Yet commemorations of the war also remember to forget certain events, issues, and experiences, as they, too, are fraught with the politics of exclusion and erasure. In chapter 6, I pursue the issue of collective amnesia in the Mariana Islands, by examining the "forgotten" history of Japan's conscription of indigenous labor in wartime Guam, from 1941 to 1944. Here I discuss the roles of those who could be understood as indigenous "collaborators" with Japan's wartime empire, namely Chamorro "comfort women," interpreters, and police assistants. In the pages that follow, the euphemisms "comfort women" and "comfort stations" are used only to signal the patriarchal and sexist dimensions of Japan's official wartime policies on forced prostitution and rape. Following the United Nations and Korean Council's official terminology, I employ the phrases "military sexual slavery," "sexual slavery," and "sex slave" to emphasize the violent nature of the so-called comfort stations and to reflect the language currently used by survivors of sexual slavery (Chung 1997, 222). As the late Filipina Maria "Lola Rosa" Henson once declared, "I had been held captive as a sex slave for nine months" in 1943 (1999, 48). Lola Rosa's story of struggle in the face of Japanese wartime sexual slavery resonates with the stories of Asian and Pacific Islander female sexual slaves elsewhere. Guam is the focus of this aspect of study because this is where the recruitment of Chamorro interpreters, police assistants, and sex slaves for Japan's wartime empire created the conditions to further fragment the intracultural relations among Chamorros. Guam is also the area where the greatest contact among "Americanized" and "Japanized" Chamorros occurred, illustrating the violence associated with colonial loyalties and disloyalties in the time of war.

In conclusion, in chapter 7 I revisit the key themes explored in this social history of World War II. I raise questions about the future of commemorative activities in the Mariana Islands, given the changing politics of colonialism and indigenous cultural agency. As a means to address these issues, I explore the life and death of Father Jesus Baza Dueñas, a Chamorro priest who worked in Japanese-occupied Guam. I examine Father Dueñas as an ethnographic and mnemonic figure, in light of the emergence of war commemorations since 1945 throughout the Mariana Islands. My intent is to demonstrate that the past is never past, and that people consciously engage in the making of history. The story of Father Dueñas provides a poetic rumination on the study of war histories and histories of war in the Mariana Islands and elsewhere. Through this kind of social history of war I hope to encourage more studies on the politics of colonialism, indigenous cultural agency, and commemoration.

Chapter 1
Loyalty and Liberation

One cannot appreciate the memories and histories of World War II in the Mariana Islands without understanding the narrative devices, or concepts, that shape their meaning and purpose. In the time before the war, which Chamorros identify as *antes gi tiempon guerra,* a variety of concepts informed the nature of economic, political, and social relations among Chamorros and their respective colonizers. Most notably, these concepts included, but were not limited to, notions of "loyalty" and "liberation." As a working definition, loyalty signifies "an abiding disposition to act with others in support of a shared commitment" (Waller and Linklater 2003, 224). The etymological roots of loyalty stem from "law," or the Latin *lex,* which has "also generated the French terms *loi* (law) and *loyauté* (loyalty)" (Fletcher 1993, 62). The idea of "liberation," on the other hand, can be described as "the action of liberating or condition of being liberated."[1] The significance of these terms for this discussion rests primarily on the broad range through which they could have been implemented and interpreted by both the colonizer and the colonized not only in the Marianas, but also throughout the colonized world of the early twentieth century.

In attempting to establish colonial rule in Africa, the Pacific, or Southeast Asia, colonial powers often resorted to acquiring the loyalty of their subjects, if not achieving outright political conquest through conflict and violence. A loyal, colonized society implied, superficially, an obedient and pacified population. As John Bodnar noted with regard to the American context, the rhetoric of loyalty has been "invented as a form of social control" (1992, 17). Similarly, European missionaries promulgated the idea of "spiritual liberation" in an attempt to convert colonized peoples to Christianity, contributing, in turn, to the rise or demise of colonial rule.[2] Historical developments of loyalty and liberation, as concepts of control and conversion, have thus varied in meaning and purpose over time. Yet these concepts find common ground in what Nicholas Dirks called the process of "securing the nation-state," that is, developing and maintaining state rule, class ruptures, world capitalism, and even international cultural, economic, and political hegemony (1992, 4).

By no means, however, did the modern expansion of European rule and settlement in the colonial periphery signal a homogenous or uniquely Western colonial enterprise (Hanlon 1994, 93). "Colonialism is not a unitary project but a fractured one, riddled with contradictions and exhausted as much by its own internal debates as by the resistance of the colonized" (Thomas 1994, 51). As opposed to the citizenry, the colonized often resided, and still do, in states of political ambivalence and uncertainty, simultaneously recognized and renounced as members of colonial polities (LiPuma 1995, 43).

Yet the questions remain: How did the colonial governments of Japan and the United States foster notions of loyalty among the Chamorros of the Mariana Islands and among their colonized subjects more generally? How did the historical development of the concepts of loyalty and liberation affect the economic, political, and social fabric of indigenous and settler societies in the Mariana Islands? And how did the establishment of two competing notions of colonial loyalty affect the cross-cultural and intracultural relations among Chamorros and, moreover, their sense of agency and collectivity? Here, I explore these questions in an effort to bring greater context and meaning to the politics of American and Japanese colonialisms in the Mariana Islands. My purpose is to examine the origins and impact of the concepts of loyalty and liberation among the Chamorro people in the time before the war.

The Politics of American Colonialism in Guam

In trying to understand the histories of the Mariana Islands in the twentieth century, it is important to "scrutinize the historical processes by which the natives have learned to work within and against the grain of . . . outsider attempts to colonize the Chamorro" (Diaz 1994, 53). The histories of Spanish Catholicism in the Mariana Islands, for example, began as violent intrusions into the worldviews and everyday practices of Chamorros in the seventeenth century. As historian Francis Hezel observed, the "progression in Spanish policy throughout this period was from conversion to conquest— but conquest only in the belief that this was necessary to achieve the Christianization of the [Chamorro] people" (1982, 132). Canonical histories of this past have also described Spanish Catholicism, and the series of debates and conflicts it spurred during its introduction, as signaling the demise of Chamorro cultural agency and collectivity (Diaz 1995, 159). Contrary to these reductive understandings of cultural change and continuity, however, Chamorro agency has proven to be incredibly resilient and adaptively responsive to adverse social, economic, and political influences, in spite of the histories of colonialism in the Mariana Islands (M Perez 2005, 588). Chamorros eventually sought meaningful ownership of a series of Catholic signs and symbols, initially associated with the Spanish Jesuits, but later "open to transformation" by competing individuals and parties (Comaroff and Comaroff 1991, 18). Thus, the Christian God became accepted as their

God (or *Yu'us*, in the Chamorro vernacular), as did a variety of prayers, rituals, and saints associated with Catholicism.

At the turn of the twentieth century, Chamorro cultural agency and collectivity reflected a strong identification with Catholicism, or more appropriately, Chamorro Catholicism (Rogers 1995, 102–105). Although histories of Christianity in the Pacific often began with violent encounters between indigenous and colonial peoples, many Pacific Islanders have been able to draw meaning from Christianity to maintain older traditions, to seek sources of wealth and power, and to construct new identities (Flinn 1990, 222). This, too, has been the case with the Chamorros of the Mariana Islands. Catholicism would serve as a foundational cultural base for Chamorro interpretations of American and Japanese notions of loyalty and liberation before, during, and after World War II.

With respect to the rise of American empire in Guam, irony resonates in Chamorro recollections of the time before the war. Because Chamorros, especially those of the older generations, tend to romanticize the prewar past of the Mariana Islands, equating the time before the war with peace, conflict and violence do not appear as dominant themes in their memories. But many Chamorros forget, or remember to forget, that this prewar past speaks to two equally significant wars: the Spanish-American War in 1898 and World War I in 1914. More important, these wars contributed greatly to the rise in American and Japanese colonial expansion and settlement in regions that extended beyond their national borders, geographically bridging Asia and the Pacific to the Americas and the Caribbean (Peattie 1984a, 18; Schoonover 2003, 34). In other words, these two wars helped to promote early twentieth-century debates about the economic, military, and political value of colonial rule outside the demarcated territories of nineteenth-century Japan and the United States.[3]

In short, these wars introduced the Chamorros of the Mariana Islands to their new "mother countries" (Hofschneider 2001, 51). As Chamorro scholar Penelope Hofschneider observed, Chamorros saw the Americans—and, by extension, the Japanese—as filling "a position established and held by the Spanish for two hundred and fifty years" (2001, 51). At the turn of the twentieth century, Chamorros expressed no collective, interisland affinity for "national" belonging to either Japan or the United States. As Michael Waller and Andrew Linklater argued, new loyalties "lack strong emotional attachment until they have survived real tests and been hallowed by time—or have been sealed by a compact, formal or informal" (2003, 13). Loyalty to a nation, religion, or ethnic group, moreover, "does not naturally find resonance within the hearts and minds of ordinary people" (Bodnar 1992, 17). The Spanish-American War and World War I generated the conditions for the United States and Japan, respectively, to introduce and attempt to make "natural" colonial loyalties among their colonized populations. Through their varied forms of governance, Japan and the United States strove to foster, in theory and praxis, loyalty and liberation as concepts of social control.

The Spanish-American War of 1898 signaled both the end and the beginning of colonial rule in Guam, with Spain exiting the island and the United States entering it. Spain's loss in the war also led to the political separation of Guam from the Northern Mariana Islands. With Guam in the hands of the United States Naval Government, Germany acquired the Mariana Islands north of Guam, including Rota, Tinian, and Saipan.[4] Germany purchased the Northern Mariana Islands from Spain, along with Palau and the Caroline Islands, for five million dollars. Germany's interest in the economic potential of these islands as sites for the production of copra or the mining of phosphate rose as quickly as it fell. The outbreak of World War I in 1914 led to the dismantling of German rule in the Pacific region and to the introduction of Japanese overseas governance. The United States, though, obtained more than Guam.

In 1898, the United States also expanded its rule to eastern Sāmoa, Hawai'i, and the Philippines in the Pacific, as well as to Cuba and Puerto Rico in the Caribbean (Levi 1948, 55). Resistance movements across both the Caribbean and the Pacific soon surfaced, if not meshed, with ongoing efforts for sovereignty, in an attempt to counter America's colonial expansionism (Kramer 2006, 89). Whether couched in the languages of class struggle, international diplomacy, nationalism, or revolution, these resistance movements encountered varying degrees of success and failure (Silva 2004, 146; Grosfoguel 2003, 55). Even the Anti-Imperialist League, established in Boston on 19 November 1898, failed to rally mass public support against the United States' expansionist desires and policies (J Smith 1994, 203). Although a variety of objectives informed the Anti-Imperialist League, one of its goals included a desire to uphold American traditions of liberty, progress, and representative self-government in the continental United States. The subjugation of other peoples in and beyond the coasts of the United States contradicted these principles (S Cook 1996, 95). It was also not uncommon for Anti-Imperialists to forward the position that "Polynesians, Asians, and Latin Americans were incapable of assimilating into Anglo-Saxon society" (S Cook 1996, 96). In terms of the economic fallibility of imperialism, Anti-Imperialists added the argument that further expansion would strain domestic trade and investment, diverting funds to the development of American colonial administration abroad (S Cook 1996, 96).

Despite the efforts of the Anti-Imperialist League, the US government ultimately favored expansion into the Pacific region, knowing that its islands and atolls would support and sustain American naval and maritime activities in the region. The US Navy erected a coaling station in Guam that served the refueling needs of visiting ships on voyages of economic and military exploration. Elsewhere in the Pacific, naval vessels made similar stops for provisions at naval stations located in eastern Sāmoa, Hawai'i, and the Philippines, creating what Samoan historian Damon Salesa called a "domain that was at once tactical and strategic, imperial and intimately local" (2007, 72).

While US policy in the Pacific showed a decidedly militarist character, neither the United States government nor its military services fortified the islands beyond Hawai'i's shores. In the years between the two world wars, the United States saw no immediate and pressing need to do so. Numerous military diplomats and strategists reassured themselves that the Hawaiian archipelago provided the sufficient land mass and distance needed to shield the US mainland from potential Asian enemies, more particularly, Japan. Although many worried about the military capabilities of the Japanese, US officials quelled such fears by arguing that Japan posed no substantial military threat. In the time before World War II, the US Navy saw the western Pacific region as an area for economic exploration, military maneuvering, and political posturing.

On Guam, the US Naval Government attempted to impart to Chamorros an awareness of American civic notions of economic and political development, while ensuring that they attained only token and trivial positions of political representation and authority. In replacing the previous Spanish colonial government, US naval authorities made no official proclamations about "liberating" Chamorros. Yet advocates for American expansion in the media, military, and government often spoke in euphemisms to the contrary, supporting the immediate "liberation" of indigenous peoples in Cuba, Guam, and the Philippines from Spanish "tyranny." The American media promoted, for example, the "conviction that only a war with Spain could free Cuba and thus fulfill the American obligation to spread freedom and end Old World tyranny" (Curti 1946, 195). Other US government and military officials used the terms "'liberate' as a code for 'occupy,' and 'pacify' for 'conquer'" in their descriptions of American colonial activities in the Pacific and the Caribbean (Schoonover 2003, 99). In matters regarding relations with the Chamorros, however, the issue of loyalty "was consistently voiced during navy discussions over" the island (Maga 1985, 171).

American loyalty in Guam, as Chamorro scholar Robert Underwood argued, "didn't spring up overnight. It was planted and cultivated by many individuals with many motives" (1977, 6). American colonial education, health policies, and economic projects attempted to garner the loyalties of Chamorros (DeLisle 2001). The US Naval Government specifically sponsored various activities, such as speech contests and village parades, to "assimilate" Chamorros to American rule. Whereas assimilationist policies in the continental United States targeted some immigrant populations to become part of an "Anglo-Saxon" community, the dynamics of American assimilation differed in Guam because of its colonial context (Gordon 1964, 77).

In Guam, the US military constituted a migrant community attempting to control an indigenous population overseas, reflecting a relatively new, underdeveloped aspect of American colonial governance. As Chamorro historian Anne Perez Hattori noted, "The Chamorro people were not immigrants to American shores, and to them so-called 'American customs' were radical foreign intrusions. As indigenous people living on their home island, it was not possible for Chamorros to assimilate into an existing American culture, as was expected of immigrants" (2004, 25). Instead, argued Hattori, "Assimilation programs on Guam were promulgated principally through the dictates of [US] governmental policy" (2004, 25). Attempts to instill the concept of American loyalty among Chamorros were a key component of the naval government's assimilation program. By the early 1900s some Chamorros had appropriated the concept of American loyalty to obtain citizenship, which was then perceived as offering greater individual and collective autonomy to Chamorros under naval rule.

On 1 July 1925, three Guam Chamorro leaders presented their views of the United States to several visiting congressmen in Hagåtña, Guam's largest village and the island's capital (map 2). They aimed to convince these congressmen that their loyalty to America warranted inclusion in America's political sphere. Don Atanasio T Perez, a chief clerk to the naval governor of Guam, noted that "the Chamorros are neither citizens nor aliens—they are truly without country. . . . I hope that Congress will see fit to retain our appreciation and strengthen our loyalty by granting us the title we would prize above all others:—Citizens of the United States" (PSECC 1993, 31). Jose Roberto added that the "middle aged natives of the island . . . assure you of their respect and loyalty to the [American] flag" (PSECC 1993, 31). Ramon Sablan reiterated these points by saying, "as political orphans, we trust, obey and appreciate the paternal protection and guidance of the American flag. As citizens, we would not betray that trust, we would not neglect our obligations; we would not decrease that appreciation" (PSECC 1993, 32).

The visiting congressmen listened to these petitions for citizenship, reassuring the Chamorro leadership that the United States Congress would soon deliberate on the issue of granting citizenship to the people of Guam (Hofschneider 2001, 67). Naval governors such as Willis W Bradley Jr also endorsed the movement for US citizenship in Guam (Hanlon 1994, 112). Yet, as David Hanlon observed, the US Navy ultimately stated that the Chamorro people of Guam were "not prepared for self-government and that, in effect, they already enjoyed many of the privileges of citizenship without any of the accompanying responsibilities" (1994, 113).

Efforts to attain US citizenship evidently failed because the issues regarding the civil rights and political status of the Chamorro people rarely attracted the serious attention of Congress or the US Navy. Yet the Chamorro movement to seek US citizenship reflected a substantial degree of success in the navy's attempts to indoctrinate Chamorros into believing in the ideals of American law and politics. Guam Chamorros had accustomed themselves to the workings of American naval colonialism in Guam. That they still attempted to achieve citizenship demonstrated, at the very

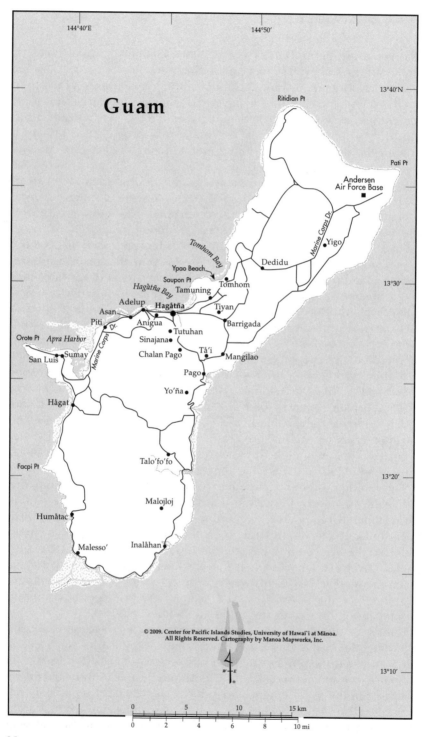

Guam

Ritidian Pt

13°40'N

Pati Pt

Andersen
Air Force Base

Tomhom Bay

Marine Corps Dr.

Yigo

Ypao Beach
Saupon Pt
Tamuning
Hagåtña Bay
Adelup
Asan
Piti
Anigua
Orote Pt   Apra Harbor
Sumay
San Luis

Tomhom

Dedidu

13°30'

Hagåtña
Tiyan
Barrigada
Tutuhan
Sinajana
Chalan Pago
Tå'i
Mangilao
Pago
Yo'ña

Marine Corps Dr.

Hågat

Facpi Pt

Talo'fo'fo

13°20'

Malojloj

Humåtac

Malesso'   Inalåhan

13°10'

W — E

0   5   10   15 km
0   2   4   6   8   10 mi

144°40'E   144°50'

MAP 2.

least, the complex layers of subjugation, resistance, and adaptation through which they interacted with the US colonial government.

The move to garner US citizenship in Guam illustrated a paradox that on the one hand represented indigenous efforts to resist US naval rule, but on the other showed indigenous acceptance of American democracy—the same democracy that supports and is supported by the US military. Loyalty, as a concept, served the needs and desires of the American colonial government and the Chamorro political elite. Despite the various interpretations of American loyalty, the idea that Chamorros should accommodate the wider needs of the American polity persisted. Holidays and celebrations often publicly reminded the wider Chamorro population of this point—to abide by and uphold American notions of loyalty, education, sanitation, and industry. The Guam Industrial Fair, for example, displayed agricultural stands, organized carabao races, and coordinated parades to encourage Chamorros to compete among themselves. The goal of the fair was to determine who could produce the most and best agricultural products.

Another holiday, called Flag Day, celebrated the American presence in Guam, specifically highlighting the infrastructural, medical, and educational contributions of the colonial government. In March 1934, Remedios L G Perez, the Chamorro principal of Dorn Hall School, in Hagåtña, praised the occasion of this holiday. Addressing US naval officials and public spectators at the Althouse Plaza, in Hagåtña, she spoke with authority and conviction. "These improvements," she began, "come to us through the American Flag, the American Government, the American People" (*Guam Recorder* 1934, 213). Raising her voice, she firmly continued, "and, does it [America] ask for a penny in return? It does not! But it is expected of all of us to appreciate the benefits we enjoy under American rule and we should always love, honor and uphold that flag and never bring it to shame" (*Guam Recorder* 1934, 213). As evidenced in Perez's comments, Chamorro loyalty to the United States had become a pressing and highly visible issue by the mid 1930s.

Throughout the island of Guam on specific occasions like Flag Day, the Industrial Fair, or the Fourth of July, US governors required Chamorros and military personnel to display the American flag in front of their homes. The colonial government likewise advised the populace to paint the trees surrounding their homes with the colors red, white, and blue (figure 1). Did these commemorative activities represent a growing interest on the part of Guam Chamorros to be loyal to the United States? And did the concept of loyalty function only within such contexts of commemoration and, in the case of the citizenship movement, political representation?

To the contrary, American efforts to garner the loyalties of Chamorros in the first half of the twentieth century were fundamentally racist, belittling Chamorros in every manner possible. With few exceptions, racism and militarism determined the scope and purpose of US naval governance of Guam. The militarist dimension of American loyalty attempted to ensure

FIGURE 1. Village scene in Guam, early 1900s. The US colonial government suggested people paint trees near their homes red, white, and blue to show patriotic loyalty to the United States. *(Baltazar B Aguon, reproduced with permission)*

that Chamorros did not challenge the naval operations on the island in particular and the role of the US Navy in general. The Guam Congress, made up of Chamorro political leaders and created in 1917, served only as an advisory board to the naval government, and held no legislative power to create, nullify, or revise laws. Elementary schools segregated Chamorro children from the children of white US military personnel; a naval policy of segregation likewise applied to the military personnel themselves, who were usually discouraged from marrying native women (Rogers 1995, 130). And naval medical policies served the interests of the military more than those of the wider Chamorro population, protecting "the health of their [American] personnel and validating their colonial presence while positioning them as the rescuers of an underprivileged race" (Hattori 2004, 25).

Further, executive orders drafted by numerous naval governors attempted to mold Chamorro attitudes and behaviors in ways deemed proper by the military government. As Chamorro scholar Laura Torres Souder asserted, these orders "dictated appropriate standards and acceptable behavior for the people of this newly acquired territory" (1992, 33). Souder added that these "edicts proclaimed who could marry whom; when church bells could ring; what language would be used; and prohibited whistling and spitting, particularly of betelnut spittle" (1992, 33).

Executive Order 5, issued on 5 September 1899, for example, prohibited the raising of "illegitimate children" by Chamorro families, an act documented by the military government as "antagonistic to moral advancement, incompatible with the generally recognized customs of civilized society, a violation of the accepted principles of Christianity, and a most degrading injustice to the innocent offspring" (Souder 1992, 33). While some Chamorro families may have shamed the parents for having children out of wedlock, the positive cultural motivations for adopting children often outweighed the negative ones. In its widest sense, *mamoksai*, or adoption, connoted more an effort to welcome children from all aspects of Chamorro society into the hands of capable and willing family members, often maintaining current or forging new reciprocal relations among individuals and clans (Iyechad 2001, 120). Above all, many of the naval orders tried to create Chamorros who, in the naval government's view, were civil, industrious, and obedient (Hattori 2005, 8).

The racist elements of American loyalty were reflected in many American views of Chamorros in Guam as well (Leibowitz 1989, 323). The United States "sought to justify domination of Guam and its people through demeaning, essentially racist description" (Hanlon 1994, 111). Many Americans who came to Guam in the early part of the twentieth century, as either sojourners or settlers, perceived Chamorros as lazy, dirty, and ignorant. The "hospitable" nature of Chamorros also garnered praise from these same people, as many noted the "generous" nature of Chamorros in providing food and shelter. Thus, numerous US military personnel envisioned Chamorros as either the "noble savage" or the "ignoble savage," drawing from a longer history of colonial discourse in the Pacific.[5] But the racial and racist dimensions of American loyalty were not just descriptive in nature; they were also prescriptive, in that American loyalty worked simultaneously to accept and distance the colonized from the colonizer.

The early historical development of American loyalty in Guam drew from a wider history of white American perceptions of and relations with colonized people in the continental United States. The strong racist undercurrents that gave shape to the promotion of American loyalty in Guam reflected histories of indigenous dispossession and slavery in the United States. In other words, the US Naval Government looked on the generic figure of the "Chamorro" by borrowing from canonical and caricatured images of the "Indian" and the "Negro." For example, Merle Curti stated that the "Indian was, like the African, of an inferior race, alien, incapable of learning the white man's ways or ever becoming an American" (1946, 90). In his assessment of the social relations in early twentieth-century America, Curti argued that the "Indian had seldom been regarded as capable of becoming a full-fledged citizen" (1946, 183). Yet the possibility of integrating Native Americans into the public sphere of American society arose as a topic of discussion in American political and legal debates. "Having at last been worsted and shoved into reservations," explained Curti, "the red men, many held, now could be integrated into American life through missionary, educational, and governmental means, made over into good Americans and trained in loyalty to the nation" (1946, 183).

Curti's observations apply to America's colonized subjects outside the continental United States in general and to the Chamorros of Guam in particular. As Walter Williams asserted, an "analysis of policies toward American Indians thus shows that the evolving legal status of Indians by the late nineteenth century was a 'subject' status that was similar to the status imposed on other colonial peoples. To be an Indian 'ward' was in fact to be a colonial subject" (1988, 247). In the time before the war, the US Naval Government employed the concept of American loyalty ultimately as a form of social control, reflecting a larger history of militarism and racism in the United States and in its newly acquired territories (Barker 2005, 6). That Chamorros began to speak English, sample American foods like hot dogs, and even develop personal and marital relationships with American soldiers and sailors did not signal total acculturation into the American political and social sphere.

The politics of American colonialism attempted to guarantee that the "Chamorro," the "Indian," the "Negro," and other colonized subjects be loyal to the United States only insofar as citizenship, or full constitutional recognition, remained beyond their reach. On the other hand, in Guam the concept of liberation did not play as integral a role as did the concept of loyalty. It surfaced only during the time of the Spanish-American War in 1898 and briefly thereafter. That would not be the case for the Chamorros of the Northern Mariana Islands, where the politics of Japanese colonialism necessitated the use of both loyalty and liberation as, first, concepts of social control and, second, concepts of "national belonging." As with the Chamorros in Guam, the Chamorros of the Northern Mariana Islands would soon comprehend the colonial dimensions of Japanese loyalty and liberation, as well as their mutability to assist indigenous needs and demands.

The Politics of Japanese Colonialism in the Northern Marianas

At the onset of World War I, German rule in the Northern Mariana Islands ceased. Germany lost the northern islands to Japan as a result of the League of Nations granting Japan a Class C Mandate to govern the islands of the western Pacific, otherwise known as Micronesia. Specifically, and without the expressed consent of indigenous peoples, the League of Nations presented Australia, Britain, Japan, and New Zealand with the sovereignty to preside over former German possessions in the Pacific. Japan received islands north of the equator, including the Caroline, Marshall, and Mariana Islands, except for the US territory of Guam. Australia took control of islands south of the equator, such as former German New Guinea and the Bismarck Archipelago. Western Sāmoa and Nauru were transferred to New Zealand and Britain, respectively.

The Japanese acquisition of islands in Micronesia reflected an extension of its expansionist policies already in effect in Asia.[6] Premised on the veiled belief in a Pan-Asian empire, Japan sought new territories in such areas as Korea and Manchuria, China. The Japanese aspired to promote what they euphemistically called *kaigai hatten* (overseas development) in an attempt to address Malthusian fears of overpopulation and poverty in Japan proper, and to resist Western colonialism in the Asian and Pacific regions. Japanese colonial authorities promoted the idea of liberation mainly because the rhetoric of Pan-Asian solidarity and national self-determination did not appeal in areas outside northeastern Asia, such as the Pacific Islands and Southeast Asia (Tarling 2001, 126). In Micronesia, the Nanyō-chō, or South Seas Government, likewise aspired to undermine, through the rubric of "liberation," Western forms of colonialism.

Coupled with aspirations to bring "modernity" and a particularly modern Japanese way of life to the Pacific, the Nanyō-chō promoted itself as a "liberator" of American, British, and German colonial rule in Micronesia (Ching 2001, 11). Under the provisions of the mandate, Japan established laws; monitored the traffic of arms, alcohol, and ammunition; and submitted annual reports to the League of Nations. These stipulations helped Japan to establish the Nanyō-chō and to govern the indigenous peoples of these islands and atolls. The Japanese language quickly became the lingua franca of Micronesia, supplanting through formal order the use of indigenous languages in official and administrative settings. Japanese entrepreneurial, trade, and scholarly interest in the region increased in scope and effort in comparison to earlier ventures in the late 1800s. The establishment of the mandate allowed these people and companies to pursue their interests with increased vigor.

The economic development of the region proved foremost on the agendas of both government-sponsored and privately owned economic enterprises. Their economic fervor led to the development of sugar plantations and processing plants in the Northern Mariana Islands, especially on Tinian and Saipan, and to the mining of phosphate in such islands as Peleliu, Palau.[7] As part of its obligations under the new mandate, Japan also built schools for the education of Pacific Islanders in Micronesia, and "saw education as a means to insure the obedient and loyal acquiescence of Micronesian peoples" (Peattie 1988, 92). It can be argued that later the American naval education in Guam served the same purpose, that is, to acquire the loyalty of the Chamorros. In addition to implementing education programs, the Nanyō-chō introduced the Shinto religion, provided opportunities for a few Pacific Islanders to visit Japan, and organized Pacific Islander youth into patriotic organizations (Peattie 1988, 104).

Historian Mark Peattie argued that these policies were not intended to "assimilate" *(doka)* indigenous peoples into Japanese society, as numerous theories of Japanization claimed.[8] Rather, their purpose was to ensure that the Japanese remained in important socioeconomic positions, reflecting the hierarchal nature of this settler society. As with loyalty and citizenship issues in US-occupied Guam, indigenous peoples throughout the Japanese empire were subjected to colonial policies and processes of "becoming Japanese and not having the rights of a Japanese citizen" (Ching 2001, 7). As Peattie remarked, Japan's notion of assimilation attempted to "remold them [islanders of Micronesia] into loyal, law-abiding subjects who could become almost, but not quite, Japanese" (1988, 104).

The concept of loyalty as perceived by Japanese colonial authorities thus functioned in the same manner as for the US administration in Guam: to shape the native to be like us, but not quite like us. Yet these concepts differed in application and in interpretation over time. What remains clear is that the Japanese notion of loyalty served to *differentiate* indigenous people from the shared cultural traditions of Asia, such as Confucianism, whereas the American notion of loyalty worked to *associate* indigenous peoples with either the noble savage or the ignoble savage (Narangoa and Cribb 2003, 17). The Japanese notion of loyalty represented the "'Confucian' . . . moral values of loyalty and filial piety [that] were resurrected [in the 1880s] to buttress the newly created emperor system and the modern military nation" (Ohnuki-Tierney 2002, 6). With regard to the indigenous people of the Pacific, "Micronesians, like their indigenous counterparts elsewhere in the empire, were second-class citizens in their own lands, and indeed were considered by the Japanese as considerably less worthy than Chinese and Koreans with whom the Japanese at least shared a common cultural heritage" (Peattie 1984b, 189). These contradictory processes of assimilation and exclusion, as illustrated in the Japanese notion of loyalty in the mandated islands of the Pacific, formed "a constant theme throughout the imperial era and were a major element in the dissatisfaction of colonized people with Japanese rule" (Narangoa and Cribb 2003, 11).

Despite the broad range of indigenous experiences under the Nanyō-chō, general statements can be made about Japan's relationship with the indigenous people of Micronesia. As preparation for war got under way in the late 1930s, for example, views on Micronesia shifted from seeing it as a region of economic possibility to seeing it as a region of military necessity. Natives contributed to Japan's economy and war effort as a "patriotic" and dependable labor force—a goal Japanese assimilation policies strove to attain in times of peace and to maintain in times of war.[9] Chamorros of the Northern Mariana Islands, like the neighboring Pacific Islanders of Micronesia, encountered these policies firsthand. Many experienced Japanese rule in the schools, in the fields, and in the everyday activities of that period.

At the level of interpersonal communication, Chamorros believed that the Japanese generally respected their customs, and, outside the school and the workplace, the Japanese rarely interfered with their daily routines. Chamorros attended Catholic mass and rituals without interruption. In the time before the war, they also continued to fulfill their familial obligations of providing food for the immediate and extended family, and tending to the elderly and sick. Tan Lucia Aldan Dueñas noted that "the living condition . . . was very good during the Japanese administration. The groceries were cheap. . . . The people were well off because there were lots of respect amongst the people. There was respect between the Japanese and Chamorros and everyone was in good terms" (L Dueñas 1994, 4). Tan Lucia suggested that mutual respect existed between Chamorros and Japanese.

Furthermore, the tolerance of intercultural marriages constituted, at the very least, an acknowledgement of the relatively peaceful coexistence of Chamorros and Japanese.[10] Friendships grew, and relations were maintained. Chamorros and Japanese, as well as Koreans and Okinawans, learned or were exposed to the intimacies of each other's culture through individual relationships rather "than through the more formalized aspects of political, economic, and educational organization" (Spoehr 2000, 57).

Although the Japanese allowed intermarriages to take place, and although they met the minimum requirements of the mandate in governing indigenous peoples, nothing detracted from the reality that their policies were racist in nature. Even though some Chamorro elders, like Tan Lucia, continue to remember the time before the war in nostalgic terms, eliding the realities of Japanese racism, Chamorro prewar memories are not all romantic. Some Chamorros recall the era in ways that appropriately reflect the official tone and temperament of the Nanyō-chō. For example, Tun Nicolas Q Muña, a Chamorro elder of Saipan, explained that "during the Japanese times there was discrimination" (1995, 3). Tun Ignacio M Sablan, another elder of Saipan, added that "the high positions in the government were held by Japanese" (1981, 52). These Chamorros testified to the reality that Chamorros were again losing their place in their own homeland.

Despite the racist nature of Japanese rule in the Northern Mariana Islands, some Chamorro leaders believed in complying with the Japanese to the point of requesting participation as Japanese nationals to defend Japan's eastern borders. Led by Jose Pangelinan and signed by 180 Chamorros, a petition presented to the Japanese government provides clear evidence of Chamorro interest in abiding by the norms of Japanese colonial rule. Dated 11 September 1938, part of the petition read:

> For twenty years we have been honored to be taken care of by Your Majesty. We have greatly enjoyed the civilization that you have brought to us, and have sought to improve ourselves. Herein, we wish to express our deepest gratitude, even though a full expression is impossible. . . . Great Emperor, we believe that we are ready to stand as Your Majesty's shield. We wish to be the protectors of our country's south sea line. We strongly wish to be Japanese nationals forever. Therefore, we humbly beseech your Majesty's permission, that we, the natives of the nan'yo (South Seas Islands) become soldiers of the Empire of Japan.[11]

In accordance with Japanese policy in its treatment of indigenous peoples in the mandated islands of Micronesia, however, Japan presumably responded negatively, as its government never granted Chamorros from the Northern Mariana Islands the status of nationals, let alone recognition as soldiers of Japan's empire. In spite of such loyal efforts, the Japanese government belittled Chamorro calls for representation in the military and national spheres of Japan.

Parallel to the US citizenship movement in Guam, the movement to attain recognition as Japanese nationals for Chamorros in the Northern Mariana Islands emerged during the time before the war. And, like the push for US citizenship in Guam, the efforts to acquire official designation as nationals and soldiers in the Northern Mariana Islands illustrated the web of colonial politics and indigenous strategies for cultural survival that have come to signify the nature of cross-cultural relations in the prewar Mariana Islands. Like the US Naval Government on Guam, the Nanyō-chō provided no positions of equal power for indigenous peoples in their colonial society. In this respect, Japan held no place for indigenous peoples in its wider endeavor to develop the region of Micronesia economically. One consequence was that Japan sponsored the importation of Asian immigrants, many of whom worked in Saipan's sugar industries.

In the early 1900s, Japanese, Korean, and Okinawan laborers and their families began to migrate to the Northern Mariana Islands. "Between 1916 and 1918 some 2,000 Korean and Okinawan farmers arrived to work in the first sugarcane fields. By 1925 there were 5,000 Japanese, Okinawans and Koreans in the [northern] Marianas. By 1930 it was well over 40,000" (Farrell 1991a, 323). In the late 1930s, a few years before the outbreak of the war, Chamorros and Refaluwasch numbered around 4,300, less than 10 percent of the total population in the Northern Mariana Islands. The Asian labor and settler population had displaced the indigenous people.

Some of the Asians came as skilled laborers for the sugar industry. Others came to support the military fortification of the islands (Denfeld 1984, 3–15). Many came under the auspices of the Japanese imperial government. On Saipan, Tatsu Sato, for example, recalled her childhood visit to "Karabera-yama," or Mt Kalabera, with her family of sugar pioneers. Once atop the hill, Sato reminisced that "father rammed the pole with the rising sun flag deep into the earth. The flag snapped wildly in the strong wind. I can still picture my father's smiling face as [he] turned to me and said proudly, 'We as Japanese marked our feet here'" (Sato 1985, 18). Sato's remarks represented the patriotic and nationalistic zeal of those times. As part of the Japanization process, a plethora of organizations, holidays, and events were launched to indoctrinate Pacific Islanders into becoming patriotic subjects of Japan (figure 2) (Joseph and Murray 1951, 344).

The Japanese created such events as a means to glorify their national "heroes" and histories, as well as to impose principles and beliefs of Japa-

FIGURE 2. Unidentified Refaluwasch celebrate the unveiling of the statue of Mat-
sue Haruji, founder of the Nanyō Kōhatsu Kaisha (South Seas Development Company). He was called the "Sugar King" for his work in revitalizing and expanding
the sugarcane industry in the Northern Marianas. Saipan, circa the 1930s. Still clip
taken from Nanyō Kōhatsu archival footage and reproduced courtesy of the Japan
National Film Center, Tokyo.

nese colonial society on the Pacific. Islanders throughout this region, especially the youth, began to identify closely and patriotically with their new
colonizers. While the youth constituted but one of the generations targeted
by assimilation policies and propaganda, Japanese officials clearly demonstrated a strong interest in changing the attitudes of the younger, presumably
easier influenced, generation. In Micronesia, "parades, uniforms, and ban-
ners, fused with imperial rhetoric and appeals to local pride, seem to have
won the loyalty and approval of hundreds of youngsters" (Peattie 1988, 108).

In the 1930s, photographs showed Chamorros, as well as Palauans,
Yapese, and other Pacific Islanders, frequenting Shinto shrines and appear-
ing to pray for the success of Japan's expansionist efforts throughout Asia
and the Pacific. Patriotic youth groups like the *seinendan* sprang up throughout the major islands of Micronesia (Peattie 1988, 106, 108). Japanese loyalty and patriotic activities infused almost every facet of daily life, from the
Northern Mariana Islands to the Marshalls, as Pacific Islanders "joined

Japanese in patriotic displays. People recall lining up behind Japanese leaders, facing Japan, listening to prayers, and singing songs dedicated to the
emperor" (Poyer, Falgout, and Carucci 2001, 30). These Japanese methods
of colonization did not differ greatly from those concurrently employed by
the Americans in Guam. The emphasis on indigenous loyalty ranked high
among the concerns of these colonial administrations in their governance
of Chamorros. By 1941, Pacific Islanders' "attitudes toward the Japanese
had been shaped by decades of colonial effort to socialize them as loyal
members of the empire" (Poyer, Falgout, and Carucci 2001, 27).

The Time before the War in Retrospect

Despite their differences in governance, the American and Japanese colonial governments were in agreement on one point. They separately con-
curred that the processes involving the colonization of Chamorros could
not be fully implemented without first securing and guaranteeing their loyalty to the nation in power. These two colonial governments interpreted
the notion of loyalty as a form of social control, perhaps even hegemony.
Farthest from their minds was the idea that loyalty designated total incorporation into the nation-state. Based on their racial notions of difference
and sameness, militarism and imperialism, the American and Japanese
colonial governments created the generic "loyal Chamorro subject" in
order to justify their establishment of colonial expansion and rule in the
Mariana Islands. Comparable to France's colonial construction of "black
Frenchmen" in the Pacific and elsewhere, the American and Japanese colonial governments fashioned the "loyal Chamorro subject" as an essentialist
ideal for Chamorros to aspire to in both Guam and the Northern Mariana
Islands (Ward, Connell, and Spencer 1988, 4). Moreover, this racist ideal
shaped the conditions, not for eventual Chamorro economic, political, and
social independence, but for continued subjugation under the structures of
American and Japanese colonial governance (Omi and Winant 1994, 71).

   In the first half of the twentieth century, Chamorros did not openly resist
colonial efforts to inculcate them as loyal subjects of Japan or the United
States. They also did not resist American and Japanese colonialisms by
way of rebellions, revolutions, and other acts of violent protest; no known
record exists of Chamorro attempts to overthrow American or Japanese
colonial rule (Mittelman and Chin 2005, 25). Instead they coped with their
everyday activities and responsibilities within the limits allowed or not prevented by American or Japanese colonizers. It can be argued, though, that
nascent forms of loyalty were taking shape in ways contrary to the intentions
of the American and Japanese colonial governments. Loyalty was indeed
an emergent concept, one of what Raymond Williams called "new meanings and values, new practices, new relationships and kinds of relation-

ships [that] are continually being created" (1977, 123). Initially a form of control, loyalty also became a mechanism for indigenous adaptation and survival, rather than being perceived as outright subjugation. Chamorro petitions for American or Japanese recognition demonstrated, at the very least, that some Chamorros saw loyalty as a means of achieving equality and, ideally, a shared sense of "nationality" with their respective colonial powers.

Political efforts by Chamorros in Guam and the Northern Mariana Islands illustrated the ambivalent nature of indigenous loyalties in the period before World War II. Calls for military or national integration evidenced a degree of colonial control, as much as a degree of indigenous adaptation and survival. But what these failed attempts for recognition ultimately demonstrated was that Chamorros, as a cultural unit of one language and shared customs, had now acquired conflicting notions of loyalty. The promotion of such ethnic divisions, both cross-cultural and intracultural, has surfaced as a common theme in colonial policies in the Pacific and elsewhere around the world (M Howard 1989, 45). Specifically, American and Japanese impositions of colonial loyalty further fragmented Chamorro interisland and intracultural relations, deepening divisions and rivalries rather than fostering unity in Chamorro cultural collectivity throughout the Mariana Islands.

Chamorros in the Northern Mariana Islands of Rota and Saipan usually developed favorable attitudes toward the Japanese, but knew very little about Americans and the United States. Conversely, many Guam Chamorros viewed Americans in more familiar terms, slowly adjusting their loyalties to the United States. Generally, Guam Chamorros interpreted the Japanese as a foreign people of no immediate significance.[12] At the same time, some Chamorros throughout the archipelago noted, with expressed dissatisfaction and resentment, the imperialist, militarist, and racist dimensions of both Japanese and American colonialism.

What these cross-cultural and intracultural relations reveal is that the politics of American and Japanese colonialisms never worked in a totalizing fashion, in the same way that indigenous agency never unequivocally yielded to or resisted colonialism. Instead, as Diaz underlined, it is necessary to understand Chamorro agency, in the present or in the past, through "discursive claims, that is, by virtue of Chamorro ways of speaking as well as unique Chamorro ways of doing things." These claims "work through the materiality of things and ideas that are non-Chamorro in origin," as in the case of American and Japanese notions of loyalty and liberation. "Where these claims are recalled, in conscious (and unconscious) ways, there is Chamorro culture in struggle" (Diaz 1994, 53). In the time before the war, Chamorros of every age and gender "struggled" to come to terms with their new American or Japanese colonizers.

Chamorro loyalties to Japan or the United States must be understood within the terms and contexts of both the colonized and the colonizer. The notion that these loyalties had strongly resonated among *all* Chamorros in Guam and in the Northern Mariana Islands also remains highly suspect (Underwood 1997, 7). Nor did the concept of liberation greatly impact Chamorro views of themselves and their colonizers; this concept, for one, never came to fruition in prewar Guam, and even Japan's rhetoric of liberation failed to take on meaningful dimensions among Chamorros in the Northern Mariana Islands. Scholars might learn something, instead, about the ambivalent, fluid, and still emergent state of colonial loyalty in the prewar Mariana Islands by listening to the words of a young Chamorro boy.

This unidentified, fourteen-year-old Chamorro boy lived on Saipan, presumably during the late 1930s, only a few years before the war. His words were put on paper by visiting American journalist Willard Price, who worked for the *National Geographic Magazine* compiling ethnographic depictions of island societies in Japanese Micronesia. When asked if he worshipped the pictures of the Japanese emperor adorning school walls, the young schoolboy responded, "Of course. They [the Japanese] put them up in the assembly room and we must worship" (Price 1944, 404). Speaking to the American journalist as an elder, the Chamorro boy quickly consented to his inquiry as if Price were his teacher, relative, or a colonial official. Perhaps the boy's extended family had raised him to respond to elders and authority figures with respect and humility. Perhaps the young boy agreed immediately, without question, to the curious inquiry of the American journalist.

But the young Chamorro boy had not finished speaking to someone he probably thought was a strange-looking white man. He continued, in a matter-of-fact way, "But I have a cross [crucifix] on a string around my neck. It's under my shirt and they [the Japanese] can't see it. I put my hand on it when I bow" (Price 1944, 404–405).

This young Chamorro boy's brief conversation with an American man, located in a Japanese colonial setting, illustrates the intricate web of colonialism and indigenous agency in the time before the war. In the years to come, the concepts of loyalty and liberation would assume greater meaning, force, and persuasion in narrating not only the histories of the prewar Mariana Islands, but also the very memories that are created by these histories.

Chapter 2
World War II in the Mariana Islands

By 1941, several decades of colonial rule had resulted in the development of separate, though ambivalent, spheres of Chamorro loyalties in the Mariana Islands. In the time before the war, Chamorro identifications with and against their colonial powers, particularly Japan and the United States, surfaced. Political movements for citizenship, educational instruction, commemorative activities and national holidays, village health and agricultural contests, and everyday interactions with the colonial governments provided venues for Chamorros to come to terms with the politics of American and Japanese colonialisms. Outside the efforts to acquire military or national recognition, Chamorros evidenced no collective, politically conscious desire to embrace or contest these colonialisms.

Throughout the archipelago, Chamorros showed little in terms of wanting to "belong" among the wider American and Japanese communities, but rather strove to survive under American and Japanese rule. Further, no mass movements for or against colonial policies and loyalties transpired; loyalty was, at best, an emergent, mutable concept of colonial control and indigenous adaptation. Liberation, too, was an idea forged by Japan and the United States, but without much success. Chamorros, quite simply, carried on with their everyday lives to the extent permitted by American and Japanese colonial policies.

The outbreak of World War II in the Mariana Islands, however, dramatically changed the politics of colonialism and indigenous agency, as the war intensified in scope what was already a heavily militarized setting. The war now required Chamorros to contemplate, if not openly accept or resist, their loyalty to their colonizers; during the war, one's loyalty or disloyalty often determined one's death or survival. Certainly, concepts of loyalty varied from place to place, changing subtly or radically over time (Waller and Linklater 2003, 6). But the war between Japan and the United States created the conditions to make visible and violent the divided loyalties among Chamorros of the Mariana Islands. Wars produce loyalties as much as loyalties manifest wars (Somerville 1981, 568). Modern nation-states draw "on the loyalty and active participation of all the people, civilian and military" in times of war (Fujitani 2001, 244). The Mariana Islands was no exception.

Japan and the United States hoped to foster loyalty and solidarity among the peoples of their respective countries. The purpose was to encourage peoples' contributions toward the development and maintenance of their respective wartime ideologies on the one hand, and military arsenal and technologies on the other. Japanese and US citizens enlisted as soldiers, worked in airplane factories, donated goods, or purchased war bonds. The fervor of American and Japanese loyalties reached its peak during this period. But what did such loyalties mean for those in the colonies and for those who were not considered citizens of these nation-states? How did the divided loyalties among Chamorros affect their perceptions of and social relations with themselves and their colonizers? In this chapter I address these questions by surveying the impact of World War II in the Mariana Islands and examining the influence of American and Japanese wartime colonial policies in reshaping notions of loyalty and liberation among the Chamorros in both Guam and the Northern Mariana Islands.

World War II in Guam

In the late 1930s, the US Naval Government of Guam began replacing the preexisting Spanish Capuchins with American Capuchins. The naval administration asserted that the Spanish priests helped to "perpetuate the Chamorro language in their sermons and writings," a philosophy that countered American efforts to institutionalize English as the primary language of Guam (Rogers 1995, 159). The Spanish endorsement of the Chamorro language challenged US naval authority. Eventually, the naval government decided that the Spaniards would no longer interfere, directly or indirectly, with their policies regarding the Chamorro people. By 1939, the Spaniards had relinquished control over Guam's diocese to a Capuchin order from Detroit, Michigan (Rogers 1995, 159).

Of all the Spanish priests, only two remained on the island—Bishop Miguel Angel de Olano y Urteaga and Father Jauregui Jesús de Begona. Father Román María de Vera, a priest revered by the Chamorros and a staunch supporter of the Chamorro language in church activities, was one of the last Spaniards to leave, in September 1941. Midway through Guam's rainy season, a group of Chamorro women followed Father Román to the Apra pier where a boat awaited his arrival. As the women wept, many recalled Father Román saying, "You are crying because I am leaving and you are wiping your tears with your handkerchiefs. But soon the day will come when not even your sheets will be enough to dry your tears!" (Forbes 2002).[1] Although Father Román spoke to a small group of women, his "words spread like wildfire, and proof of that is the fact that so many Chamorros have repeated this anecdote up to the present time, even though they were not actually present at the pier" (Forbes 2002). His brief gesture of farewell provoked caution and alertness among Chamorros who believed that war was imminent.

Those who heeded Father Román's prophecy noticed that there were "bad signs in heaven" (P Sanchez 1979, 9). According to local histories, animals became restless throughout the island, and the sunsets appeared redder than usual. Sanchez noted that "some predicted a big typhoon, or a tidal wave, or an earthquake, or all three. There was prediction of a famine. Some of those who remembered the dreadful influenza of 1918 saw another epidemic on the horizon. Because it was outside their experience, no one predicted war" (Sanchez 1979, 9). Neither Father Román's ominous warnings nor local predictions of disaster prepared Chamorros for the Japanese attack on Guam or for the years of Japanese military occupation.

Some may have taken the admonitions seriously, but the majority of Chamorros on Guam cared little about international politics, let alone a possible conflict between Japan and the United States. Except for the naval government and a few local leaders, Chamorros failed to recognize the increasingly severe degradation of relations between the United States and Japan. For its part, the naval government contributed greatly to local misunderstandings of US and Japanese political and economic relations, as it rarely fully informed Chamorros of the impending dangers. The "U.S. Navy had long abandoned any plans for defending Guam, and had concluded in 1938 to let the island fall to the Japanese in the event of an attack. Guam was simply too far away from American supply lines to be properly defended" (Ballendorf 1997, 221). On 17 October 1941, American military dependents of the naval government departed for Hawai'i on board the USS *Henderson,* leaving approximately 160 military personnel and local men of the Insular Force Guard to defend the island (Rogers 1995, 162).[2]

Not many Chamorros knew of the American evacuation or of the US government's view that the island was not defendable. Undisturbed by world politics, Chamorros attended to their farms and family matters and spoke little about war. If the topic ever arose, they assumed that the United States held superior military forces that not even Japan, a newcomer to the colonial powers of the world, could sway. For Chamorros "in the late 30's and early 40's the talk of war among the powers of the world was of no particular concern. They did not believe for even a moment that war would actually touch them. For one thing, they felt quite strongly that war with Japan would not last long—perhaps two weeks [but] not over a month" (Sanchez 1979, 4). Instead, numerous Chamorros were preparing for the approaching religious celebration in honor of Santa Marian Kamalen, the Virgin Mary, on 8 December 1941 (see Jorgensen 1984; D Tolentino 1999). People caught fish, gathered foodstuffs, and slaughtered pigs in preparation for this Catholic ritual.

The Japanese invasion of Guam, on the feast of Santa Marian Kamalen, coincided with the Japanese attack on Pearl Harbor (Pu'uloa), O'ahu, surprising the residents of both islands. As Japanese planes flew over Guam's villages of Hagåtña, Sumay, and Piti, strafing military and civilian buildings, Japanese soldiers landed on the island's southernmost and centrally located beaches. Chamorros hurriedly gathered family members and scattered to take shelter at their ranches and nearby family dwellings. As they tried to come to grips with the reality of war on Guam, they sought refuge in their spirituality. Praying to Yu'us (God), many recalled Father Román's "prophetic" words: He was right, as "war came . . . not even sheets were enough to dry their tears" (Forbes 2002).

During the early weeks of December 1941, Japan invaded Guam as a part of a larger effort to militarize the western Pacific region. Japanese army and navy combatants moved forcefully and swiftly, from Pearl Harbor to New Guinea. Reviewing the organization and efficiency of the Japanese military, Stewart Firth wrote, "The air strike against the United States fleet at Pearl Harbor on 7 December 1941 initiated a blitzkrieg against other targets in the Pacific and South-East Asia, all rapidly taken. . . . Japan's Greater East Asia Co-Prosperity Sphere, now vastly extended, encompassed not only most of South-East Asia but also the Gilbert Islands, the Solomons, Australian New Guinea and parts of Papua" (1997, 294, 296).

As in each of these island invasions, the Japanese assault on Guam, under the command of Major General Tomitara Horii, was conducted with machinelike precision and calculation. The Japanese assault battalions and naval forces, numbering over five thousand, quickly overcame the ill-equipped US military defenses of Hagåtña.[3] The Japanese Imperial Army wasted no time in establishing its presence and military superiority. The first few days of occupation witnessed the death of several Chamorros, some of whom had worked for the naval government as Insular Guards. Among those killed were Vicente Chargualaf, Teddy F Cruz, Angel Flores, Larry L Pangelinan, and Jose C Untalan. Approximately thirteen US servicemen and ten Japanese soldiers died as well. Others killed were innocent bystanders. Unfortunately, the exact number and identification of native and foreigner deaths remains unknown because of poor records for the invasion of Guam.

On 10 December 1941, only two days after the initial bombing of the island, US Naval Governor George J McMillin surrendered the island to the Japanese occupation forces. Thereafter, the Japanese renamed Guam "Omiya Jima" (Great Shrine Island); they renamed all of Guam's villages as well. "At this point, the Japanese capture of Guam was seen as a relatively small action within the context of the entire Pacific War. But, for those living on Guam at the time, it was a fierce and frightening engagement" (Ballendorf 1997, 231). That the Japanese violently invaded Guam, and that the Americans did nothing to counter the Japanese, largely explained why Chamorros increasingly became wary, even fearful of the Japanese. Unlike the Chamorros of the Northern Mariana Islands, who had been under Japanese colonial rule since 1914, and who had become accustomed to Japanese traditions and laws, the Chamorros of Guam were, in large part, ignorant of Japanese society.[4]

Based on their unfamiliarity with the Japanese, Chamorros in Guam could not anticipate what awaited them from the Japanese military. "We Chamorros," wrote Tun Ben Blaz, "simply did not know what to expect from our new masters" (1998, 88). Chamorros also shared no preconceived prejudices about the Japanese or Japan, other than that they were a weaker nation than the United States. Even when the Chamorros of Guam expressed their loyalty to America, they rarely demonized and dehumanized Japanese as did the racist propaganda of the US media and military. In other words, Chamorros lacked a political will and cultural vocabulary to portray Japanese along the lines of dominant American views of Japanese "Others," that is, as "inherently inferior men and women who had to be understood in terms of primitivism, childishness, and collective mental and emotional deficiency" (Dower 1986, 9). However, toward the end of the war in Guam, during the early months of 1944, Chamorros began to despise the Japanese military for the cruel treatment many of them experienced.

In acquiring Guam, the Japanese Imperial Army viewed the island as another country "liberated" from Western rule, reflecting the wider goals of the Greater East Asia Co-Prosperity Sphere. The Japanese military sought to achieve and maintain peace and order, acquire natural resources, and establish military self-sufficiency on the island (Higuchi 2001a, 19). To achieve these goals, they needed an obedient and industrious indigenous population, something ideally akin to the Japanized Chamorros of the Northern Mariana Islands and the Japanized Pacific Islanders of the Caroline and Marshall Islands. As a necessary first step, the Minseisho, the civilian affairs division of the Japanese Imperial Army's South Sea Detachment (Nankai Shitai), initiated a census of Chamorros and others living on the island. In March 1942, the Keibitai, a security force of the Imperial Navy, and the Minseibu, the Department of Civilian Affairs, replaced the Minseisho, whose administrative power was not restored until the return of the army in March 1944. For almost three years, until the US invasion of Guam in the summer of 1944, these three agencies, composed of Japanese civilians and army and navy personnel, attempted to Japanize the Chamorros of Guam.

In her assessment of the Japanese occupation, Japanese historian Wakako Higuchi noted that the Japanization policy "was intended to place Chamorros in the same group as the other races ruled by Japan. The purpose was to mobilise Chamorros as a labour and fighting force for carrying out national policies" (2001a, 34). Although the Japanese administration wanted to place Chamorros on "the level of Japanisation which the islanders in the Japanese mandate had achieved during 28 years of Japanese rule," the circumstances of war and the fact that Guam was a former US territory meant that Japanization was more about military occupation (Higuchi 2001a, 34).

It was not just a matter of "educating" them about things Japanese; for the Japanese military and its civilian benefactors, the main goal of Japanization was eradicating forty years of American symbols, values, and, ultimately, loyalty among the Chamorros.

The Japanese recognized that as long as the Chamorros identified with America, Guam could never be fully transformed into an effective Japanese military outpost as part of Japan's eastern defense perimeter. The Japanese military aimed "to eliminate all influences implanted by the American administration. . . . The political-social dynamics required that the Japanese language replace English, and the Japanese spirit and work ethic overturn American ideals of democracy and rationalism. Furthermore, Chamorros were required to share with the Japanese hostile feelings toward the Americans" (Higuchi 2001a, 34). Higuchi effectively suggested that the Japanization policies implemented by the various military and civilian Japanese agencies tried to change Chamorro attitudes, from ones sympathetic to the United States to ones favorable toward Japan. However, the implementation of these policies placed Chamorros in an ambiguous position, wherein the Japanese regarded them as both ward and foe.

Because of the Chamorro affiliation with America, the Japanese found it difficult to view Chamorros outside the parameters of the "enemy," even though the Japanese perceived them as "non-whites" and thus part of the Greater East-Asia Co-Prosperity Sphere. Consequently, the Japanese often treated Chamorros with suspicion, reflecting the militarist dimension of their overall assimilation program. For example, during the first year of occupation (1941), the Japanese administration issued passes or *lisiensan ga'lago* (dog tags) as a means of identifying Chamorros. With the assistance of Chamorro interpreters from Rota and Saipan (also called Rotanese and Saipanese, respectively), the Japanese immediately established police personnel throughout the island to survey the activities of Chamorros and to arrest anyone who challenged Japanese authority. Militant in their form of investigation, the Rotanese, Saipanese, and their Japanese supervising officers interrogated, punished, and executed some Chamorros for failing to yield to Japanese wartime rules and laws.

Allegations of being American spies or sympathizers abounded during the war, and because of them, Guam Chamorros suffered dearly and, in many ways, innocently. Some of the most severe examples occurred as a consequence of the search for the only unaccounted-for American sailor on island, a radio-man named George R Tweed.[5] Soldiers also raped indigenous women, though no written records or oral testimonies exist as to how many suffered these violent acts.[6] Similarly, Chamorro women, as well as Japanese, Korean, and Okinawan women, served as sexual slaves throughout the island. Japanese soldiers also demanded that Chamorro families provide them with vegetables and livestock.

More often than not, however, the Japanese tried to assimilate Chamorros in as "peaceful" a process as possible. While examples of physical violence and abuse occurred, especially during the early months of 1944 leading up to the US invasion, the Japanese civilian administration made every effort to incorporate the Chamorros into their segregated society. As in their past interactions with Pacific Islanders under the mandate, the Japanese sought the peaceful incorporation—a euphemism for wartime colonization—of Chamorros into the empire. In their view, the Japanese wanted Chamorros to "uplift" their "spirits" and to appreciate and respect Nihon Seishin (the Spirit of Japan). Kiyoshi Nakahashi, a former Japanese teacher in wartime Guam, claimed that Japanization policies did not exploit or oppress Chamorros, but instead worked to "'awaken the Chamorro mind's eye to some aspects of East-Asia and the Orient'" (Higuchi 2001a, 24). Education and instruction in the Japanese language especially typified the paternalistic character of Japanization policies.

Japanese language schools emerged all over the island "as the Japanese language was considered to be fundamentally important as the first step in Japanisation" (Higuchi 2001a, 24). Some Chamorros served as teachers and assisted the administration whenever they were called on. Yet competence in the Japanese language was just one aspect of Japanization, as the Japanese also focused on "school ceremonies which centered on Japan's Emperor, the nation state, history, and war events" (Higuchi 2001a, 24). To this extent, instruction in the Japanese language coincided with the observance of Japanese commemorations, which occurred during "national holidays, such as Kigensetsu (Anniversary of the Emperor Jinmu's Ascension), Tenchosetsu (Emperor's Birthday), and New Year's Day" (Higuchi 2001a, 24).

In their attempt to mold Chamorros into loyal subjects, Japanese officials promoted the knowledge of Japanese culture and history beyond the classroom. They lectured Chamorros in churches about the virtues of Japan, showed propaganda films about Japan's military conquests in Asia, and forced Chamorros to partake in their military celebrations. For example, the fall of Singapore to the Japanese Army on 15 February 1942 led to a celebration in Hagåtña attended by both Chamorros and Japanese. Chamorro "men, women and children were given Nihon flags. Then they were forced to march through the main streets of [Hagåtña] to celebrate the victory over the British Army. Every few hundred yards, at the urging of the gun-toting troops and Samurai-sword wielding officers, the marchers shouted 'banzai!' 'banzai!' 'banzai!'" (P Sanchez 1979, 67). Chamorro educator Tun Tony Palomo noted that "most elderly Chamorros who witnessed these events remembered . . . the inevitable float showing a young nisei boy wearing a Japanese military uniform and pointing a rifle at another boy dressed in American navy attire, with the nisei youngster stepping on an American flag" (1991, 139). Such celebrations of Japanese wartime successes provided one of the few times when Chamorros and Japanese assembled together. Despite the promotion of Japanese assimilationist policies, no systematic attempt to join the two groups was made. Efforts to integrate Chamorros into the Japanese public sphere were impeded by preexisting Japanese segregationist and racist attitudes toward the *tōmin,* or Pacific Islanders. Japan's nationalist rhetoric of "Asia for Asians" did not fully apply to Pacific Islanders, who were considered inferior subjects in Japan's socioeconomic and racial hierarchies.

In Guam, most interactions between Chamorros and Japanese occurred in official settings and on official terms set by the Minseibu. Any personal relationship that developed did so in secrecy. Overall, though, Chamorros kept to themselves in much the same way as the Japanese did. Social activities like the trading of goods and attendance at segregated games briefly brought them together. Even so, the Japanization policies disturbed many Chamorros, who saw them as strange, intrusive, and disrespectful. Forced to live under Japanese rule, Chamorros grudgingly accepted their subjugated roles. Whenever possible, they resisted the policies by simply refusing to obey them. When there was no choice, many Chamorros honored the policies, such as bowing to Japanese officials, just so they could move on with their daily lives and familial obligations. Chamorro parents also discouraged their daughters from developing relations with Japanese soldiers and sailors and, as a result, "there was no known marriage between Chamorros and Japanese during the occupation" (P Sanchez 1989, 225). From the level of individual interaction to that of the family, Chamorros distanced themselves from the Japanese and their policies whenever they could.

One of the most powerful and popular forms of resistance was musical expression, as Chamorros sang prewar American melodies whenever they were by themselves, especially during family gatherings. During the war, "Islanders composed a huge medley of songs to comment on remarkable experiences and transformations in their lives" (Lindstrom and White 1993, 192). In Guam, a commonly cited English song personified the United States as "Uncle Sam," an approachable symbol that Chamorros looked to for moral guidance. They saw Uncle Sam as a figure of "courage, thrift, simplicity, an ability to carry more than a fair share of the load, a capacity to labor and to make lightning decisions, and an optimism not to be floored" (Curti 1946, 142).[7] Sung to the melody of "Sierra Sue," some of the lyrics were:

> Early Monday morning
> The action came to Guam,
> Eighth of December,
> Nineteen forty-one.
>
> Oh, Mr Sam, Sam, my dear Uncle Sam
> Won't you please come back to Guam?

Our lives are in danger,
You better come.
And kill all the Japanese
Right here on Guam.

Oh, Mr Sam, Sam, my dear Uncle Sam
Won't you please come back to Guam?

We don't like the sake,
We like Canadian [whiskey],
We don't like the Japanese.
It's better American.

Oh, Mr Sam, Sam, my dear Uncle Sam
Won't you please come back to Guam?

So long with corned beef,
With bacon and ham,
So long with sandwiches,
With juices and jam.

Oh, Mr Sam, Sam, my dear Uncle Sam
Won't you please come back to Guam?[8]

Another equally well-circulated tune ridiculed the authority of Japanese teachers. Pedro C Sanchez recorded some of the lyrics, which were based on the tune of a Japanese patriotic war song. Originally sung in the Chamorro language, one of the translated English verses goes:

Teacher, teacher
what do you eat?
Soy sauce and soybean soup.
Seems that you like that very much.
No wonder you are ugly. (Sanchez 1979, 77)

The last line cut to the point.

Songs like these illustrated the creativity of a Chamorro resistance that often took the form of sarcasm. Music provided a discursive means for Chamorros to express their frustrations with the Japanese occupation, as well as their desire for the return of the United States. Outmatched by the Japanese military, Chamorros possessed no technical or military means to overthrow them. They instead resorted to these passive forms of resistance—what James C Scott called "everyday forms of peasant resistance"—such as song, prayer, and humor, whose overall content could be described as a kind of politicized spirituality (Scott 1985, xvi). With regard to the Malaysian context, Scott explained that peasant forms of resistance "require little or no coordination or planning; they make use of implicit understandings and informal networks . . . [and] they typically avoid any direct, symbolic confrontation with authority" (1985, xvi). In many ways, Scott's analysis of peasant resistance can be extended to everyday Chamorro forms of resistance under Japanese rule in Guam.

For example, Chamorros frequently drew on the supportive and reciprocal networks of the immediate and extended clans, strongly embracing, in song and story, their collective belief in the guidance of Yu'us and in the supremacy of America. They often repeated the phrase, "We are in God's hands. God knows better. Only God disposes" (P Sanchez 1979, 101). Reiterating this point, educator Jose Q Cruz stated that many Chamorros believe that "whatever has happened Yu'us will take care of it, Yu'us will take care of it in good time" (2002). Chamorros intricately intertwined these beliefs to the point where the distinctions between church and state became blurred, resulting in a spiritualism deeply couched in the Catholic faith and in the perceived political, military, and humanitarian power of the United States. For the Chamorros of Guam, principles espoused by the United States, such as democracy and freedom, provided a dramatic counterpoint to the oppressive Japanese administration.

Although Chamorros held a variety of views of the United States during the prewar era, the outbreak of World War II in Guam radically suppressed criticisms of the United States in general and the US Navy in particular. Perhaps in reaction to the implementation of the Japanization policies, Chamorros further embraced their loyalties to God and America. The Japanization policies "did not bear any fruit in Guam. One important, but unanticipated result . . . was the creation among the Chamorros of a stronger pro-American feeling and political identity" (Higuchi 2001a, 35). Further, the Japanese eventually recognized "the difficulty of replacing religion with a political ideology and the figure of Jesus with that of the Japanese Emperor" (Higuchi 2001a, 26). "One of the most difficult things for the Chamorros to accept was the edict that the Japanese Emperor was both the temporal and spiritual leader of the empire. This was contrary to their religious upbringing because at least 95 percent of the people of Guam were Christians, the great majority Catholics" (Palomo 1991, 139).

Flawed from the outset, the Japanese colonial project in Guam did not entirely succeed. Partly because of the intrusive, militarist, and violent nature of their assimilationist policies, the Japanese failed to fully transform Chamorro society. Chamorros contrasted the wartime Japanization policies with what they remembered of a "peaceful" prewar period of Americanization. They concluded that American rule was simply better than that of the Japanese. No matter how problematic and romanticized they appeared, these political and spiritual convictions gave Chamorros strength as they entered the most turbulent times of the Japanese occupation.

That period of tragedy and despair began in the spring of 1944. By then, the Japanese were conscripting Chamorro men "between the ages of 12 and 60 . . . to work on projects related to the Japanese defense of Guam" (Ballendorf 1997, 232). These young and elderly men, with the assistance of Korean and Okinawan laborers, helped to build roads and runways, coastal canon fortifications, ammunition storage shelters, and other military facilities. The Japanese administration also mandated that Chamorro women over the age of twelve participate in an aggressive campaign to produce agricultural goods and livestock for consumption by Japanese soldiers and sailors. As US military forces moved into Micronesia, capturing first the islands of the Gilberts and the Marshalls in March 1944, the Japanese Imperial Army hastily worked to fortify the Marianas "as part of Japan's inner perimeter of defense" (Ballendorf 1997, 232). That same month, the Japanese military "sent some of its best troops to Guam—seasoned combat veterans from Manchuria commanded by Lt. General Takashina" (Ballendorf 1997, 232).

Yet no amount of training and experience prepared these soldiers for the war in Guam. Some became restless and hungry (Rogers 1995, 176). They knew of the rapidly approaching US forces, who had already landed on nearby Saipan in June 1944, and of their earlier military victories in the Pacific. The Japanese believed in the overall might of their war empire, but they also realized that Guam was nowhere near sufficient as a military base. Some of these soldiers unleashed their anxieties and frustrations on the Chamorros, a people whose loyalties they understood as more American than Japanese.

Despite Chamorro contributions of labor, albeit forced, in the construction of military fortifications and in the production of food, numerous Japanese soldiers, as well as some of their Chamorro interpreters from the Northern Mariana Islands, abused, punished, and murdered Chamorros from Guam. "From Yigo in the north to Merizo in the south, scores of men, women and children met untimely death [at] the hands of the Japanese police and troops" (P Sanchez 1989, 222). Approximately five hundred Chamorros "met death through Japanese atrocities," which included the indiscriminate beating, bayoneting, and shooting of individuals in caves, shallow graves, and other jungle areas (P Sanchez 1989, 222). One survivor, Jose F Mendiola, pleaded, for example, "You have to be patient with me. You see my tears come out? This comes from the Japanese. They beat me, they clubbed me during the Japanese times" (*Pacific Daily News* 1990). The Japanese also executed Chamorros such as Father Jesus Baza Dueñas, a priest whom they accused of withholding information on the whereabouts of the US Navy sailor George Tweed. Indeed, Japanese military behavior "degenerated into a kind of destructive nihilism" (Rogers 1995, 181). Such erratic conduct increased as the Americans approached Guam. The Japanese forced most of the Chamorros into concentration camps in the villages of Yo'ña, Malesso', and Malojloj. Instances of humane and generous behavior on the part of the Japanese were few and far between.

The way of war held no place for compassion and sympathy in Guam, as several Japanese massacres of Chamorros in the villages of Hågat, Malesso', and Yigo attested (Rogers 1995, 180). However, survivor Joaquin Cruz recalled a rare incident in which an unknown Japanese soldier befriended his family in the Manenggon concentration camp in Yo'ña. The soldier provided them with desperately needed food items, such as rice and candy. In return, Cruz told the soldier how to make coconut oil, a versatile oil used as medicine and food (Oyen 1990). That friendship lasted briefly, risking the lives of the soldier and the Cruz family. In another instance, survivor Maria Cruz talked about an unidentified Japanese male who helped her family to avoid harm during the US invasion. "When morning came," she recalled, "this one Japanese told us to go to a different place than the others. He wrote a note and gave it to us and said, 'if you meet a Japanese soldier give him this note because you people are good'" (Ray 1994a, 41, 60). Cruz did not indicate where the "others" went, recording only her indebtedness to the Japanese soldier for protecting her family.

Among the two Cruz families, no one knew what happened to these considerate soldiers, as bombs from above quickly forced many into hiding. From early June to mid July, the US Navy bombarded the island, focusing on Japanese coastline defenses and on the city of Hagåtña. During the war, many Chamorros interpreted the dropping of bombs as *bindision Yu'us*, or "God's blessing." For example, Tun Antonio "Min" C Babauta, who was a young child during the war, recalled that his "mother and grandmother used to pray to the Blessed Virgin Mary to spread her cape, saying *'Baba nai i copamu yan protehi ham,'* or 'open your cape and protect us.' I didn't know what it meant at that time. . . . Now I know more about what they're praying for" (Babauta 2002). God's blessing thus signaled the return of the Americans and the hoped-for end of Japanese rule.

The bombing finally ceased with the US invasion of Guam, code-named "Operation Stevedore," on 21 July 1944.[9] After days and nights of armed conflict, the US military declared Guam secure on 10 August 1944. About sixteen thousand Japanese, Korean, and Okinawan soldiers and laborers, as well as nearly two thousand US infantrymen, lost their lives in an island far from their homes and families (Rogers 1995, 194). The Chamorros of Guam, on the other hand, surfaced from the debris of almost three years of war under Japan's rule. For them, the war began with the Japanese invasion on 8 December 1941 and continued under the Japanese military and civil administrations, ending with the US military victory in the summer of 1944. Treated as both enemy and subject by the Japanese soldiers and administrators, the Chamorros of Guam never received or sought recognition as loyal minorities of Japan. Instead they directed their spiritual and political allegiances to the United States and judged the Japanese as enemies.

However, their relatives to the north, especially in the islands of Rota and Saipan, held different and generally favorable attitudes toward the Japanese that "had been shaped by decades of colonial effort to socialize them as loyal members of the [Japanese] empire" (Poyer, Falgout, and Carucci 2001, 27).[10] For those in the Northern Mariana Islands, World War II also began on 8 December 1941, when the Japanese "instituted martial law in the Marianas, giving the military full authority over the islands and their people" (Farrell 1991a, 329). While the Japanese military were implementing policies to fortify the entire Mariana Islands, Chamorros of the northern islands prepared for war. They readied themselves for encounters with what they had come to know as "evil" and "violent" white men.

World War II in the Northern Marianas

From 1941 to 1943, the Japanese government militarized Chamorros of the Northern Mariana Islands in ways different from the intimidation and harm experienced by their relatives in Guam.[11] Chamorros, as well as Refaluwasch, Koreans, and others, built military fortifications and runways, learned basic military skills, and participated in fire drills. They worked together with the Japanese government and military, reflecting a stronger level of acceptance and cooperation than the Chamorros of Guam. Tan Consolacion C Guerrero remarked that "when the invasion of Saipan was about to happen, the natives were taught. They were gathered up, Chamorros and Carolinians. They were taught about what to expect from the war. . . . We were made to carry the bucket so that once the war ensued, we will scoop the water and spray it to control the fire. All of those were taught by the Japanese before the war" (Guerrero 1994, 5). Although the Japanese seldom conscripted Chamorros as soldiers, they required them to aid in military operations. For example, Tun Vicente T Camacho learned semaphore signaling, or *hōkukutai,* for the National Service Corps. He noted that "every morning in the *hokukutai,* it was exercises and drills; every morning [Sergeant Nakano] trained us in the things that Japanese soldiers did. . . . We learned how to shoot rifles, how to dive into air-raid shelters, all the things that regular soldiers did. Even how to dig air-raid shelters, how to make them—everything" (V Camacho 1992, 23). Between twenty and thirty Chamorros worked as police assistants in Saipan and Guam. Chamorros, especially male laborers and interpreters, participated in these military-sponsored activities as they prepared for impending war.[12] Pacific Islanders throughout Micronesia contributed to Japan's war efforts in the Pacific. They "served the Japanese military directly as lookouts and quasi-military servicemen of various sorts; as loyalists who passed information and enforced local security rules; or rarely and most dramatically as recruited members of the military services" (Poyer, Falgout, and Carucci 2001, 159). With military activity on the rise, the Japanese called on Pacific Islanders across the region of Micronesia to show their loyalty to Japan by working in these capacities.

Public opinion about the war naturally sharpened with the involvement of so many Pacific Islanders in the construction of military fortifications and projects throughout Micronesia. Chamorros of the Northern Mariana Islands saw Japan as the eventual victor of the war in the Pacific. They asserted that the Japanese "were unbeatable, especially with the events of the early part of the war and with Guam being lost and . . . the fact that the United States was thrown out without much of a fight and all of the early victories" (Russell 2002). The few Chamorros who questioned the exact meanings and motives of the war remained silent or discreet, fearing Japanese punishment. Even the mere mention of *beikoku* (America) served as grounds for Japanese disciplinary measures. Tun Vicente Atalig Inos, a Chamorro elder from Rota, observed, "We never said anything about the Americans during the war because . . . I don't know their customs. . . . But you never would say these words in front of the Japanese because if they heard you saying that, they would hit you or kill you because they don't want local people to talk about [Americans]" (1981, 64).

Although many Chamorros knew that they could not talk openly about Americans, they continued to wonder about their attitudes toward Chamorros. In part, Chamorro interest in Americans stemmed from Japanese descriptions of "America" as one of the Western countries opposing Japan's "liberation" campaigns in Asia and the Pacific. Based on accounts of relatives in Guam married to Americans, several Chamorro families thought that Americans were decent people. However, the majority of Northern Mariana Islands Chamorros accepted Japanese characterizations of the Americans as "imperialist murderers." For example, Tun Ignacio M Sablan reflected that the Americans "were a bunch of killers . . . . That's what the Japanese told us" (1981, 56). Throughout the war, the belief in Americans as "killers" endured in the Northern Mariana Islands, in contrast to that of Americans as "saviors" in Guam. Chamorro loyalties to Japan undoubtedly prospered, but the question of their continuity loomed on the horizon.

Beginning in February 1944, several Japanese military units arrived in Saipan, including the 29th Infantry Division, the 9th Tank Regiment, and the 43rd Infantry Division. Most of these divisions came from Manchuria. Many of these soldiers entered Saipan ignorant of the relationships that had developed over the years between Chamorros and Japanese. Tun Vicente T Camacho, himself an aid to the Japanese military and police, noticed that the Japanese soldiers "weren't friends anymore. So many soldiers came to Saipan; they came in droves" (1992, 25). The stress of war affected these soldiers, making it difficult for them to perform their military assignments, let alone interact with indigenous peoples. The success of US and Allied naval attacks on Japanese shipping undermined the confidence of these soldiers, and many of them displaced their increasing anxiety on the Chamorro communities (Peattie 1988, 297).

Throughout the Northern Mariana Islands and other battle sites of the western Pacific, Japanese soldiers caused some of "the most profound dislocations in the patterns of civilian life" (Peattie 1988, 297). The arrival of the Japanese army divisions—the final warning that war with the United States was imminent—marked a key turning point in Chamorro relations with the Japanese. Historian Scott Russell stated in an interview (2002), "When the military came in things changed. The military was pretty brutal. People didn't like them. People tried to avoid them. . . . And a lot of the disillusionment that came with the Japanese came with the Japanese military in that period. The Japanese military did not care about the people. . . . They had a mission and the mission was to hold the homeland."

That these particular Japanese soldiers cared little about Chamorros immediately affected indigenous understandings of the Japanese. As Tan Escolastica Tudela Cabrera observed, "When the fighting started the Japanese became mean" (Petty 2002, 27). Tan Lucia Aldan Dueñas recollected, "The new soldiers who came . . . were very strict with the people of the islands. They slapped people who did not help and whenever they passed by you had to stand up and salute them regardless of their appearance. You had to salute them" (L Dueñas 1994, 6). In the spring of 1944, therefore, the violent attitudes of the newly arrived Japanese soldiers, some of whom were veterans of battles in Nanjing and Shanghai, further undermined the relationships between Chamorros and Japanese.

Not able to attend Mass and displaced from their homes in Garapan, Saipan, now occupied by the soldiers, Chamorro families, laborers, and civilians rushed to the caves in the mountains and valleys for protection from the war (Farrell 1991a, 328). To the south, in Rota and Tinian, the Japanese military instructed civilians to seek shelter as well. In mid-eastern Rota, many Chamorros stayed in the village of Tatachok under orders from the Japanese military. Others feverishly worked to complete fortifications, scores of which failed to meet the standards of the military since "panic and exhaustion ruled the way things were constructed" (Peck 1983, 6).

Panic and a general sense of chaos characterized the atmosphere of the southernmost islands of the chain, as soldiers prepared their military defense strategies and as Chamorros scrambled for protection. With most of the army stationed in Saipan, the Chamorros there experienced the force and pressure of the soldiers' demands. Although the Japanese did not erect internment camps for the Saipanese, as they did in Guam, they required Chamorros to dig holes near their homes. The Japanese military never stated its exact intention for these holes, but many Chamorros suspected that they would be buried in them. Tan Lucia Aldan Dueñas remarked, "What scared the Chamorros here on Saipan was at every house the Japanese dug big holes for everyone to hide. Then my father was suspicious of what was happening" (1994, 6). Chamorro fears about these holes and of the possibility that they might be executed by the Japanese reflected suspicions held by other Pacific Islanders in Micronesia.

These Pacific Islanders also "suspected that the Japanese planned to exterminate them—perhaps to alleviate the critical food shortage, in retaliation for disloyalty, to cheat the enemy of his prize, or as a final attempt to achieve honor in a lost war" (Poyer, Falgout, and Carucci 2001, 10). Fortunately, no mass exterminations occurred in the Northern Mariana Islands. "There [weren't] the atrocities that you had in Guam" (Russell 2002). Having grown accustomed to dealing with the Japanese over more than three decades of colonial rule, northern Chamorros cooperated willingly with the Japanese military. Such cooperation may have tempered some of the anxieties and prejudices of the soldiers and helped to ease the wartime tension between Japanese and Chamorros.

Even with the American bombing of Saipan in early June 1944, culminating with the US invasion of the island code-named "Forager," Chamorros in the Northern Mariana Islands assisted, however unwillingly, the Japanese military in its needs. In doing so, Chamorros risked their own lives and those of their families. As the Japanese soldiers fought the invading US forces through different valleys and terrain, they often sought food and shelter in caves where Chamorros and civilians were hiding. There, the soldiers took pleasure in helping themselves to food, water, and rest. Many families resented such disrespectful behavior, as it reflected shameful acts, what Chamorros call *taimamalao*. All Chamorro families could do was watch as the coming and going of the soldiers depleted their supplies. Chamorros also guided the Japanese soldiers around the villages and through the jungles and, in some instances, fought alongside them. Many prayed to Yu'us and their favorite saints to stop the war. Overhead, the bombs fell incessantly on Chamorros, Japanese, Koreans, Okinawans, and Refaluwasch alike, but they were definitely not seen as a sign of God's blessing, as in Guam. Chamorros in the Northern Marianas may instead have interpreted the bombs as signs of God's wrath, or even as evidence of the "evil Americans." The arrival of US forces in the Northern Mariana Islands brought violence and destruction. As the bombs rained on them, Chamorros feared the Americans and, increasingly, the Japanese.

With the war at its height in Saipan, Chamorros tried to protect themselves from the fighting. "Immediately after the [American] invasion, I was with my family. We were wandering around not sure of what was happening. I was most concerned about the safety of my family, most of whom were not with us. The invasion itself did not bother me too much because I was on the Japanese side and I was sure the Japanese would win against the Americans. [But] as the invasion continued, and as the bombs were dropped, I became worried about my family, about their safety, and about the island itself. Everything was being damaged, and it looked like the Japanese might not win. Everybody was out of the village, at the farm, hiding from both the Japanese and the Americans as the war progressed" (Taitano 1981, 10). Chamorros "thought that both sides were our enemies. That was the worst time of all. If we turned to the left there were enemies, if we turned to the right, there were enemies. No matter where we turned, up, down, east, west, it was enemies everywhere" (V Camacho 1992, 29). Indeed, everywhere in the Northern Mariana Islands, Chamorros began to question the strength of the Japanese empire and, in turn, their loyalties to that empire.

On Rota, Tun Lewis Mangloña excitedly recalled a battle between Japanese and American aircraft. "Now I'm not sure why my friend and I were for the American plane for we had been told that the Americans' sole purpose in coming to Rota was to cut off our ears and tongues, but it was the American plane we were cheering for." Amazed at the skill of the American pilot, he continued, "Suddenly [the American airplane] seemed to have been hit for it rolled over in the air and started to fall. But it was only a stunt, for as soon as the Japanese plane turned its tail it recovered, came at the Japanese plane and shot it down. . . . We almost went crazy laughing and clapping and shouting until a Japanese soldier heard us and came running at us with his sword raised. That settled us and we bowed to him and tried to look as if we had been crying" (Peck 1983, 6). Tun Lewis's "tears" demonstrated the ambiguous nature of Northern Mariana Islands Chamorro loyalties to Japan toward the end of the war.

The power and cohesiveness of Japanese loyalty slowly deteriorated among Chamorros, who wondered if Japan would even win the war. In addition, Japanese military acts of disrespect and violence disturbed and offended many Chamorros. Unwittingly, Japanese soldiers created the conditions for Chamorros to think more critically about their colonial status as indigenous subjects of the Japanese empire. Although Chamorros supported Japan's war effort on the surface, they began to question to what extent their loyalties guaranteed their safety and survival. Some of them continued to aid the Japanese military during the war, at times hesitantly and at other times willingly. But the majority protected their own families in the confines of caves and underground dwellings. There, they thought deeply about their lives and the outcome of the war in the Northern Mariana Islands. Uncertain about their future, they pondered the increasingly fragmentary nature of their loyalties to Japan.

Various Asian populations in Rota, Saipan, and Tinian shared concerns similar to those of the Chamorros. Japanese, Korean, and Okinawan civilians hid in natural and artificial shelters. They, too, feared the war and its outcome, not knowing their future under either the Japanese or the US militaries. Apprehensive about that future, they sometimes contemplated surrendering to two kinds of "death." One required that Japanese subjects pay tribute and honor to Japan in the form of *gyokusai,* an "honorable death" (*Shogakukan Progressive Japanese-English Dictionary* 1986, 453). "The idea of gyokusai was to force a Japanese soldier to destroy his most precious possession—his own life" (Y Tanaka 1996, 195). This was the patriotic way to die. The other form of death, the dishonorable one, came from contact with the relatively unknown American enemy. As a result of Japanese wartime propaganda, some Asian civilians believed that encounters with Americans would lead to torture and, finally, execution. Despite the severity of these fears and stresses, only a small number of Japanese, Koreans, and Okinawans, civilians and soldiers alike, chose *gyokusai*.

Small numbers of people jumped from cliffs and ridges located on the northern coasts of Saipan and Tinian during the humid month of July. Facing north to Japan, with the salty wind in their faces, these civilians and soldiers died in the direction of their "motherland." US military forces and the media often misconstrued these deaths as "mass suicide,"[13] while effectively noting the patriotic and nationalist zeal behind them. Recounting a dramatic encounter with *gyokusai* on Saipan, Lieutenant Robert B Sheeks observed, "Some civilians and troops crowded at the end of the island, swam out to the high outer edge of the submerged reef, and most drowned themselves when our boats or amphibian tractors approached in an effort to rescue them." Others "banded together at the top of cliffs, sang patriotic songs, and leaped into the sea" (1945, 112).

The losses associated with *gyokusai* constituted only a fragment of the total number of deaths in the Northern Mariana Islands. Many more people, especially the elderly and the young, died either from starvation or from the violence inflicted on them by the US and Japanese armed forces. Those who survived chose to trust the words of enlisted nisei, or Japanese soldiers in the US Army, as well as some of their kin who had already passed over into American lines. Working as interpreters, the nisei traveled through stretches of jungle, cliffs, and caves where many civilians took cover during the war. Speaking through megaphones, they offered food, water, and medical treatment for civilians and promised them safe refuge. The presence of relatively healthy civilians and captured prisoners of war during these excursions encouraged others to surrender, easing further suffering and death.

Memory and Meaning in World War II

The capitulation of civilians to the US forces continued long after the Americans declared the Mariana Islands secure on 10 August 1944, though most had turned themselves over by the end of that summer.[14] Not until the end of the war, a year later in September 1945, did the Japanese give up Rota, an island the Americans had earlier declared nonthreatening because of its lack of sufficient military resources.[15] Once the campaign to secure the Mariana Islands had ended successfully, the United States used the islands as bases for aircraft bombers and as refueling stations for submarines (Farrell 1991a, 371). "Guam, along with the Mariana Islands of Saipan and Tinian, became huge airbases from which daily bombing attacks were launched against Japan" (Ballendorf 1997, 235). These assaults included the US atomic bombings of Hiroshima on 6 August 1945 and Nagasaki on 9 August 1945.

Following Japan's surrender on 15 August 1945, the United States "set out upon an imperial course to guarantee its future security in the Pacific and East Asia by taking direct control over the Pacific Islands from Japan" (Friedman 1995, 339). In 1947, through the United Nations, the United States established a strategic trusteeship that enabled them to govern not only the Marianas, but all of the formerly Japanese-held islands in Micronesia. This trusteeship allowed "the United States to deny the area to foreign powers and guarantee that Pearl Harbor–style attacks were never again inflicted on the United States" (Friedman 1995, 341). While US policy makers in distant capitals negotiated for the colonial acquisition of Micronesia, Pacific Islanders at home struggled to recover from the ravages of the war.

The major atolls and islands in Micronesia had witnessed some form of military activity or warfare. Melanesian Islands, such as Papua New Guinea and the Solomons, had also borne the brunt of numerous air raids and land invasions. It made perfect sense, then, that survival temporarily superseded all other priorities. Pacific Islanders contacted relatives, hastily built shelters, and salvaged food, working feverishly to rebuild their lives. Even though the war was declared over in 1945, "the meaning and the memory of the war would never end" for these people or for other survivors and veterans (Poyer 1991, 86).

In the Mariana Islands, memories of the war are complicated by the histories that preceded it. Histories of nearly half a century of American and Japanese rule greatly inform how Chamorros came to remember and understand the war. "From one island group to another the local meanings of the war frequently depended upon the prior history of colonial experience" (White 1991, viii). The political language of loyalty infused the everyday lives of Chamorros and became the main medium of communication between them and their colonizers. "For colonial powers, relations with 'native' peoples during the war were often framed in terms of 'loyalty' . . . Islanders whose relations with colonial 'masters' were ambivalent at best prior to the war often did not regard the conflict as *their* war" (White 1991, vii).[16] This assertion generally ran true for most Pacific Islanders, such as those in Papua New Guinea and the Solomon Islands (Nelson 1980, 255).

However, the Chamorros of the Mariana Islands are an exception. To some degree, they increasingly knew about the cultural, ideological, and political stakes involved in suppressing or revealing their loyalties; the war became their war, though in ways not entirely of their own making. For example, by patriotically supporting Americans during the war, Guam Chamorros resisted Japanization. They invariably looked to the figure of Uncle Sam, whose principles of freedom and liberty fused nicely with indigenous understandings of spiritual providence and cultural perseverance. They suffered dearly for their loyalty, as numerous innocent Guam Chamorros died at the hands of Japanese soldiers.

In similar fashion, Chamorros in the Northern Mariana Islands took strength from Yu'us, as they, too, wanted the war to cease. But in Guam, in effect, the Chamorros from Rota and Saipan represented symbols of Japanese militarism—as interpreters, soldiers, and workers for Japan's empire— a collective image of Japanese militarism and "collaboration" contested by the Chamorros of Guam. Thus, while Chamorro loyalty to Japan meant betrayal and distrust in Guam, it simultaneously meant loyalty and, ultimately, survival in the Northern Mariana Islands. As the war came to a close, however, the increasingly militant behavior of Japanese soldiers caused Chamorros in Rota and Saipan to lessen their loyalties to Japan, a change in social behavior that occurred elsewhere in Japan's wartime empire (Poyer, Falgout, and Carucci 2001, 223).

In all respects, then, the war deepened the intracultural divisions among Chamorros, especially in the contexts of colonial loyalties in the Mariana archipelago. As one American correspondent observed in 1946, "To speak of Saipan and Guam—which are about 100 miles apart—is almost to speak of black and white. The atmosphere, scenery and morale on the two islands is that much in contrast" (*Christian Science Monitor* 1946, 139). Unlike the Spanish-American War in 1898 and World War I in 1914, World War II affected Chamorros in ways that left wounds of profound magnitude. How would the postwar period of American reconstruction and rehabilitation address these issues of war, colonialism, and agency? If the outbreak of the war generated the conditions to make visible and violent colonial loyalties, how would the war's "end" shape their meanings in the future? The attempt to assess these questions involves another historical period fraught with the politics of US militarization in particular and the rise of the Cold War in general.

Chapter 3
The War's Aftermath

The years immediately following World War II have been referred to, inter-changeably, as periods of "reconstruction" and "rehabilitation" (Gaddis 1972, 96). These terms have been used to describe the dismantling of the military industries of Germany and Japan, respectively, and of the Allied rebuilding of local and regional economies affected by the war (McCormick 1991, 27). In the Pacific theater, the dropping of the atomic bombs on Hiroshima and Nagasaki by the United States on 6 and 9 August 1945 killed thousands in those cities, compelling Japan to surrender a few days later, on 15 August. The bombings instigated a new sort of war (Hein and Selden 1997, 4). More than a militarist act of profound violence, America's use of the atomic bomb on Japan demonstrated to the world, and particularly to the Soviet Union, America's capacity to exert its newly acquired economic and military power on a global scale (Henriksen 1997, 15).[1]

As an ideological war between American democracy and Soviet communism, the early stages of the Cold War greatly shaped the policies and politics of Allied rehabilitation efforts in Asia, Europe, and the Pacific Islands (Gaddis 1972, 361).[2] Of particular relevance is US President Harry Truman's "Truman Doctrine," outlined in 1947, which required the United States and its allies to "contain" communism by spreading democracy. In US-occupied Japan, from August 1945 to April 1952, the campaign to demilitarize and democratize Japan and its people took on, ironically, the militarist dimensions of the Cold War (Dower 1999, 23). Comparable to the Allied rehabilitation of Germany, the American rehabilitation of Japan served to deter Soviet communism and to revive an East Asian regional economy that granted the United States access to its resources (Cummings 1993, 38).

Just how, though, did the different peoples of these war-torn countries respond to and interact with the Allies and their attempts to "rehabilitate" them and their physical surroundings? More broadly, how did the Cold War affect these so-called rehabilitation policies? How did the Allies, the "victors," and the "defeated" portray themselves? And, if the concepts of loyalty and liberation applied to wartime contexts, did they likewise apply to the war's aftermath? For some people in Europe, liberation "meant welcoming Allied soldiers while for others the Nazi occupation was replaced by another occupation by the Soviets" (Duchen and Bandhauer-Schöffmann 2000, 1). Elsewhere, in Japan and Okinawa, the United States presented itself as a "liberator" of regions once under Japanese wartime fanaticism and militarism (Fujitani, White, and Yoneyama 2001, 12). In Micronesia as well, the American rehabilitation campaign invoked the rhetoric of liberation. Moreover, the arrival of US military forces in 1944 provided indigenous peoples and even Asian settlers with opportunities to compare and contrast the Americans with the Japanese, in terms of both wartime militaries and peacetime societies.

In this chapter I explore the impact of the American rehabilitation project on the Chamorros of the Mariana Islands, with a particular emphasis on Chamorro views of and responses to American notions of loyalty and liberation. I suggest that Chamorros, like their neighbors elsewhere in Micronesia, used the postwar period as another time to assess their relations with the Americans and the Japanese. From this perspective, the American rehabilitation project did not merely generate tremendous changes in the physical, economic, and political landscape of the Mariana Islands. It also greatly shaped Chamorro memories of the war period and of the colonial histories that preceded it. These two periods—the war and the postwar rehabilitation era—would later serve as key historical markers for the commemoration of World War II in the Mariana Islands.

Liberation Sought, Liberation Received?

Shortly after the Japanese military assault on Guam on 8 December 1941, rumors about the return of the Americans circulated among the Chamorro population. "Like their fellow Americans on the Mainland, the people of Guam believed that war with Japan would not last over a month or two. This strong belief in the immediate recapture of the island provided hope to the islanders from the day the war broke out" (P Sanchez 1979, 99). Chamorros imagined that the American return invasion would occur on a national holiday. They knew that American commemorations played a large role in the naval administration of the island. Commemorations, as the navy had sometimes proclaimed in the prewar era, signified important days of remembrance and reflection in America. Agricultural fairs, parades, and US national holidays instilled such values as cooperation and loyalty among Chamorros. In a world suddenly challenged by the foreign presence of the Japanese, it made perfect sense that Chamorros drew inspiration from the then widely held belief that Americans would reappear on a day of significance—that is, on a day of commemoration.

The earliest rumor indicated that the US military planned to attack Guam on 25 December 1941 as a "Christmas gift" to the Chamorros (P Sanchez 1979, 99). That rumor proved false. Further, Japanese officials, assisted by Chamorro interpreters from Rota and Saipan, punished anyone accused of spreading such rumors as part of an overall attempt to eradicate

Chamorro loyalties to the United States. However, the threat of punishment and the erroneous nature of previous rumors did not prevent Chamorros from speculating about the return of the Americans. During the first year of the Japanese occupation, 1941, these rumors flourished, again focusing on national holidays as possible dates for an American military invasion. As Tun Rafael J M Reyes stated, "I thought of the upcoming 4th of July . . . when perhaps the American troops would liberate us. They were long overdue, I told myself, as we marked each national holiday since the Japanese invasion as the day the Americans would free us" (1991, 10). Teresita Perez reiterated these sentiments; throughout the war period, she said, "never have we doubted the return of the Americans to us but at desperate moments we wondered just how long it would take them to cross the vast ocean that lay between our liberation and the place of our suffering."[3] Japanization policies placed a heavy toll on the indigenous population's moral, spiritual, and political loyalties to America. As the years under Japanese rule progressed, the prospect of American liberation seemed to grow more bleak.

Although Chamorros on Guam generally refused to accept their subjugation to Japan, the delay in the US military's return to the island with each passing holiday disheartened them. When the Americans did not appear on New Year's Day in 1942, "rumor had it that the [US Navy] fleet was detained elsewhere in a battle with the Japanese Navy" (P Sanchez 1979, 99). As each rumor of another American return proved untrue, Chamorros moved the date of their presumed liberation from one holiday to the next. Eventually, "the rumor mill stopped [because] its credibility suffered from so many liberation rumors which went sour" (P Sanchez 1979, 99). By the time the US military did return, in the summer of 1944, the "rumor mill" of American liberation was exhausted. Nearly three years of false rumors had tested Chamorros' optimism. The sight of American planes overhead and navy ships outside the island's reefs steadily increased Chamorro morale. But they still waited for concrete evidence of a US land invasion. As Marian Johnston exclaimed, "Sometimes [Chamorro scout patrols] would return and tell us Americans had landed, but we had heard that so often in the past two years that we didn't believe it. . . . We finally were convinced when some of the boys came back to camp with Lucky Strike and Chesterfield cigarettes. We knew then that [the US landings] were true" (McManus 1944, 11). Excited by the reality of US land invasions, Chamorros again spread stories throughout the island that the Americans had finally arrived.

As the US armed forces swept across the island, they came across a fatigued, malnourished, and emotionally distressed people. US Marine correspondent Alvin M Josephy Jr wrote, "We encountered [Chamorros] in small groups, here and there, as they emerged from the caves and broke free from Jap concentration camps" (1946, 72). He described them as "old, gnarled men with sticks; crones with wispy white hair, lace dresses, and no shoes; young girls in mud-stained rags, carrying naked babies; little boys and girls holding onto each other's hands fearfully" (1946, 75–76). Tun Manuel Cruz Diaz, one of the few Chamorros serving in the US Navy at that time, recalled his return to Guam on the USS *Essex* in 1944. His early impressions of Chamorros reflected their sense of despair. Cruz stated, "People's faces were different. You [could] see the struggle they went through. They were dazed" (Braley 1994, 16). As Guam historian Paul Carano explained, "The people were overjoyed, but they were too weak and tired to engage in avid celebrations" (1973, 5). However, Chamorros' physical and emotional exhaustion did not deter them from welcoming American soldiers enthusiastically.

In large part, Chamorros eagerly conveyed their appreciation for the American invasion. Unlike neighboring Pacific Islanders in Micronesia, the Chamorros of Guam "knew what to expect and were eager to get into American hands" (Poyer, Falgout, and Carucci 2001, 251). The Chamorro reunion with the American military was therefore "more unequivocal and emotional than American arrivals in former Japanese colonies" (Carano 1973, 251). Chamorros presented homemade American flags to soldiers, thanked and hugged them profusely, and sang patriotic songs. "There was never any question of [Chamorro] loyalty to us: They were hysterically glad to see us" (Josephy 1946, 72). After arriving at a civilian camp in Hågat, for instance, the Reverend Joaquin Flores Sablan remembered that the villagers "hoisted the American flag with bursting hearts, singing the national anthem with gusto. There was not a person in the group with dry eyes. It was a day never to be forgotten by my people. Our cup simply ran over with joy" (J Sablan 1990, 160; Forbes 1997). Another survivor of the war, Don Pascual Artero, described his family's emotionally charged meeting with Americans: "'It is impossible to describe those moments . . . we started to cry for sheer joy and to embrace each other. . . . Our clothes were soaked and torn, but who cared? We bubbled with happiness to find ourselves among the American soldiers'" (Palomo 1984, 215). Such expressions initially surprised American soldiers, many of whom knew nothing about Guam Chamorros and their political affiliation with the United States.

While some soldiers rudely described Chamorros as "gooks," many Americans sympathized with Chamorro stories of struggle under the Japanese occupation (Brooks 1994, 6). Cynical soldiers and sensitive combatants were astounded by the spectacle of ragged Chamorros overwhelmingly in "love" with America. As soldiers, some Americans identified with the wartime pain and suffering of Chamorros. Indigenous tales of perseverance and especially loyalty provided a common ground to bridge the cultural, political, and economic differences that separated Chamorros from Americans. Sometimes survivors and soldiers fostered solidarity.[4] Both parties identified with the United States, and both groups resisted Japanese colonialism.

Describing these cross-cultural exchanges, Quentin Reynolds stated, "Thousands of soldiers and sailors respect [Chamorros], many marry them, and a great many more swear they will return to this green friendly island when the war is over" (1945, 5). These stories and the emotions of war forged friendships across ethnic lines and inspired a renewed sense of loyalty for all. As one American combatant declared, "I didn't have anything to do with rescuing these people. . . . I'm just a goddam spectator here, but I was so proud to be wearing an American uniform that I damned near bust" (McManus 1944, 10). American soldiers were impressed, saddened, and stirred by the war stories of the Chamorros. Troops provided Chamorros with chocolate candies, canned goods, field rations, cigarettes, and almost anything that could be easily delivered by hand. Chamorros thankfully acknowledged these gifts by treating the Americans with the utmost respect and admiration.

As a result, numerous Chamorros felt deeply obliged to the families of American soldiers whose sons had sacrificed their lives. The return of American soldiers, as personable and symbolic representations of America, convinced Chamorros of the perceived humanitarian dimension of US military expansion into the Pacific. They consequently viewed the American invasion in cultural and spiritual terms, integrating the deeds and deaths of Americans into indigenous and Christian systems of respect and reciprocation. Felix Torres Pangelinan wrote, for example, that Chamorros "owe an everlasting debt to these gallant [American] men; a debt that we can never repay, but that we can show, in our humble gratitude, by being loyal, faithful, and patriotic to the United States of America"; in Pangelinan's judgment, Chamorros "were ready at any time to lay down their lives for American principles of democracy."[5] Grateful for their renewed sense of freedom, Chamorros created a collective sense of obligation to the United States, thus strengthening the bonds of reciprocation between Chamorros and Americans. Many Chamorros internalized the liberation of Guam into their ways of thinking, receiving, and sharing. At the end of the war, they committed themselves to perpetuating the liberal aspects of American democracy, and to "aiding" Americans at some point in the future.

Military Government and Rehabilitation in Guam

On declaring the Mariana Islands secure in August 1944, US military officials transformed the islands into forward deployment bases.[6] The primary purpose for obtaining these islands was "to further the successful prosecution of the war."[7] As Don A Farrell pointed out, "The decision to capture the Marianas was not based on any American commitment to liberate the people of Guam from the Japanese. Nor was it to liberate the American servicemen who had been stationed there when Guam was taken by the Japanese on December 10, 1941. . . . The decision to capture the Marianas was based solely on strategic military objectives" (1991a, 345). The secondary role of the military in the Mariana Islands was to function as a government for the people, and to reestablish the island economies. The execution of this policy was achieved by "relieving combat forces of the care of civilians, by restoring law and order, by encouraging agriculture, fishing and industry for the purpose of making the civilian population self-subsistent and thereby relieving shipping."[8] In addressing both military and civilian concerns, the naval government strove to support the war effort without further aggravating the already stressful conditions of the various Chamorro, Japanese, Korean, Okinawan, and Refaluwasch populations.

In preparing and implementing these policies, American military officials intended to "win the goodwill, cooperation and loyalty of the native peoples" (Richard 1957, 165). With respect to the Chamorros of Guam, military officials felt optimistic about the future of military and civil affairs on the island. Island Commander Major General Henry L Larsen proclaimed, "The success of the administration of this island by the U. S. Navy cannot be illustrated any more forcefully than by pointing out the supreme patriotism of the natives of Guam which has been shown in innumerable ways during the Japanese occupation and since our reoccupation."[9] In tune with Larsen's observations, military officials often repeated that Chamorros were "extremely happy with our return and can be depended upon to cooperate in our efforts toward early rehabilitation, consistent with military necessity."[10] Others similarly commended Chamorros for being "most cooperative with Military Government," again adding that "their devotion and loyalty to the United States is of the highest order."[11] That the island was a former naval outpost further encouraged military policy makers to ensure that Guam remained under American jurisdiction.

From August 1944 to May 1946, the military government imposed martial law in Guam. The military government enforced curfews, restricted travel, and rationed food (Leon Guerrero 1996, 91). Chamorro families remained in refugee compounds scattered throughout the island, as required by the military government, which discouraged them from visiting neighboring ranches, villages, and extended family members. The isolation of Chamorro families limited and constrained daily communication and contact among clans. Despite the imposition of martial law, and the everyday hardships it generated for Chamorros, the military government tempered such acts with celebratory references to prewar colonial rule in Guam. Accordingly, military officials interpreted the island's prewar government as a "successful" naval colony.

In a letter to the judge advocate general in 1944, Chief of Naval Operations F J Horne stated, "The natives of Guam have been wards of the Navy since 1898 and have learned during that period to look first and only to the Navy." Praising the naval administration's relationship with Chamorros, Horne reasoned that the "Navy is familiar with the people, with their needs, and with the values on the island."[12] As one naval report concluded,

"In the half century from 1899 to 1950, the Guamanians have, with gradually awakened but accelerating ambition, become cohesive and progressive
people, capable of self-discipline and of adapting the instruments of modern civilization to their own advancement" (USDN 1951, 1). In managing
the rehabilitation project in Guam, military officials continually professed
their familiarity with the Chamorros of Guam. Conversely, these officials
reassured others, such as the media, that the Chamorros understood American government in general and naval jurisprudence in particular.

By drawing on the island's naval past, military officials wanted to demonstrate, above all, that the Chamorros of Guam knowingly re-accepted them.
Military officials seized this opportunity to represent themselves as humanitarians familiar with indigenous issues and needs. The image of a "powerful" navy helping, once again, a "weak," though Americanized, indigenous population surfaced, providing military officials with the moral and
political license to proceed relatively unimpeded with their specific military
agendas. Military correspondents, for example, painted a picture of a grateful yet physically impoverished indigenous population. Describing one of
the camps in Yo'ña, Josephy wrote, "Among the trees they had built miser-
able lean-tos and thatched huts, and crowded together on the mud banks
on both sides of the brackish stream. . . . By the time our troops reached
the camp, most of the people were in rags. They were weak and coughing
and ridden with malnutrition, dysentery, and tuberculosis" (1946, 78). Josephy's depiction of the state of Chamorro health and well-being was not far
from the truth.

Given the demanding and violent conditions of war, Chamorro families were hungry and sick. The military government responded by providing them with food, medicine, and shelter. "Food was provided free to all
Chamorros by the military government through a rationing system" (Rogers 1995, 200). Temporary shelters, or "tent-cities," were erected throughout the island. The military government introduced Tabasco®, Spam®,
and canned corned beef—food products that Chamorros quickly adopted
into their diets. Construction on military airfields, ports, and roads began.
Schools and desperately needed medical centers also surfaced throughout
the island. For the most part, Chamorros appeared to anticipate a brighter
postwar future. "The natives of Guam do not talk of the past; they talk of the
future when their . . . cities will be rebuilt" (Reynolds 1945, 5).

Optimism about a brighter economic and political future also emerged
for the navy and the political elite. Enthusiastic about the perceived success
of the rehabilitation project, Major General Henry L Larsen declared that
the "results of Naval administration of Guam stand as a monument to the
wisdom and effectiveness of this form of government here and may well
stand as a pattern model for other similar territory under the American
flag." Larsen boasted that "the record of achievement already established by
the Navy on Guam in the rehabilitation of the natives in these few months

since reoccupation of this island, it is believed, will compare most favorably with any other corresponding endeavor by the United States or its Allies."[13] Considering the magnitude of destruction on the island, the US military government deserved praise for its altruistic efforts to restore Chamorros to a physically more comfortable and secure life. In large part, Chamorros appreciated the time, effort, and money that government provided.

However, civilian Japanese, Koreans, and Okinawans did not embrace the return of the American military forces. Nor did Chamorros with Japanese spouses or relatives. They did not subscribe to the image of the generic "loyal Chamorro subject." Rather than face capture by the Americans, "individual Japanese civilians on Guam did kill themselves out of fear of the Americans. Some Japanese civilians simply disappeared, presumably killed in the whirlpool of war that swirled around them" (Rogers 1995, 192). As did Asian inhabitants of the Northern Mariana Islands, Japanese, Koreans, and Okinawans on Guam worried about what the American military might do to them. Toshio Francisco Kishida recalled, "There was no time nor day in our existence. We never knew what to expect or whether we [would] live or survive. We did not have any direction nor were we knowledgeable of where we were. All we knew was the constant sounds of battle and the cries of the dying" (Ramirez 1984, 58).

Many Japanese soldiers, civilians, and laborers were frightened and confused, and some even "accepted the propaganda in reference to the evil of the Americans" (Maga 2001, 47). Fearful of persecution by the American "barbarians"—an image popularly circulated by Japanese wartime propaganda—some Japanese fled into the jungles of Guam. "Many Japanese still eluded capture, and islander homes and property were always in peril from raiding parties of these 'stragglers'" (Maga 2001, 47).[14] It has been reported that some Chamorros died as a result of these "raiding parties," yet the stragglers were not sufficiently well equipped to pose a military threat. What they sought was food and safe refuge from the anticipated "horrors" of the US military.[15]

The Japanese who surrendered to the American military or to Chamorro scout platoons were imprisoned in internment camps in the villages of Hågat, Tamuning, Tutuhan, and Yigo.[16] These camps were set up for "several hundred Japanese soldier and civilian POWs, plus Saipanese, Rotanese, and a few local Chamorros suspected of Japanese sympathies" (Poyer, Falgout, and Carucci 2001, 252). Some Chamorros from the Northern Mariana Islands were also imprisoned because the American military considered them a "racial problem" in Guam.[17] The racial problem related, of course, to Japanese soldiers and their supporters, some of whom happened to have been Chamorro interpreters and police officers during the war. At the camps, the American military separated soldiers from civilians as a means of aiding the investigation of alleged war criminals and maintaining peace. Chamorro interpreters and police officers, as well as others accused of war crimes, were arrested for "collaborating" with the Japanese military.

Many more innocent people faced prison time because of their Japanese heritage. Peter R Onedera, a Chamorro with three generations of Japanese ancestry, stated in a 2002 interview that Chamorro-Japanese families were "corralled and sent off to stockades in Hågat . . . and many of these families were subjected there in the stockades for even up to two years after the war." On numerous occasions, Chamorros "would pass by these stockades and hurl insults and rocks." Onedera remarked that these Chamorro-Japanese families "were never compensated for that humiliation. . . . Many of these families also lost their livelihood, their businesses" (Onedera 2002).[18]

Likewise, Catherine Okada Rivera, another Japanese descendant, said that "many Japanese civilians and their families on Guam began to be mistreated by both the native and the American population" (1984, 83). Rivera recalled that on release from these camps, her family members had to replace their Japanese surnames with Chamorro ones. "For this reason, several of my grandfather's sons were forced to change their names. They took their mother's maiden name of Santos in place of Okada. This enabled them to get much needed jobs in order to support their families" (Rivera 1984, 83). Chamorro-Japanese families thus struggled to rebuild their lives after the war. As Rivera noted, many Japanese descendants changed their names in order to survive among an island people whose understanding of Japanese society had become limited to and tainted by Japan's wartime militarism.

The racist imprisonment of Chamorro-Japanese families in postwar Guam was not an isolated event. The internment of Japanese in Guam paralleled the wartime confinement of Japanese and Japanese Americans along the Pacific coast of the continental United States (Kurashige 2002, 70). There, Japanese families were segregated and placed on Native American reservations located in such areas as California and Arizona, mainly because of American racism and xenophobia. Elsewhere, governments in Canada and South America created and enforced similar anti-Japanese segregation and relocation policies during the war. For example, in British Columbia the Canadian government forcibly displaced up to twenty-three thousand Japanese residents to remote camps in areas like the subarctic; many of them did not return to their homes until 1949 (Pike 2001, xxxiii).

Japanese civilians and soldiers in Guam were imprisoned for racist and xenophobic reasons, too, but most notably they were accused of facilitating wartime atrocities. Regardless of the rationale, the US government and military unlawfully incarcerated Japanese civilian families. It did not matter whether or not these families had supported the American war effort; they were the "enemy." By virtue of their Japanese ethnicity or perceived association with the Japanese military, these families witnessed Americans justifying their dehumanization as the Japanese "enemy" in Guam and in the continental United States.

On Guam, many Chamorros continued to reject public affiliation with Japanese, Chamorro-Japanese families, and Chamorros from the Northern Mariana Islands. For example, the term, "Guamanian," emerged during this time as a way to distinguish Guam's "Americanized" Chamorros from the Northern Mariana Islands' "Japanized" Chamorros (P Sanchez 1989, 264). Profound feelings of distrust and hate came to characterize most relationships between Chamorros and Japanese in Guam. In contrast, equally intense emotions of joy and praise typified intercultural relations between Chamorros and Americans. Numerous Guam Chamorros expressed their loyalties to Americans in terms of cultural obligation and survival.

American Liberation and Loyalty Reconsidered

Elsewhere in Micronesia, the concepts of "liberation" and "loyalty" continued to dictate, in part, the terms of cross-cultural relations among the colonized and the colonizer. Even before World War II erupted in the Pacific, Japanese officials frequently assured indigenous peoples of their liberation from such Western powers as Australia, Britain, Germany, and the United States. The general intent of the rhetoric of liberation—to attain the loyalties of indigenous peoples—persisted relatively unimpeded throughout the war and postwar periods. In the case of the United States, Americans "expected that their role as liberators would secure a welcome reception and an extended period of goodwill from grateful, needy, and debilitated populations" (Hanlon 1998, 24). In large part, Americans believed that they were liberating former European colonies from Japanese wartime rule. However, not all island populations viewed Americans as "liberators." In most cases, Micronesians did not "regard the Americans as liberators who saved them" from the awful fate of war (Useem 1945, 100). Micronesian experiences "of the war's end were far from uniform" (Poyer, Falgout, and Carucci 2001, 230). Even if Americans assumed that the indigenous peoples were nonhostile, "it yet was inaccurate to suppose that they would be cooperative out of spite or out of any dislike of the Japanese who had ruled them" (Richard 1957, 2:5). Initial wartime encounters between indigenous peoples and Americans were burdensome to say the least. Information about Americans came from Japanese propaganda, or from limited contact with American missionaries, traders, and whalers in the nineteenth century. Neither group had much experience with the other, nor did the limited use of interpreters and sign language prove effective means of communication.

During the period of transition from Japanese to American rule, cross-cultural relations among Americans and Japanese were certainly fraught with problems of communication. Also, Japanese loyalties to their emperor and nation did not necessarily create a suitable environment for such cultural exchanges. Some Japanese, for instance, completely refused to believe anything redeeming about the Americans. The Japanese "have not been won over to a deep and abiding love of all things American. They are not reconciled to defeat and assume that the Japanese armed forces will some day restore them to their earlier status" (Useem 1945, 100). In Saipan, interned Japanese spread "rumors about the Japanese navy shortly coming to liberate Saipan and to drive the Americans into the sea." When the Japanese navy failed to arrive, the rumors shifted to stories about "imminent, surreptitious landings from Japanese submarines bent on committing devastating sabotage" (Meller 1999, 3).

Belief in the invincibility of the Japanese empire and in the spiritual strength of its military forces legitimized these rumors for the Japanese. Like the Chamorros of Japanese-occupied Guam, who often longed for the arrival of the American military, the Japanese similarly hoped for the return of Japan's army and navy. Even if the rumors of Japanese liberation never came true, it was clear that such stories lasted well into the first few months of the American occupation of Micronesia. For the US military forces, one task at hand was to eradicate any and all forms of loyalty to Japan, especially notions about Japanese liberation. By demonstrating to indigenous populations the "generous" character of the US military government, American military officials hoped to eliminate loyalties to the Japanese. On Guam, the military encountered no substantial difficulty in promoting this image of generosity. The Chamorros of Guam generally embraced the Americans and thanked them profusely for their salvation. But in the neighboring islands of Micronesia, previously Japanese-ruled, Americans generated a new set of problems.

Outside Guam, the loyalty of indigenous peoples and civilians had to be acquired in order to sustain the American war effort in the western Pacific. Policy dictated that Americans be as courteous as possible to these peoples, especially in their initial proclamations of the principles of liberation, democracy, and freedom (Poyer, Falgout, and Carucci 2001, 278). "Relations with the people of the islands were handled with great care. . . . Service personnel were ordered to show the islanders all possible consideration, to refrain insofar as possible from disturbing their normal existence, and not to intermingle with them" (Richard 1957, 1:165). At times, military personnel were even advised to suspend temporarily their moral and racial understandings of the Pacific region, its peoples, and its histories. Any prejudices on the part of Americans had to be suppressed, many argued, for the purpose of achieving peaceful social relations among peoples believed to be "pro-Japanese."

For instance, John W Vandercook of the National Broadcasting Company suggested that "the strictest orders—and of course this goes for the whole Pacific area—be issued that neither American officers nor men should ever be allowed to show any hint of racial prejudice." Vandercook reasoned that "even a wrong tone of voice [would] instantly be reported to tens of thousands—and would color their attitude toward us accordingly."[19] If the appearance of "brotherhood" was not maintained among all, he asserted, especially between black and white soldiers, then indigenous populations might question the benevolent attitudes and intentions of Americans.

This semblance of brotherhood affected Pacific Islanders throughout the Pacific region. The appearance of black soldiers working alongside white soldiers had a significant impact on Pacific Islanders in Melanesia, where a "positive image of military others" emerged; Melanesians "saw for the first time skilled [black] American servicemen looking at least superficially similar to themselves: made, as it were, in their own image, but already possessing the knowledge and accoutrements of Western culture" (Lindstrom and White 1989, 18).

Throughout the Pacific, the American military attempted to present itself as a cooperative, homogenous, and peaceful multiethnic mass. Although they were soldiers first with military missions, they were now required to work as civil servants in the war-torn communities of Micronesia and Melanesia. Cognizant of pan-ethnic antiracist coalitions in wartime America, military postwar policies in the Pacific thus aimed to repress resistance and solidarity movements on the part of the indigenous and civilian populations (Lipsitz 2001, 364). At least at a policy level, the US military did not desire to fight another "enemy," nor did they aspire to be perceived as invaders, let alone as overseas extensions of white racism. The American military, then, strove to generate support from the rather sizable indigenous and civilian populations of the former Japanese mandated and wartime-occupied islands.

It has been estimated that in 1944 the three major archipelagos of Micronesia—the Carolines, the Marianas, and the Marshalls—were inhabited by "approximately 56,600 civilians, of whom 31,000 are natives, 22,000 are Japanese, and 3,600 are Koreans" (Useem 1945, 94). Many of these people, originally sugarcane laborers, were located in the Northern Mariana Islands. Saipan alone hosted the largest pool of Asian civilians and indigenous people, with a projected population of 17,880 in the summer of 1944 (Meller 1999, 2). Japanese, Koreans, and Okinawans vastly outnumbered Chamorros and Refaluwasch in Saipan, as well as in the neighboring islands of Rota and Tinian. Japanese and Koreans also hid on the smaller islands of Aguiguan, Anatahan, Pagan, and Sarigan, some of whom surrendered to American military forces as late as 30 June 1951.[20] In the Northern Mariana Islands, the American military confronted a population whose loyalties to Japan were either clearly defined or somewhat ambivalent.

The Chamorros of the Northern Mariana Islands certainly did not run from the hills to welcome the Americans, nor did rumors of salvation and liberation circulate among them. However, the main cause of concern for

US military officials was Japanese armed resistance, disobedience, and sabotage. Americans considered the Japanese "enemy aliens, with all the negative connotations that designation engendered" (Meller 1999, 33). Okinawans, often mistaken for Japanese, were also subjected to American military surveillance and psychological assessments. For instance, military personnel took great interest in noncombatant Japanese "because the capture of Saipan afforded the first opportunity of studying enemy civilian attitudes toward both the United States and the Japanese homeland" (Richard 1957, 1:466).

Furthermore, the United States had no experience abroad "with Japanese civilian populations and no definite information as to how they might affect" a military operation (Sheeks 1945, 112). By assessing Japanese attitudes, the US military reached a general understanding of the wartime roles of Japanese civilians in the Northern Mariana Islands. They found that many believed in the naval superiority of Japan, feared capture by the Americans, and in a few instances resorted to "honorable deaths" as a form of resistance. But what many American intelligence personnel sought in studying Japanese attitudes were ways to improve American propaganda. In the event that the United States might invade Japan, American intelligence personnel wanted to develop propaganda—from flyers detailed with instructions for surrender to nisei offerings of peace—that would guarantee the capitulation of enemy civilians (Bosse 1945, 176–182). On Saipan and Tinian, American efforts to encourage surrender were successful, as illustrated by the large number of survivors.

The non-Japanese fared no better in the initial days of encountering the Americans in the Northern Mariana Islands. Despite their designated status as "liberated peoples," Chamorros, Koreans, and Refaluwasch were still treated with suspicion. Not until camps were fully established, monitored, and self-governed by "loyal" subjects did the American military government lessen its control over civilian affairs. As a means to consolidate its resources, the military government decided to erect two internment camps, which, as in Guam, provided much-needed medical care, food, and shelter to the indigenous and Asian populations. However, in certain instances the rehabilitation of the Northern Mariana Islands did not completely parallel the situation in Guam.

In Rota, Saipan, and Tinian, American military officials believed they were dealing with an "Oriental" or Japanized population. As a result, the civilian populations had to be treated even more "carefully" than those in Guam, many of whom were already familiar with the Americans. With regard to Chamorros and Refaluwasch in Saipan, some argued that the people needed "time to recover from the shock of invasion, time to adjust themselves to their new situation, and time to gain enough confidence in [Americans] to make known their needs as they see them, not merely as they think we wish them to be" (Joseph and Murray 1951, 318–319). The

FIGURE 3. A lieutenant of the US Marine Corps and Vicente Deleon Guerrero, on the left, watch as Juan M Ada plants the US flag in Saipan, 4 July 1944. The photo's original caption reads: "Lt. Colonel Donald T. Winder, USMCR, of 2121 Virginia Avenue, N.W. Washington, D.C. reads and explains the Declaration of Independence to Chamorro natives of Saipan in first internment camp set up on island by Marines." *(National Archives at College Park, Maryland; photograph 97613)*

internment camps provided ample "time" for indigenous people to make sense of their new American colonizers, and vice versa. The largest of the camps, Camp Susupe, was located in Saipan; the second, Camp Churo, in Tinian. In addition to supplying provisions to the detainees, the official purpose of the camps was twofold—to protect the indigenous and nonindigenous populations from the violence of war beyond the campgrounds, and to protect American personnel from the possible violent nature of those interned (figure 3).

The apparent separation of US military personnel and civilians was but one of numerous divisions in the camps. In Camp Susupe, the US military government assigned three dwelling areas: Area One for Chamorros and Refaluwasch, Area Two for Koreans, and Area Three for Japanese and Okinawans (map 3). "Each area had its own internal administration which provided basic services headed by an elected mayor. The mayors, in turn, reported to a military government officer who was responsible for the local

affairs of his respective area" (Russell 1983, 21). The village of Chalan
Kanoa, once the exclusive domain of Japanese residents, housed Area One.
Prior to the war, Japanese law had prevented indigenous people from visiting this restricted site after dark. With the relocation of Chamorros and
Refaluwasch to the village, the prewar rules of Chalan Kanoa changed. Not
only were Japanese prohibited from entering the village, now reinhabited
by the indigenous population, but they also could not fraternize with Americans and Koreans. Americans themselves were not exempt from such rules.
The men in particular could not interact with the women of the camp, as
interethnic relationships were strongly discouraged.[21]

The military government appointed US military officers and indigenous
policemen to enforce segregationist camp rules and regulations. In the
interior, Japanese civilians were assigned to monitor domestic activities.
They had some form of authority but it was limited in comparison to that
of their indigenous counterparts. Entrusted with guarding the periphery
of Camp Susupe, Chamorros and Refaluwasch served as policemen who
inspected all visitors to the camp. They held considerable symbolic power
since, for the first time, they could oversee the doings of their former Japanese colonizers. In extreme cases, indigenous police officers "treated Japanese and Korean civilians rather roughly, even striking them on occasion"
(Embree 1946, 6). Physical abuse of internees was not an unfamiliar disciplinary tactic for Chamorros and Refaluwasch. It was highly likely that
a few of them had worked as policemen for the Japanese during the war,
when the physical punishment of "criminals," from alleged spies to petty
thieves, was one way of demonstrating the officers' loyalty to their Japanese
supervisors. Interestingly, Chamorros and Refaluwasch may have internalized these strategies and continued them in their roles as police officers for
the Americans, thereby illustrating a shift in allegiances.

The granting of such powers to Chamorros angered the internees, most
notably the Japanese, who frequently considered indigenous peoples inferior. The Japanese also deemed the Okinawans inferior, and disliked the
idea that they shared the same housing area. American military officials
knew about the increasing social tensions among the groups in Susupe, but
they did not implement any policies to alleviate them. Nor could they transform the camp into an ideal living space for every ethnic group. Military
practices and notions of governance, rather than what some might have
erroneously perceived as democracy, administered the camp. The entire
logistical setup for Camp Susupe "mirrored the military government's eth-
nically distinctive containment policies" (Meller 1999, 34). Consequently,
the Japanese racial hierarchies of the Greater East Asia Co-Prosperity
Sphere were turned upside down, with the Japanese situated at the lowest
social echelon of the camp.

In northern Tinian, rehabilitation efforts at Camp Churo mirrored those
in Saipan. But because of the small, almost entirely Japanese population,

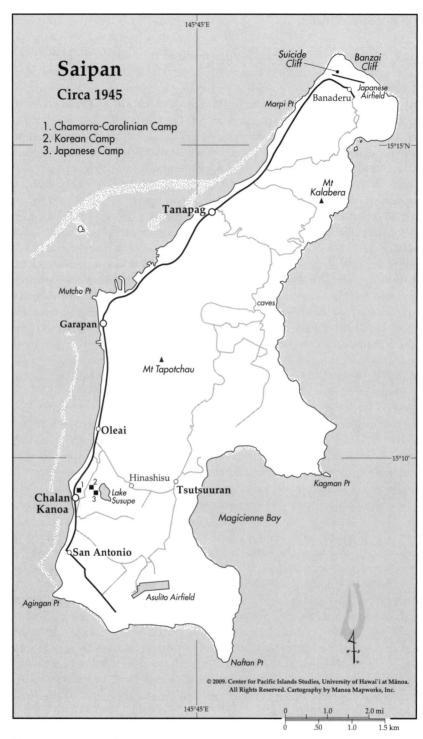

Saipan
Circa 1945

1. Chamorro-Carolinian Camp
2. Korean Camp
3. Japanese Camp

145°45'E

Suicide Cliff
Banzai Cliff
Marpi Pt
Banaderu
Japanese Airfield
15°15'N

Mt Kalabera

Tanapag

caves

Mutcho Pt

Garapan

▲ Mt Tapotchau

Oleai

Hinashisu
15°10'

1 2
3 Lake Susupe
Chalan Kanoa

Tsutsuuran

Kagman Pt

Magicienne Bay

San Antonio

Agingan Pt

Asulito Airfield

145°45'E

Naftan Pt

0   1.0   2.0 mi
0   .50   1.0   1.5 km

MAP 3.

"a situation was avoided that might [have led] to the sharp discriminatory treatment which existed at Susupe" (Embree 1946, 34). In the absence of Chamorros and Refaluwasch, Camp Churo operated relatively peacefully. The camp was "less constraining, families afforded more privacy, and the Japanese civilian administration there exercising greater power over and concomitantly sharing responsibility for matters relating to camp governance and internee welfare" (Meller 1999, 27). From the military viewpoint, the establishment of internment camps in Rota proceeded without serious harm to the people, except for damage sustained from a typhoon in the autumn of 1945. As in Saipan and Tinian, the Asian populations lived in dwellings separated from the Chamorros, many of whom later settled at the village of Songsong, located in western Rota (Bowers 2001, 65). English instruction classes, religious services, and menial employment opportunities—all postwar manifestations of American overseas colonialism—gradually surfaced as the basic needs of the camps were met. To the degree they were allowed, people resumed their daily, though monitored, routines of fishing and farming. Before long, public fears of being tortured by Americans began to fade (figure 4).

FIGURE 4. Unidentified Korean women prepare rice balls for meals in the Korean camp area of Camp Susupe. The photo was taken on 10 July 1944 by a soldier in the 73rd Bomb Wing. *(Collection of Northern Mariana Islands Museum)*

As the US military government continued to provide goods and services to the civilian populations, some concluded that the Americans were not the "barbarians" portrayed in Japanese propaganda. Liberal provision of food, shelter, and medicine greatly shaped, at times in positive terms, how indigenous peoples and others came to view the Americans. "The Americans could have done nothing more calculated to ingratiate themselves with the Micronesian people than to offer them generous amounts of food—something that has always had a sacramental quality for Pacific peoples—after what many called 'the year of the famine'" (Hezel 1995, 244). Humbled by these perceived gestures of goodwill, some Pacific Islanders supported the American and Allied war effort by enlisting in scout platoons, assisting injured personnel, and providing information about Japanese military activities. In the Northern Mariana Islands, some advanced the war effort through monetary means. As a way to show their appreciation, Koreans at Camp Churo, Tinian, gathered money in the amount of $666.35 and donated it to the US Navy in November 1944 (*New York Times* 1945). Equally concerned about the struggle for Korea's independence, Koreans at the camp contributed $2,433.15 to the Korean National Association of Honolulu toward that effort (Richard 1957, 1:567).

Chamorros of the Northern Mariana Islands also shared their thoughts regarding the American military government. "Regardless of nationality, the Americans provided assistance by giving people water to drink first, then they gave people food to eat. The services provided by the Americans [were] good" (Guerrero 1994, 8). The Americans "were really nice because they treated the sick people and the injured people, and they gave Chamorro people food. They also took the local people to serve and to work in the public works department" (V Inos 1981, 64). Many clearly expressed thanks for what they interpreted to be "free" American food and services— aid believed to have come from the compassionate hearts and hands of military government officials. Increasing numbers of Chamorros thus felt a "deep gratitude for the disinterested and unselfish help provided by the American government" (Puyo 1964, 64). Many Chamorros were particularly moved by American assistance to the elderly and the sick. These exchanges and acts of goodwill attracted Chamorros to their American benefactors. According to Chamorro cultural traditions, the sharing of food, labor, and medicine may be interpreted as acts of *chenchule,* or forms of assistance bound by reciprocal relationships and obligations (Cunningham 1992, 121). When they interpreted American rehabilitative efforts through such cultural norms, Chamorros could make better sense of the Americans.

Overall, Chamorros in the Northern Mariana Islands were still not familiar with American military attitudes, behaviors, and goals. American military officials understood that various cultural obstacles hindered their progress in establishing relationships with not only Chamorros but also other Pacific Islanders in Micronesia. Abiding by their projected image as "liberators,"

American military officials strove to convey simple, seemingly altruistic and progressive principles to the Pacific Islanders of this region. One of these principles was the American idea of "freedom." Micronesians "recall that the first U.S. officers they saw proclaimed the arrival of 'freedom,' but they had little context in which to interpret that announcement." In encountering Americans, Micronesians began to realize that the American notion of freedom, as illustrated in the efforts of the American rehabilitation project, "opened new options in work, leisure, and status relations." During the first weeks of the American military rehabilitation of Saipan, for example, Chamorros understandably could not grasp the significance of "freedom," let alone comprehend the English language (Poyer, Falgout, and Carucci 2001, 279). But after a few months of receiving aid and living in conditions superior to those experienced under Japanese rule, Chamorros began to make sense of the term.

Tun Ignacio M Sablan acutely observed, "When the Americans came, you know, they were so friendly, so nice, you [could] tell them what you want, as opposed to under the Japanese rule whereby you [had] to be very careful in what you're saying. Here you can say everything you want as long as it is true. And that's the difference. We live as a free man, and this is the first time that we realize" (1981, 55). It was common for Chamorros like Sablan to arrive at these conclusions after interacting closely with Americans. Ideas such as "freedom" and, in turn, "liberation," steadily became part of the new English political vocabulary of Chamorros in the Northern Mariana Islands. The appropriation of these terms reflected more than an increased understanding of the American military government and the English language. More important, the use of such terms revealed that Chamorros had acknowledged the defeat of Japan and had resigned themselves, however unwillingly, to American colonial governance. As Tun Ignacio stated, a "change in feeling" engulfed him, on realizing that the rising sun had finally set (1981, 55).

Problems of Military Government in the Marianas

In the first few years of the American military occupation, Chamorros throughout the Mariana Islands experienced a variety of feelings. US military officials hoped that loyalty to the United States would become the primary sentiment of all Chamorros. But due to the fragmentary nature of Chamorro cultural identities, as well as their separate colonial experiences, there was no single, unifying sense of loyalty directed toward the United States. Nevertheless, the American military government attempted to shape popular opinion about the United States in the western Pacific. In Guam, the navy described a prosperous, homogenous, and loyal postwar community. In particular, they commended the prewar naval administration for producing a people and environment conducive to US military and political control.

In the Northern Mariana Islands, the navy encountered a different set of conditions and peoples—the "civilian," the "enemy," the "native," and the "oriental"—whose loyalties remained in question. The task at hand seemed challenging from the military's standpoint, as the navy had no prior experience in "rehabilitating" large wartime populations. Even Stanford University's School of Naval Administration, which trained junior naval officers as civil administrators, did not adequately prepare military personnel for addressing the variety of social, political, and economic issues affecting the inhabitants of the Northern Mariana Islands (Hanlon 1998, 35–50). Still, as months passed, the navy claimed to have transformed a Japanized population into a society supportive of the American war effort. The media legitimized these assertions, often noting that "Saipan is the showplace of naval military government, one of the few places where the results of war-caused American rule in the Pacific are apparent—and on the happy side" (Coontz 1946b). The Saipanese, a reporter observed, were "hardworking and grateful for the American direction that has brought them to this independence and prosperity. The exchange of war has been to their advantage—work in the sugar cane for the Japanese versus work in their own fields . . . for their own future" (Coontz 1946b). In some respects, the American military granted Chamorros specific freedoms and opportunities not allowed under the Japanese wartime governments. The appearance of liberation from colonial rule gave rise to an image of the navy as generous, kind, and ultimately democratic.

But the American rehabilitation project was a severely problematic venture, as evidenced in part by its racist treatment of those interned. Comparable to earlier forms of internment of Japanese Americans and Native Americans in the United States, the American overseas rehabilitation campaign in the Mariana Islands illustrated another case of segregating populations for reasons of fear, hatred, and racism, if not outright economic, military, or political exploitation (Saito 2007, 84). Despite military proclamations of administrative benevolence or ethnic pluralism, American officials could not repress the colonial and racial prejudices that underlay the so-called rehabilitation project. "Military rule is contrary to our entire democratic political philosophy. . . . Because [naval officers] represent an autocratic tradition they are more likely than civilian administrators to manifest race prejudice and institute social discriminations. [Military officers] have not chosen their careers through an interest in civil administration, and are likely to find such activities uncongenial, if not, indeed, an actual barrier in the path of normal promotion" (Murdock 1948, 4). Critical of the military's "missionary zeal," American anthropologist George Peter Murdock cautioned others about the consequences of Americanization. He raised the issue of American historical contacts with Native Americans and feared that the indigenous peoples of Micronesia might suffer similar problems of "chaos, bewilderment, helplessness, and stagnation" (1948, 3).

Murdock's observations accurately characterized the entire structural makeup of American military governments in Micronesia. More often than not, navy officers who administered indigenous affairs possessed "no military government training" and frequently knew "little or nothing about the local population and culture" (Rachlis 1946, 756). Military officers, some of whom claimed to know the islands' customs and values, failed to implement "culture-sensitive" policies. In rehabilitating the islands, these officials employed policies that often reflected white American values rather than indigenous ones. "Much of the language used in planning documents and public statements was permeated with racist and cultural assumptions about the alleged superiority of mainland, Caucasian-American values. . . . American officials perceived the Pacific Islanders as helpless children who needed paternalistic guidance from the United States in their every thought and action" (Friedman 2001, 117–118). American military officials treated Chamorros in the Mariana Islands in corresponding fashion.

The military's supposedly well-intentioned rehabilitation policies proved devastating for the islands and the people. Due to the heavy militarization of the archipelago, American uses of property under wartime conditions dominated the ways in which land came to be governed. For example, North Field in Tinian developed into perhaps the largest military runway in the western Pacific. The B-29 *Enola Gay,* the airplane responsible for dropping the first atomic bomb on a civilian population, departed from Tinian for Hiroshima, Japan, on 6 August 1945. Apart from North Field and a few bases in Saipan, the American military eventually chose to develop most of its bases in Guam. The strategic value of Guam, now hailed as the next "Pearl Harbor," dramatically increased; the island was transformed from a prewar coaling station to a postwar military fortress (Dudley 1947, 18). Military strategists believed that Guam's southerly location protected it from periodic Japanese airplane raids from the north, possibly from Iwo Jima (Farrell 1991a, 395). The island also had a larger land base and deeper harbors.

It was apparent that the strategic needs of the military in the islands far outweighed civil objectives for the indigenous population. Military control of the islands had always been explicitly stated in the American rehabilitation project, but it was not an immediate concern for many Chamorros, who were still recovering from the war. With increasing land dispossession, the colonial nature of rehabilitation became strikingly evident. In Guam, "the appropriation of land by the military intervened in Chamorro lives unlike any other imposition of the U.S. government. By 1947, a total of 1,350 families had lost their land and homes due to military policy" (Hattori 2001, 190).[22] These violent acts of displacement were raised in the Guam Congress (Hattori 1995, 1–27), which often informed the naval government of rising Chamorro discontent regarding the taking of their lands by the military. Others, such as John Unpingco from the village of Tomhom (also spelled Tumon), took matters into his own hands. Recalling Unpingco's protest of American postwar militarization, Chamorro attorney Michael F Phillips stated that Unpingco "stood in front of U.S. military personnel and their bulldozers with his gun and refused to leave his family land in Tumon. Rather than risk an embarrassing news story, the U.S. military retreated and allowed Unpingco to keep his land" (1996, 7). Despite these examples of resistance, few Chamorros were able to protect their lands from exploitation by the American military (J Aguon 2006, 32).

Given Guam Chamorros' overall appreciation for America's liberation of the island, indigenous resistance seemed futile at times. Although it was important to protest military land condemnations, numerous Chamorros did not want to seem ungrateful to Americans for their liberation. "For the most part, Chamorros did not dispute the need for military bases. With the war experience so fresh on their minds, Chamorros welcomed bases as signs of future protection against foreign invasion" (Hattori 2001, 190). Chamorros "gladly turned over large tracts of the island to the military— thinking it would be returned when the war ended or when the military no longer needed it—and they did so gladly because they felt it a debt of the heart" (Blaz 1998, 110). Bound by cultural values of obligation and sometimes ignorant of American Cold War interests, some Chamorros lent their lands to the military government. "In deeply felt acts of Chamorro reciprocity, our people extended the most valuable of their possessions, albeit the only possessions they had to give—land and their very spirits—to Uncle Sam" (L Souder 1994, 193).

As a result of these forms of militarization, a wage economy was also introduced to support the infrastructure of the military, presenting another challenge to Chamorros throughout the archipelago, whose livelihoods were premised on farming and fishing. In Guam, most of the island's prime agricultural lands became air force and naval bases in areas such as Tiyan, Sumay, and Yigo. "Farming [on Guam] was not allowed on any large scale; it would not have been possible anyway, because of the widespread devastation and the loss of the island's best farmlands to the new military bases. . . . Without access to their *lancho* [ranch], Chamorros were forced to seek other ways to make a living. This was the beginning of their economy's rapid transformation from subsistence agriculture and bartering to a system of wage employment and monetary exchange" (Leon Guerrero 1996, 91). After the war, Guam's "land use pattern changed radically. Farm lands became airfields and supply dumps, land taxes were suspended, and residents of land acquired by the military, or whose homes were demolished by the American bombardment, were moved into temporary camps" (P Souder 1971, 196).

In the Northern Mariana Islands, Chamorros and Refaluwasch also encountered problems in reclaiming lands for agricultural and residential use because the military considered the northern islands to be strategically located.[23] As in Guam, the construction of military airfields and bases in Saipan and Tinian used large amounts of coral, which covered valuable top-soil. "So after the war, that's what happened to Saipan. We could have been very productive today if [the major farm lands] were not buried under the coral" (I Sablan 1981, 57). Further, the American designation of formerly "Japanese-owned" lands in the northern islands as "public lands" prevented families from staking legal claims to lands they had traditionally farmed (McPhetres 1993, 16). While the naming of lands as public space some-times condemned indigenous efforts to resettle their lands in the postwar era, the policy also permitted the American military to repatriate Chamor-ros from the neighboring islands of Yap and Pohnpei, from as early as 1945 to as late as 1948. The policy enabled Chamorro individuals and clans who had previously been dispersed under Japan's empire in the western Pacific to be reunited.[24] At the same time, thousands of Asian civilians from camps Susupe and Churo were repatriated to their respective countries in 1946, as were others from Micronesia. Some stayed with their families on Rota, Saipan, and Tinian. Other Asians left willingly, but some family members were forcefully separated and never saw each other again (Farrell 1991a, 472–473).

In this time of land displacement, militarization, and resettlement, Guam remained an American territory and the Northern Mariana Islands soon fell under the Trust Territory of the Pacific Islands. Despite the dif-ferent political systems of the two territories, for the first time in almost fifty years they were reunited under one colonial power. During the war, Guam, Saipan, and Tinian briefly entered American popular conscious-ness as "stepping stones" for the possible invasion of Japan. The image of a generous navy, coupled with attempts to gain the loyalties of Chamor-ros, demonstrated the initial level of the United States' investment in these islands. But in the minds of military officials the islands became permanent strategic sites for the militarization of the western Pacific. The United States had entered the Cold War with the Soviet Union, and American military strategists viewed the Pacific region as a vast unprotected area throughout which Soviet communism could establish itself. Soviet communism had to be "contained" by developing what military officials termed a "deterrent" posture in the region.[25] The demands of the war, the rehabilitation project, and subsequent Cold War posturing turned the Marianas into America's westernmost line of defense.

As the islands adapted to or resisted the contours of the American mili-tary, new and familiar notions of loyalty and liberation were introduced. For the Chamorros of the Northern Mariana Islands, the American rehabilita-tion project was a time for comparing American understandings of loyalty and liberation with those of the former Japanese mandate. Given language barriers between Americans and Chamorros, however, Chamorros grasped at best only the rudimentary objectives of the American colonial govern-ment. It was highly unlikely that most of them fully comprehended Amer-ican narratives of loyalty and liberation. However, it can be argued that American acts of material generosity gave Chamorros a favorable impres-sion of the United States—and laid one of the historical foundations for succeeding forms of war remembrance in the Northern Mariana Islands.

On the other hand, the return of the American military forces to Guam reinforced most Chamorro loyalties to the United States. Although the American rehabilitation project posed numerous problems, especially the dispossession of Chamorros from their lands, many Chamorros continued to showcase their loyalties toward the United States and their faith in Yu'us. The notion of American liberation soon became entrenched in the English political vocabulary of Guam Chamorros, as did memories of Chamorro appreciation for the American elimination of Japanese occupational forces. In the next chapter I examine the commemorations of World War II that emerged in Guam during this period of profound turmoil and change.

Chapter 4
From Processions to Parades

During the first half of the twentieth century, American and Japanese colonial administrations in Guam and the Northern Mariana Islands sometimes used commemorations as a means to encourage the loyalty of the Chamorro population. These cultures of commemorations would grow in number in the decades following World War II, albeit in ways increasingly dictated by Chamorro memories of their wartime and postwar experiences. In this chapter I explore the historical development of Guam's central commemoration of the war, Liberation Day (21 July 1944), from its inception in 1945 to the fiftieth anniversary of the war in 1994. I examine the processes through which colonial and indigenous memories of the war contend for public representation in the commemoration of Liberation Day.

Agueda I Johnston and the "Rebirth" of Liberation Day

More often than not, women do not occupy prominent positions in the commemoration of war. In Western societies, for example, women have long been celebrated in war for their roles as mothers and mourners (Gillis 1994, 10). Their deeds and doings as members of different wartime societies have not been memorialized in ways equal to those of their male counterparts. Relegated to the domestic sphere, women often continue to be commemorated as caretakers, nurses, and wives. Although it can be argued that nowadays more women throughout history are being remembered for their social contributions, rather than their assumed domestic roles, this has not been the case in the commemoration of war. The late Chamorro educator Agueda Iglesias Johnston is one exception.

In the 1940s, Agueda Johnston had gained a reputation as "one of the island's most respected school teachers and administrators" (PSECC 1995, 64). She earned this status from her long record of public service working as a teacher and administrator from the early 1900s. Johnston cooperated with the American and Japanese colonial governments and sought ways to ease the troubles that plagued island residents. She may not have succeeded in all of her endeavors, but she contributed much to the well-being of her fellow Chamorros. Local leaders, journalists, educators, and even colonial officials hailed her in innumerable ways. Over the years, she has been called the "Queen Bee of Guam," "Guam Leader," "Guam Heroine," "First Lady of Guam," "Guam School Expert," and "Guam Matriarch" (Anderberg 1966). More than a public servant, Johnston also helped many people survive to see the end of the war, including the American navy radioman George R Tweed.

Risking her life and those of her family members, Johnston secretly provided food and guidance to Tweed, as she did to numerous others. After the war, she received the title "courageous patriot" for her wartime heroism (PSECC 1995, 64). Her wartime valor and public service culminated in the creation of Liberation Day in the summer of 1945, on 21 July, the first anniversary of the US invasion. She celebrated Liberation Day because of her belief that Chamorros deserved their day of remembrance. Initially, logistical concerns regarding the lack of transportation and shelter nearly canceled the event. Further, the island was still recovering from the ravages of war. However, with the assistance of the military government, Johnston saw her plans for Liberation Day come to fruition (Murphy 1983). Other makeshift memorials, impromptu ceremonies with speeches by military officials, and floral grave decorations characterized the immediate postwar period (figure 5).[1]

As the wife of a former naval officer, Lieutenant William Gautier Johnston, Agueda Johnston had entered the social scene of the island's elites at an early point in her life. Her privileged status enabled her to participate in a whole host of civil, educational, and religious activities. Even prior to World War II, she helped to coordinate numerous patriotic festivities, such as the Fourth of July celebration (*Guam Recorder* 1927, 85). In 1945, one year after the war ended in Guam, she envisioned another commemoration that highlighted not only loyalty to America, but specifically the wartime experiences and loyalties of Chamorros. Liberation Day fulfilled this goal by remembering that "the people of Guam fought the Japanese in their own way, risking their lives, losing their land, hampering their future" (Coontz 1946a). Much as she wanted a day of remembrance, though, Johnston also felt that some memories and histories of the war should be "forgotten." Referring to the war, she claimed, "What happened yesterday has been forgotten. I only look to tomorrow and the future" (*Los Angeles Examiner* 1955).

In shaping the initial themes of Liberation Day, Johnston envisioned a commemoration that suppressed the painful memories and histories of the war. Because she wanted to forget the vivid descriptions and experiences of wartime atrocities, rape, and violence, she eschewed narratives of Chamorro sexual slaves from Guam, Rotanese and Saipanese interpreters and police officers, and other controversial wartime figures in her description of Liberation Day. Instead, Johnston saw the commemoration as an occasion for new beginnings. As she explained, "I'd consider the liberation of Guam a rebirth for all its people, and all those who showed delinquencies should be forgiven and be given another chance to really live again."[2]

FIGURE 5. Catholic mass service, Talo'fo'fo, Guam, 20 October 1944. The original caption reads, "Reverent Guamanians kneel at the village of Talofofo as a Navy chaplain says mass for them. Not many months ago they were gathered in the same place, before the same platform. But the purpose was different. Then they were herded there to watch the Japs publicly flog the Guamanians who had broken a rule of the 'new order.' Today, this same flogging platform is used to support the altar for divine service. The villagers said the Japs staged public floggings on this platform frequently and that they were required to watch. Sgt. H. W. Rohland." *(National Archives at College Park, Maryland; photograph 100076)*

Johnston's notion of "rebirth" permeated the original contours and connotations of Liberation Day in the late 1940s. The reconciliatory aspect of rebirth was about moving beyond the antagonisms and prejudices created by war. As Martha Minow would argue, Johnston's reconciliatory stance also reflected a broader view shared by diverse religious traditions that see forgiving "offenders" as a way to end the cycles of hate, vengeance, and violence created by wartime atrocities (1998, 14). Yet, as Minow suggested, acts of forgiveness by peoples and institutions are historically known for exempting from punishment, pardoning, or simply forgetting about those accused of perpetuating violence of all kinds (1998, 15). Although these may not have been Johnston's intentions, she clearly saw Liberation Day as offering ceremonial time to reflect on past conflicts and resolve them peacefully. This effort to achieve harmonious social relations was a key factor in Johnston's understanding of rebirth. In addition to the cathartic features of liberation, she believed that notions of spiritual salvation, national sacrifice, and cultural obligation should take center stage in Guam's commemoration of war.[3]

Johnston's notion of spiritual salvation rested on the broader Chamorro historical relationship to the Catholic faith, including the theme of forgiveness, which Liberation Day festivities of the late 1940s strove to portray. During this period, the liberation celebrations resembled Catholic rituals more than civic ceremonies. In 1945, the first year, Johnston organized festivities that included not a customary civic parade but a religious procession at the Plaza de España in Hagåtña, adjacent to the island's Catholic Cathedral. In addition to the ceremonial line of altar boys and priests, this Liberation Day procession included at its core the iconic representation of Santa Marian Kamalen (figure 6). As Chamorro anthropologist Dominica Tolentino stated, "Guam's patroness is the same Virgin Mary, but is locally revered as Santa Marian Kamalen, or Our Lady of Camarin" (1999, 5–6). She noted that the Chamorro veneration of Santa Marian Kamalen bears similarities to the Catholic worship of the Virgin Mary in France, Portugal, and Mexico. Catholics from these areas pray to her as Our Lady of Lourdes, Our Lady of Fatima, and Our Lady of Guadalupe, respectively. In Guam, Chamorros believe that the Virgin Mary protects them "from natural disas-

FIGURE 6. A statue of Santa Marian Kamalen is carried in a religious procession in Hagåtña, following a special mass on Guam Liberation Day, 21 July 1945. *(National Archives, College Park, Maryland)*

ters, war and oppression" (Tolentino 1999, 7). Out of respect for the Virgin Mary, the government of Guam observes an official holiday and Catholic residents annually celebrate a fiesta in her honor on 8 December, the Feast of the Immaculate Conception.

Coinciding with the beginning of the war, the date of this feast and the icon of the Virgin Mary have gained greater meaning and relevance among Chamorros in Guam. "Many people of all ages emphasize the fact that war came to Guam on the day of December 8th, the Feast of the Immaculate Conception of the birth of its patroness. . . . The coincidence of December 8th being both the Feast of the Immaculate Conception and the beginning of World War II (December 7 in Hawaii) is, in fact, considered to be important enough from a cultural standpoint in Guam that it was cited in the legislation enacted in 1971 which made December 8th a legal holiday on the island" (Jorgensen 1984, 83). The legalization of 8 December as a civil and religious holiday reminded Chamorros of the time when war came to the island. In contrast, Liberation Day's invocation of Santa Marian Kamalen was a reminder of their deliverance at the war's end.

Religious images and views saturated the early commemorations of Liberation Day in Guam. As Roman Catholic priest Father Eric Forbes noted during a 2002 interview, "The first Liberation Day celebrations right after the war . . . were largely religious in nature. There were no . . . parades or carnivals in the first Liberation Day celebrations." Instead, as Forbes remarked (2002), "people gathered for Mass, to give thanks to God for deliverance from Japanese occupation, and to pray for those who died in the war" (figure 7). Many attended mass in the various villages. Young boys and girls took flowers to the graves of soldiers and prayed. Masses and processions often concluded with reception dinners and dances at George Washington High School in Sinajana, a village located near the capital, Hagåtña. The annual themes of these commemorations were appropriately named "thanksgiving," in honor of the return of the Americans (*Navy News* 1947).

For Chamorros, however, the meaning of the Catholic religion extended beyond material celebrations and religious rituals. The relationship between religion and war in Guam differed vastly from their historically perceived roles. Ideally, "the spread of religion will develop such hostility to war as to make universal peace a certainty" (Mathews 1918, 80). Shailer Mathews suggested that this conventional view of the relationship between religion and war rarely existed in history. "As a matter of fact, none of the great religions has been in practice frankly anti-militaristic. As a rule religion has been the support of the warrior" (Mathews 1918, 81). Rather than promote warfare, the religious beliefs of Chamorros helped them to persevere and survive throughout the war. Chamorros held "a bright glow of trust in the Omnipotent God burning in the hearts of the people. . . . Surely God will not turn away at such a terrible time as [war]" (G Camacho 1952, 34).

FIGURE 7. Unidentified Chamorro woman and girl praying, Saipan, 13 July 1945. The original caption reads, "The very young and the very old on this liberated Pacific Island offer their thanks to God for deliverance from Japanese rule—and PEACE." *(National Archives, College Park, Maryland; photograph 129098)*

On a deeper level, and at a level reflected in Liberation Day, Catholic spiritual concepts shaped Chamorro interpretations of the war and their involvement in it. Chamorro views of God and the Virgin Mary assisted Chamorros in making sense of the war. Catholic religious values and political loyalties to America became synonymous with antiwar and anti-Japanese sentiments. Further, Catholic notions of liberation and salvation fused with political loyalties. Chamorros prayed to Uncle Sam as if he were a religious figure, a special mediator between the people, the nation, and God. They sought his help, his protection, and his salvation.

After the war, Chamorro prayers extended to Uncle Sam's American soldiers. As Rear Admiral C A Pownall declared in a 1947 Memorial Day address, "Nowhere on earth are the Americans' war dead more highly cherished than on Guam" (1947, 3). "The worshipping of the Americans by the Chamorros underscores the religiosity of the event, a solemnity and piety of which there was plenty to go around" (Diaz 2001, 161). On the occasion of the second liberation commemoration in 1946, island leaders presented a message to US President Harry S Truman. The letter illustrated the spiritual, cultural, and political values of liberation. Capturing the original themes and values of Liberation Day festivities, part of the text read:

> Inspired by love of home and country; the memories of the recent past; the faith and loyalty that sustains even under extreme adversity; the hopes of the future; the re-occupation of Guam by the Armed Forces of the United States D-Day July 21, 1944, which won victory for justice and right, and for our people freedom from the yoke of tyranny; and reverence for the noble and honored heroes who here gave their lives that the nation might live—we,—the people of Guam,—on this second anniversary of our liberation pause, from our daily tasks to thank: (1) the almighty God, in whose keeping right has triumphed and ever shall triumph over might; (2) those brave men living and dead, who struggled to set us free; and (3) the entire nation whose individual and collective sacrifices have justified our faith in salvation. (USDN 1946, 4–5)

Presentations like this were clear evidence of the interconnected nature of spirituality, identity, and nationality in postwar Guam. While gratitude to God is prominent in the letter, these Chamorro leaders also expressed appreciation for the American nation. Their patriotic expression of gratitude is couched in terms of American sacrifices that "justified our faith in salvation." This final sentence reveals that even in the context of loyalty to America at that time, Chamorro Catholic ideals of faith and redemption persisted. Others reiterated these points during Liberation Day festivities. They spoke to peoples at home and abroad about the island's unique wartime relationship with the United States.

The idea of an oppressed indigenous population saved by a humane liberating force continued to warrant special status and attention. Americans who

lost family members in Guam were especially moved by the island's liberation narratives. Iris Weehorn Dodd of Tyler, Texas, was one example. In coming across news coverage of postwar Guam, Dodd recalled the death of her
son, Marine Sergeant Frederick Weehorn Dodd. Representing a generation
of mourners, she related to the wartime sufferings of Chamorros. Impressed
and emotionally moved by indigenous accounts of wartime survival, Dodd
praised Chamorros for being "a brave people."[4] Instead of grieving only for
a person close to home, she now grieved for a people far away. Perhaps this
shared sense of bereavement helped her to find closure and consolation.
Her moving response to war in Guam showed that Liberation Day's narratives of suffering crossed ethnic, political, religious, and class lines.[5]

The Rise in Civil Ceremony

For Americans, liberation narratives of Guam were particularly recogniz-
able because of the enduring Chamorro loyalty to America, which was demonstrated in multiple actions. They resisted Japanese assimilation efforts,
coped with the violence of war, sustained faith in Yu'us and the American
nation, praised the bravery and sacrifice of American soldiers, and fostered
or renewed cultural systems of reciprocation and indebtedness with the
United States. As it had been during the war, the language of loyalty continued to be the primary medium of communication between the colonizer
and the colonized. Ideally, after the war Chamorros could have chosen
another medium of communication with foreigners. However, colonial
powers had often considered their interactions with Chamorros in terms
of loyalty and disloyalty. Chamorro wartime experiences were expressed in
terms of loyalty to the United States because "this was the only political language available to the Chamorros that could be heard and understood by
the Americans" (Diaz 2001, 165). The language of loyalty continued to suit
Chamorro needs because of its political and spiritual power and appeal.
Given the historical significance of commemorations in Guam, it seemed
inevitable that Liberation Day would become the "focal point" of Chamorro
loyalty (Underwood 1977, 6).

From the 1950s onward, Liberation Day festivities adopted loyalty as a
key commemorative theme. The general narrative of Chamorro loyalty
to America set the terms for how those in Guam should interpret, understand, and remember the war, establishing the conditions for history and
memory making, especially in regard to the war. Vicente M Diaz (2001),
Cecilia T Perez (1996), and Robert Underwood (1977) have all emphasized
how the patriotic fervor of Liberation Day mediated Chamorro memories
and understandings of the war. Their opinions clearly refer to the power of
Liberation Day as an occasion for the public representation and interpreta-

tion of war. Although Agueda Johnston saw liberation as a "rebirth" for the island and its people, much of which included a spiritual sense of liberation and salvation, she did not intend that its celebration should be simplified into a civic display of Chamorro loyalty.

Yet the idea of Chamorro loyalty did not persist unchanged throughout the years of commemoration. "The decision of how and where 'Liberation' Day would be observed has never been a simple matter of practicality. Each action has been dictated by political motive and explains the changes in the celebration of 'Liberation' Day over the years" (C Perez 1996, 73). The concept of Chamorro loyalty changed over the years according to the desires and needs of the island's leadership and population. In the continental United States, loyalty to the nation also shared an essential, though changing, role in the shaping of commemorations. "The need to sustain loyalty to the nation during World War II and during the earliest days of the Cold War obviously did not diminish the enthusiasm of authorities in the federal government and the states to use commemorations to foster patriotism" (Bodnar 1992, 250). State centennials in the Midwest in the late 1940s and 1950s were evidence of this official desire to foster loyalty among Americans. "These activities always honored patriotism and governmental institutions in an unquestioning way. But they also celebrated numerous vernacular interests—ethnic groups, pioneers, material progress, business, women" (Bodnar 1992, 250).

Guam's Liberation Day indeed celebrated everyday as well as official interests. As John Bodnar suggested, vernacular and official narratives of loyalty meshed in ways that helped to commemorate the past in various parts of the United States. Guam's Liberation Day festivities did not differ. As the commemoration shifted from an intensely spiritual festivity to a civil one, the politics of loyalty changed. During and after the war, Chamorro spiritual and political loyalties to God and the American nation became apparent. By the late 1940s, the political currency of loyalty in Guam intensified in the wake of a renewed movement for civil government and US citizenship. This movement demonstrated that indigenous narratives of loyalty could achieve political recognition and power at home and abroad. "Chamorros hit upon an irrefutable argument for civil government. The Chamorros were patriotic. They survived the [war] ordeal. They proved their loyalty. In fact, the Chamorros not only deserved political rights, the U.S. owed it to them. . . . The war experience soon became a hammer to obtain political rights, and, subsequently, to obtain federal funds. In order to assure its success, the war experience and Liberation Day became expressed with American symbols" (Underwood 1977, 8). "Now that [Chamorros] had unquestionably proven their love for and loyalty to the Mother Country, the indigenous inhabitants deserved the rights and privileges of American citizenship" (Hofschneider 2001, 115).

As with commemorations elsewhere, Liberation Day and the general narrative of loyalty were used by Chamorros not simply as ways to remember the past, but also to "support their claims for greater political power and social equality" (Bodnar 1992, 27). After the war, they sought an end to the oppressive features of US military rule and strove for equality within the American body politic. At the time, the lure of American citizenship seemed to answer long-standing questions of civil governance and political representation. "Citizenship and all that it symbolized had powerful appeal to a stateless people struggling to recover from the brutalities of Japanese occupation and the devastation" of war (Dames 2000, 1997). To Chamorros, citizenship "would bring not only some limitation on untrammeled Naval authority but also a sense of dignity and equality with the rest of the United States, the security of permanent political union, and finally an acceptance by the national government of their political loyalty and willingness to share the obligations of the U.S. Federal system" (Leibowitz 1989, 330). With the passage of the Organic Act in 1950, Chamorros finally attained a congressional form of US citizenship. A civil government surfaced, ending half a century of naval rule.[6] In accomplishing this change in government and citizenship, Chamorros were reassured that their loyalties to America were heeded by peoples beyond the island's shores. Now a part of the "American family," Chamorros rejoiced in their newfound political identity.

Liberation Day captured more than the celebratory mood of that period. Although President Truman signed the Organic Act on 1 August 1950, it took effect retroactively on 21 July of that year. In time, both the Organic Act and Liberation Day came to be celebrated on the same date as a legal government holiday.

> (a) Liberation Day is a legal holiday declared in commemoration of the anniversary of the liberation of Guam from the Japanese Occupation on July 21, 1944 and the inauguration of civil government in Guam on July 21, 1950. (b) The Governor is authorized and requested to issue annually a proclamation calling upon the people of Guam to observe Liberation Day by displaying the flag at their homes or other suitable places, with appropriate ceremonies and festivities expressive of the public sentiment befitting the occasion. (*Guam Code Annotated* 1996, Title 1)

Beginning in 1950, Liberation Day changed into a grand celebration of Chamorro loyalty. The inauguration of civil government and the granting of American citizenship to Chamorros further strengthened the narratives of loyalty in the commemoration of war.

While the Catholic Church continued to participate in the commemoration, it would never again achieve the prominence it had held during the immediate postwar years. Editors of the *Umatuna Si Yu'us*, Guam's weekly

Catholic newspaper, witnessed with some unease the transformation of Liberation Day from a spiritually laden commemoration to a civil-minded one. "The annual observance of Liberation Day is a civic expression of gladness at the return of Guam to American possession and gratitude towards the United States Congress for the establishment of civil law and the granting of a local constitution for the territory" (*Umatuna Si Yu'us* 1954b, 1). Recognizing the increasingly marginalized role of the Church in the commemoration of the war, the editors asserted, "No special religious observance has been part of the celebration for the last few years" (*Umatuna Si Yu'us* 1954b, 1). In response to the increased civic nature of Liberation Day, they reminded readers that "Liberation Day is not just an occasion for floats and flowers, for queens and crownings, for games and gimmicks, it is a time for soul-searching to see whether we have honestly tried to make ourselves worthy of the sacrifices of those who died for us" (*Umatuna Si Yu'us* 1954b, 5).

Whenever possible, priests and parishioners alike infused Liberation Day with spiritual themes strongly reminiscent of the war and with the wartime experiences of such survivors as Agueda Johnston. Liberation Day planners always welcomed these views. But by the 1950s, different approaches to remembering the past competed for centrality as the official public representation. Peoples and organizations from different secular and religious circles seized the opportunity to use Liberation Day as an occasion to interpret the past and the present. Liberation Day illustrated its potential as a marker and maker of island history. It also possessed tremendous flexibility as a platform for local and national politics, and even economics.

In the Name of Economic Progress

After 1950, now that the island had its own form of civil government, local leaders and developers saw the need to "rehabilitate" Guam once again. Unlike the military's notion of rehabilitation, this form exemplified modernization rather than militarization. Liberation Day festivities of the 1950s reflected the island's move toward a "modern" society. For example, in 1953 the commemorative theme was "post-war progress and future of Guam" (*Guam Daily News* 1953a). The governor of that year, Ford Q Elvidge, remarked, "Guam emerges from the past, reconstructs and rehabilitates itself. A new government is born. A new territory takes its place among the component parts of the American nation" (*Guam Daily News* 1953c). Others echoed Elvidge's comments about the new, modern Guam. Supportive of the local and military economies, the editors of *Guam Daily News* observed in 1954 that "businessmen have pioneered in the rehabilitation of home and the rebuilding of a shattered economy" (*Guam Daily News* 1954). They listed the various economic accomplishments on the island, such as the development of agricultural nurseries, banks, insurance firms, subdivisions, radio stations, and restaurants (figure 8).

However, prominent businessman Eduardo T Calvo cautioned others to be receptive and careful of the economic future of Chamorros in particular. As part of his Liberation Day remarks in 1955, he stated that Chamorros "must constantly strive to lessen our dependence upon the military and to develop wherever possible an independent economy from such of our resources as remain to us" (*Guam Daily News* 1955). Despite these concerns, many touted what they believed to be economic prosperity and progress. Economic growth, they claimed, derived from the island's patriotic history and renewed political ties with the United States.

As expected, the economic and political strides of the 1950s affected the commemoration of Liberation Day in ways that further fostered its growth as a civic celebration. The commemoration now featured floats, marching bands, and parades rather than the Catholic processions of the immediate postwar years. Young women throughout the villages enthusiastically competed to become the next Liberation Day queen. They sold tickets as a means of fund-raising for the commemoration, with the candidate who sold the most tickets becoming the next Liberation Day queen. Furthermore, the former one-day event now included activities that spanned three days. Held at the Paseo de Susana, an artificial park built on the wartime debris of Hagåtña, the festivities ranged from fireworks displays to sport competitions to public addresses. Engulfed in the political achievements and economic materialism of the decade, Liberation Day had been transformed into a commercialized celebration of the war. Even the 1959 commemorative theme, "Old Guam," appeared to signal less a nostalgic call to the past than a warm welcome to the economic future of the island (Palomo 1959).

In the late 1950s, several local voices raised the question, once again, of why Chamorro narratives of survival and salvation so central in defining the earlier Liberation Day commemorations were no longer figuring prominently in the celebrations. Refusing to be silenced by the pomp and pageantry of Liberation Day, Chamorro Protestant minister and University of Guam Professor Dr Joaquin Flores Sablan voiced points raised earlier in the decade: "The meaning of the day has been growing dimmer and dimmer each year as indicated in the way we have been celebrating it. Gambling, heavy drinking, music and dancing, and other forms of entertainment have obscured the meaning and importance of the occasion.... [Liberation Day] should be a day of thanksgiving and sober thinking. It is fitting and proper for all of us to pause and look upward and recognize where our help is coming from" (1957, 7).

Editors of *Umatuna Si Yu'us* also reminded Chamorros of the spiritual significance of Liberation Day. "The temptation to overdo it in the pursuit of sport, entertainment, eating and drinking on occasions of this kind, to place ourselves into dangerous occasions of sin, and to act as though the

FIGURE 8. Liberation Day, Hagåtña, Guam. *(Guam Daily News, 21 July 1954)*

laws of God were suspended for the duration of the celebration, leads us
to issue the word of warning, and to call for a safe and sane observance
of Liberation Day" (*Umatuna Si Yu'us* 1959). Both Sablan and the editors
expressed consternation over the increasingly secular dimensions of the
commemoration. However, they lamented not so much the form of the
commemoration as its content. As members of the generation of war survivors, Sablan and others stressed the need to see the commemoration as a
somber ceremony of appreciation and gratitude—a commemoration that
served to remember a tragic time in the war histories of the island. The
generations of the late 1950s, in their opinion, had lost all understanding
of the war and its violent impact on the island.

Overall, these reactions indicated a level of discomfort felt by the
manamko', the elder generations of Chamorros who survived the war. The
excessive attention paid to sports and parades, rather than to Christian
activities, offended the elder survivors and seemed to trivialize their war
experiences. For the elders, memories and histories of a violent war con-
flicted with the idea of festive war commemorations. Even Agueda Johnston
tempered her celebrations with a strong commitment to the spiritual reflection on the war in general and the forgiveness of individual antagonisms
in particular. In his ironic lament over the secular changes in Liberation
Day, Rev Joaquin Sablan had described the Chamorro appropriation of the
commemoration as a fiesta (1957, 7). The fact that merrymaking persisted
suggested that a growing number of people, especially those of the postwar
generation, accepted the nature and direction of the commemoration. By
the late 1950s and early 1960s, Liberation Day had assumed what anthropologist Ross Crumrine called the "Guamanian fiesta complex" (1982,
89–112). Although Crumrine's study is about village celebrations of saints,
or fiestas, her argument regarding Chamorro forms of celebration extends
to this analysis of Liberation Day. The fiesta complex is an "extremely flex-
ible and adaptive" system that absorbs popular symbolism and reflects interpersonal and intersocietal relations (Crumrine 1982, 89). Far from being a
meaningless celebration, Liberation Day, then and now, offers insight into
symbol-making, social interaction and social perceptions, feasting, enter-
taining, and, above all, remembering and interpreting the war in Guam.

As more Chamorros embraced Liberation Day as one of their special
occasions, they not surprisingly celebrated it in special, fiesta-like, ways. Liberation Day has "become a Chamorro tradition, families set up tents along
the parade route and camp out the night before preparing 'mini-fiestas' to
enjoy during the parade. Large amounts of food are prepared to feed families and friends who may pass by" (C Perez 1996, 72). The enlarged festive
nature of Liberation Day indicated that increasing numbers of Chamorros
accepted the commemoration as an important day and event in their cultural calendar. The festivities still commemorated American and Chamorro
war experiences, but elders such as Sablan believed that Liberation Day's

forms of entertainment detracted from what they perceived to be the true meaning of the commemoration, that is, a day of "thanksgiving" for God and the American nation.

As Sablan's response showed, Liberation Day elicited contestations on the part of the *manamko'* because it catered to a generation of people who did not much understand the war, let alone people who had experienced it. As the editors of a local newspaper in 1962 remarked, "There are thousands of islanders who do not remember the liberation of Guam eighteen years ago. There are thousands more who were not born at the time but who have seen our celebrations of this historical anniversary in the past years" (*Guam Daily News* 1962). The civil dimensions of Liberation Day were bolstered, in part, because of this new generation of nonsurvivors and non-veterans. Without experience, postwar generations did not "remember" the battles and conflicts that occurred on the island. However, songs, stories, and commemorations passed on increasingly disembodied memories and histories of the war from one generation to another.

Certainly, some *manamko'* simply wanted Liberation Day to pay closer attention to their horrific experiences and to take note of their appreciation for the United States. It always did so, if to a lesser degree with each passing year. But the concerns of local and national politics, competing loyalties, commercial entertainment, and regional economies were influential and, at times, unpredictable. Consequently, no single person, organization, or commemoration could, for any extended period of time, narrate a dominant and unchanging war history of the island. The commemoration of Liberation Day could never be only about Chamorro wartime experiences, always a central and long-standing cultural and historical feature of the celebration. The general narrative of Chamorro loyalty held various shades of meaning and implications for the different generations. The challenges facing *manamko'* perceptions of how the war should be remembered had only begun.

Tourism, Japan, and the Commemoration of the War in Guam

In the 1960s, it became evident among island leaders and the wider business community that tourism was the economy of the future. Yet at that time, most Chamorros did not know what "tourism" meant. As Bert Unpingco recalled, "The word 'tourism' was foreign to Chamorros and islanders and no one knew how Guam would benefit from tourism" (Borja 1980, 8). Still, American military and federal officials, consultants, and corporate representatives encouraged island leaders to consider tourism as a viable economy.[7]

The enthusiasm for the development of tourism in Guam stemmed from the opening by the United States Navy of the island's ports, airways, and trade routes to the region in 1962. Previously, the navy had regulated and enforced what was called the Naval Security Clearance Policy,[8] which restricted travel into and out of the Mariana Islands, with the exception of Rota. A product of the Cold War, the policy strove to maintain a level of secrecy regarding the US military fortification of such islands as Guam, Saipan, and Tinian. With the construction of military facilities in the islands completed, President John F Kennedy abolished the policy on 21 August 1962, thereby allowing tourist industries to develop in both Guam and the Northern Mariana Islands.

With the termination of the Naval Security Clearance Policy, the once marginal tourist industry began to thrive as foreign hotel developers, businesses, and entrepreneurs came to the island. Given the great distance separating Guam from the continental United States, as well as the prohibitive air travel costs, island leaders saw dim prospects for attracting American tourists. Further, Americans already saw Hawai'i as their premier Pacific Island tourist destination, a place where many of them sought temporary escape from the problems of urban life and industrial capitalism (Imada 2004, 135). Guam's leaders instead looked west to Japan, where they recognized a potential tourist market.

As might be anticipated, elder Chamorros did not openly welcome this new industry, which catered primarily to Japanese visitors. Yet, despite their reservations, the wartime generation did not publicly object to the idea of a Japanese-oriented tourist industry in Guam. Torn between promises of a modern island economy and unsettling memories of the past, the *manamko'* reluctantly accepted the turn of events. As Tan Urelia Francisco remarked, "When I think of those times, I hate the Japanese . . . . I know people say we need a strong economy, but I don't care. We did just fine before they came and we don't need them now. . . . I do forgive the Japanese for what they did, but I will never forget" (Bassler 1991, 16). At issue was the role of tourism in generating discussion about the remembrance of the Japanese.

Prior to the 1960s, Liberation Day festivities rarely incorporated Japanese veterans and survivors of the war as honored guests, heroic symbols, or patriotic figures. The few Chamorros who maintained relationships with the Japanese frequently remained quiet, hidden behind a veil of embarrassment and shame. For the most part, Chamorros felt no need to celebrate the histories of their wartime occupiers. The postwar commemorative representations of the Japanese that did surface featured Japanese as faceless victimizers and obedient followers of imperial ideology. Many Guam Chamorros therefore tended to view the Japanese as a homogenous group of militarist murderers and rapists. But as the tourist industry promoted an image of the island as a hospitable island paradise, its supporters asked Chamorros to perceive the Japanese in contemporary terms. Public leaders asserted that Japan had changed from a country of violent war to a peaceful nation embracing the world economy. For example, in 1966 editors of the *Guam Daily News* appealed to the public to "turn away from the thoughts of the bloodshed and the occupation to the better days that lie ahead" (*Guam Daily News* 1966a). Some even argued that Chamorros should outright suppress the violent memories and histories of the war.

The political elite of Guam knew that indigenous memories of the war could jeopardize or at least destabilize the new tourist economy. For instance, as a means of spreading support for tourism, educator Katherine B Aguon reasoned that in order to "clear" antagonisms created by the war, Liberation Day activities should "be played down gradually.... There is widespread agreement that Guam must recognize its economic alignment with Japan. It is said by many others that our relationship with Japan, our former foe, is fundamental to Guam's future growth" ([1971?], 2). The economic survival of Guam, she argued, was in part dependent on the reshaping of war memories and commemorations suitable for a Japanese tourist audience. As a means to distract Chamorros from remembering the violence of the Japanese, Aguon proposed that the island should instead commemorate the Organic Act rather than Liberation Day. Although her recommendation was never implemented, others maintained the belief that Chamorro memories of the Japanese as a violent people should be "played down."

The debate surrounding Japanese wartime violence in Guam told Chamorros, especially those of the older generations, that tourist industries catered to a different, "peaceful" group of Japanese. Yet these discussions had little impact on the ways Japanese would be remembered and commemorated among Chamorros. In the first place, Chamorro loyalties to America would appear meaningless without reference to wartime antagonisms to the Japanese military. Further, Liberation Day festivities rarely addressed Japanese memories and histories of the war in ways that provided context for Japanese imperialism and propaganda. Sadly, rather than moving toward critical understandings of Japanese—or American—colonialisms, the discussions of the role of Japan in Guam's tourist economy generated another caricature of the Japanese people.

The wartime image of the Japanese as "victimizers" was now juxtaposed with their postwar image as "tourists." Proponents of tourism in Guam were not the only ones who attempted to refashion interpretations of the Japanese during the war and postwar periods. The emerging peace movement in Japan and the gradual proliferation of "bone-collecting" missions and peace memorials all contributed to producing representations of the Japanese as peaceful, proud, and prosperous people. By the early 1960s, the Japanese government, itself a key contributor in reshaping images of the nation's wartime past, established annual memorial services "to encourage pride in Japanese accomplishment and raise awareness of nationhood" (Orr 2001, 138).

These memorial services stretched from the Japanese mainland to Japan's former wartime territories. In Guam, the Japanese government cooperated with American military officials in planning for the memorial services, a major part of which entailed the collection of human remains believed to be Japanese in origin. Separated from the pageantry of Liberation Day festivities, these bone-collecting missions grew in the 1960s with the arrival of elderly Japanese veterans and war survivors.[9] As Chamorro activist and former Senator Hope Cristobal elaborated, "When the tourist industry opened up, a lot of Japanese started coming up here. One of the first things they did was to organize Japanese tour groups and comb through the jungles and collect all the bones of the Japanese people" (dé Ishtar 1994, 75). The Japanese tour groups then performed religious services and cremated the bones. These memorial services continued largely undisturbed and without much public attention until 1967.

In January 1967 members of the South Pacific Memorial Association arrived on Guam to initiate the construction of a peace memorial. Representing the Buddhist and Catholic faiths, the association dedicated the memorial to the war dead. It gave equal recognition to the spiritual efforts of both past and future bone-collecting missions and cremation ceremonies. Mitsunoti Ueki, one of the founding organizers for what came to be known as the Guam Peace Memorial, believed that the shrine symbolized peace, friendship, and goodwill (*Guam Daily News* 1966b). Catholic Bishop Senuemon Fukahori of the Kyushu Diocese stated, "We are here to bring consolation to the relatives of the deceased of all races and of all nations. . . . [The purpose of the memorial is to] foster the beginning of peace and friendship between nations in this part of the world" (Butterbaugh 1967, 11). The association envisioned a tall, white memorial with "two hands clasped folded in prayer and meditation." It would be situated alongside a pool, fountain, and statue of two boys, an American and a Japanese, whose hands would be "clasped in 'eternal' friendship" (Butterbaugh 1967, 24).

The association chose a parcel of land in Mataguac, Yigo, previously owned by the Chamorro family of the late Joaquin Borja Leon Guerrero y Palomo, as the location for the shrine. It was also the area where the last military conflict between American and Japanese forces took place in August 1944. Members of the association gathered there to commemorate Japan's war past. In the words of Mitsunoti Ueki, they came not as soldiers or tourists, but as "newly born" Japanese in search of peace (*Guam Daily News* 1966b).

At the outset, the South Pacific Memorial Association seemed to garner all the support it needed, receiving encouragement from the Japanese Ministry of Foreign Affairs, the US Department of State, and several of Guam's local leaders and organizations. Even Father Oscar L Calvo, a prominent Chamorro priest and spiritual figure, openly endorsed the project and ensured that the association was warmly welcomed in Guam. Perhaps in part because of his involvement, no public protests by Chamorros developed. But the process to recognize the legitimacy of the peace memorial did not come without heated debate and conflict. Only a few months after the inauguration of the memorial, disapproval and criticism surfaced.

Some of the most outspoken critics were expatriate Americans. One group identified themselves as members of "The American South and Central Pacific Society," whose mission was to preserve peace and to defend American interests in the western Pacific. This society of American "super-patriots," as they called themselves, circulated propaganda in an effort to deter the increasing proliferation of Japanese memorials in American jurisdictions.[10] For example, member Herbert P Beyer vehemently exclaimed, "NEVER BEFORE IN HISTORY, has a group of private citizens of a FOREIGN COUNTRY . . . ever conspired to USURP, CIRCUMVENT, and SUBVERT, the prerogatives and function of our government in the erection of War Memorials to their war dead on our soil" (Goodwin 1967, 14). On hearing of Japanese efforts to construct a memorial, various United States congressional representatives also voiced their concerns. Congressman L Roudebush, a Republican from Indiana, protested that the United States "lost some 100,000 American servicemen in the Pacific theatre in World War Two—7,083 were either killed, missing or wounded during the Guam campaign and we don't even have a memorial on Guam honoring our own war dead" (*Guam Daily News* 1967b). Shortly after, in July 1967, a resolution that insisted on the removal of the Japanese shrine was submitted to the US House of Representatives. Although it did not pass, many continued to argue that the Japanese peace memorial stood as "an affront to those American servicemen who fought and died in the Pacific theater" (*Guam Daily News* 1967a). As these Americans attested, Guam was an American territory and key battleground in the war. In their eyes, the island signified a sacred war site of valor and loyalty. Once again, the creation of a Japanese memorial had ignited some Americans' wartime convictions about their military sacrifice and superiority (figure 9).

The objections to the peace memorial were even more weighty in the absence of a nationally recognized American war memorial on the island. Indeed, American memorials already existed throughout the island in the form of bomb shelters, plaques, tanks, and other military markers of the war, but none had been designated as an American National Historic Landmark, as Pearl Harbor, on O'ahu, had been in 1964 (Adams 1996, 58). Later in 1967, however, the Advisory Board on National Parks, Historic Sites, Buildings and Monuments approved a proposal to create a "War in the Pacific National Historic Park" in Guam. The advisory board indicated that pressure to develop the War in the Pacific National Historic Park increased "following the announcement of plans of a private group to set up a Japanese memorial in the island territory" (*Guam Daily News* 1967c).

These statements lessened most American criticisms; in truth, however, studies to build a nationally registered park in Guam had actually begun

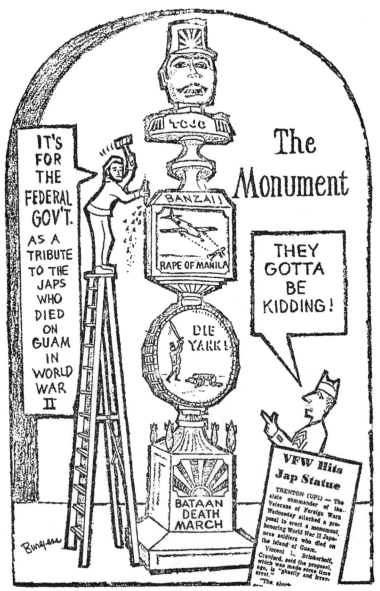

FIGURE 9. Cartoon of Japanese war monument. *(Atlantic City Press, 27 October 1966. Copy in Manuscript Collection, RFT Micronesian Area Research Center)*

in 1965, two years before the formal dedication of the Japanese peace memorial (Hewlett 1969, 1). The War in the Pacific National Historic Park would register the American invasion sites in Hågat and Asan as a National Historic Landmark. The park was to commemorate "the epic story of that phase of World War II, between the debacle of Pearl Harbor and the formal surrender of Japan, which involved the conquest of island strongholds on the road to victory in the Pacific Theater," as well as the recapture of Guam and its strategic importance as an American territory (NPS 1969, 7).

On 18 August 1978, a decade after the inauguration of the Japanese peace memorial in Yigo, Guam, plans for the War in the Pacific National Historic Park were realized. Organizers for the park anticipated that "such a park would be a source of pride to Guamanians and to other Americans and would be of considerable interest to foreign visitors not only for its historic significance, but as an example of an American institution—the National Park System" (NPS 1969, 7). The enthusiasm and pride attached to the War in the Pacific Park may have been shared by veterans and survivors of the war, but it was not as widespread among Chamorros as some assumed. As with the unveiling of the Japanese peace memorial, the majority of the indigenous population paid little attention to the new turn of events. As Vicente L G Perez observed, "There has been an extreme lack of interest for the Second World War Monuments and markers by the local people" ([1970?], 43). Part of this apathy toward the memorials stemmed from the reality that they often commemorated Americans and Japanese rather than the indigenous population. At that time, the War in the Pacific National Historic Park simply represented another example of how a national government, and its affiliates, could commemorate the war.[11]

As the criticisms surrounding the construction of the Japanese peace memorial demonstrated, numerous issues were involved in Guam's "national" commemoration of the war. Japanese organizations, for example, saw the development of peace memorials, at home and abroad, as a way to appease both the dead and the living. On the other hand, some American veteran groups strongly defended what they believed was their sole stewardship of American wartime sites and burial grounds. Both groups envisioned Guam as an island intimately part of their own individual lifetime experiences and memories; their interactions further illustrated the entangled and contested nature of war commemorative activities at the peripheries of both the American and Japanese empires. Ultimately, the propaganda leveled against Japanese war commemorations demonstrated another instance in which some Americans attempted to set the terms for war remembrance in Guam. They may not have succeeded in deterring the influx of Japanese peace and bone-collecting missions, or other efforts on the part of the Japanese to commemorate the war. But the public effort to silence Japanese responses to these attacks, as well as the immediate approval of the War in the Pacific National Historical Park, revealed one outstanding truth. Some American veterans and politicians in the 1960s possessed the emotional, political, and social license to determine how the war should be commemorated at a national level in Guam.

New Visions for Liberation Day

The exclusive nature of American efforts to memorialize the war on the island was not unique. The Japanese often performed their peace ceremonies privately among friends and families. Liberation Day itself catered mostly to those sympathetic toward the US Armed Forces and Chamorro war experiences. However, the rise in tourism and the overall changing local and international environment of the 1970s affected the meaning and direction of Liberation Day. Earlier commemorations had praised the American military as interpreted through the wartime memories of Chamorros. Religious interpretations of liberation and salvation were later meshed with civic and secular traditions of commemoration. As the island developed a military and tourist economy, large numbers of migrants also arrived as educators, laborers, and professionals.[12] Cultural critic Teresia Teaiwa has theorized this phenomenon as "militourism," a process "by which military or paramilitary force ensures the smooth running of a tourist industry, and that same tourist industry masks the military force behind it" (1999, 251). Guam now stands as one of several Pacific Island economies, from Hawai'i to French Polynesia, that draw on the productive and polluting elements of the military and tourist industries (Teaiwa 1999, 251). As a consequence of an economy dependent on these industries, the increase in migration to Guam broadened Liberation Day's intended audiences. Rather than being mainly for Americans and Chamorros, Liberation Day celebrations expanded their audience to include Japanese tourists and the diverse groups of people who now called Guam their home.

Of all those who contributed to the shaping of Liberation Day, former Governor of Guam Ricardo J Bordallo emerged as one of the few who worked to make it more inclusive and pluralistic. During his two terms, from 1975 to 1978 and from 1983 to 1986, Bordallo transformed Liberation Day into a multicultural celebration. The story of the American liberation of Guam still figured prominently. But the charismatic Bordallo, himself a survivor of the war, wanted the commemoration to represent the elements of what he called "fiestan Guam." The central ideas of fiestan Guam included cooperation, friendship, and, of course, celebration. As Bordallo explained in 1977, "to 'fiesta' means to enjoy and celebrate. . . . We can emphasize this special festivity as the one time during the year, when all the people of Guam cannot only gather together and celebrate in commemoration and honor, but also as a time to show our off-island and tourist friends that we can, as a homogenous and assimilated people do this in spirit, friendship, and harmony" (1977, 3). Aware of the emerging postwar communities on the island, such as the Chinese, Filipinos, and Koreans, Bordallo also ensured that Liberation Day would welcome these groups into its festivities. "Our ethnic communities," he noted, "have even taken the time to plan cultural programs to both acquaint our [Chamorro] people with these different lifestyles, and to provide our visitors with a little touch of home while here on Guam" (1977, 3).

This promotion of a multicultural commemoration of war reflected a part of Bordallo's overall philosophy as a governor. He believed that Liberation Day extended his emphasis on togetherness, tolerance, and tradition. Liberation Day was about modern Guam and the future of its diverse peoples. The commemorative themes during Bordallo's separate administrations illustrated his commitment to a productive and prosperous Guam. A few of these themes were "Peace Through a Brotherhood of Man" (1972); "I Famaguon Guinaiya" (Children are Love) (1975); "Dinaña" (Cooperation) (1977);[13] and "Partners in Progress: A Salute to the Year of the Handicapped" (1981). Others recognized these new focal points of Liberation Day, including its value as an occasion to raise important economic, historical, political, and social issues. This was no surprise to the Chamorros, especially the political elite, many of whom used the celebration to voice their specific concerns regarding the island's past and future.

Bordallo's pluralistic worldview challenged the notion that Liberation Day was a holiday only for American veterans and Chamorros. He continually sought ways to incorporate the island's different ethnic groups into the commemoration, allowing others to share their crafts, foods, traditions, and views. By the early 1980s, it was quite common for residents to partake in the festivities of cultures not indigenous to the island. People not only celebrated the time off from work, but a few even reflected among themselves on the significance of the war. Parallels between one ethnic group's war experiences and those of the Chamorros were frequently mentioned.

In 1972, Kyon Shik Kim, consul for the Republic of South Korea, noted, "When liberation is mentioned, our Korean people come to have a feeling of sympathy, for Korea was also once occupied by an enemy for a long time" (K Kim 1972, 13). On another occasion, Philippine Consul General Jose S Estrada acknowledged the historical affinity of Filipinos and Chamorros, who were "stumbled across by Magellan in 1521 in search of a shorter gateway to the east; colonized under the flag of Castille for almost four centuries; ceded to the United States under the Treaty of Paris; overrun by the Japanese in 1941 and liberated by the United States in 1945." He concluded, "We know you well enough to say that you will carry on" (Estrada 1968, 4).

In certain respects, the Liberation Day commemorations of the 1970s and 1980s attempted to present Guam as an island utopia of ethnic diversity. Governor Bordallo's efforts to unite the island's population and to make Liberation Day a multicultural commemoration reflected lofty ambitions. He understood that Guam was in a state of economic, political, and social crisis. The enthusiasm he brought to Liberation Day served to sanitize the growing problems of the island, such as domestic violence, increasing theft, and pollution. Modernization, he argued, threatened the environment and the very survival of the Chamorro culture. "In the name of progress," he wrote, "man has destroyed his environment, ignored the good of all for his own good. On Guam we often attribute the roots of the problems of delinquency and crime to the identity crisis—born out of confusion about who we are and what we want to become" (Bordallo 1977, 1). As the consequences of modernization became more apparent, Chamorro educators and leaders questioned the value of the island's economic and political systems. Groups such as Para' Pada Y Chamorros (Stop Slapping the Chamorros) and the Organization of People for Indigenous Rights were formed in direct response to what some were now publicly calling "American colonialism."

For the most part, the commemoration of Liberation Day remained beyond the criticisms of Chamorro political activist groups. Bilingual education, political representation, and cultural sovereignty were some of the issues advocated locally and internationally by these organizations.[14] It was not until the early 1990s that one group decided to publicly protest the celebration of Liberation Day, pointing to its colonial dimensions. In a letter to the *Pacific Daily News* in 1991, the late Angel Santos, then *maga'låhi* (male leader) of the United Chamorro Chelus for Independence Association, denounced the commemoration of Liberation Day.[15] "The Chamorros of Guam must stop paying homage to a government that has never cared for us—the indigenous inhabitants of Guam" (Santos 1991). Santos urged Chamorros to abandon the idea of the American liberation of the island, and to rethink their historical and political relationship with America. No liberation exists, he noted, as long as America retains full political control of the island's peoples and resources. Instead, Santos opted for renaming Liberation Day: "As painful as the following statement may be, the 21st of July should be more appropriately called 'Reoccupation Day'" (Santos 1991).

Among the examples of American colonialism provided by Santos, one in particular stood out. He said that if America sincerely felt concern for Chamorros, then why did the navy refuse to evacuate Chamorros with its military dependents on 17 October 1941, a few months prior to the Japanese invasion? (Santos 1991). Santos reasoned that the navy knowingly withdrew its families without due consideration for the remaining Chamorro population. The war generations of Chamorros undoubtedly recalled this incident. Members of Santos's organization, later renamed Nasion Chamoru (Chamorro Nation), similarly believed that such questions should be posed to the public, and especially to the older wartime generations. As Eddie "Ed" L G Benavente explained in an interview (2002), certain questions "beg answers."[16] He noted that in order to publicize their efforts, Nasion Chamoru waved signs at Liberation Day festivities. Their preferred site was the annual Liberation Day parade on Hagåtña's main throughway, Marine Drive (now called Marine Corps Drive). At the parades, they bore signs that read, "Are we truly liberated?" or "Are we liberated or reoccupied?" The wording of the questions, he added, prompted "bystanders to look at that sign and reflect, 'What does he mean by reoccupied?' But, you know, those were the questions that we wanted our *manamko'* to answer, our elderlies to answer, consciously or unconsciously." Benavente added that "some of the questions were just blatant like, 'Liberation, how could that be? They stole our lands.' So, we wanted directness. We believe in direct action as well" (Benavente 2002).

Whether their views were phrased as questions or statements, Nasion Chamoru played an important role in informing the island's public, Chamorro elders, and the US military about the lingering problems of American colonialism in Guam. The activist group chose an important occasion, Liberation Day, to stage its protests, knowing that the celebration received much attention and publicity. In contesting Liberation Day, Nasion Chamoru focused on examples of American colonialism such as land dispossession during the war and the degradation of Chamorro culture. As Benavente argued, part of the organization's goals included "educating" others about the contradictions of American foreign policy. Much of the knowledge gained in understanding these contradictions, he noted, stemmed from the individual experiences of the group members who were veterans of the US armed forces. According to Benavente, these men, approximately three quarters of the organization, initially joined the US military as a means to spread the precepts of democracy. Many even served in the Korean and Vietnam wars. But later, commented Benavente, "they awoken themselves to that reality, 'why am I fighting a war for liberty of peoples in foreign places?' When I come to Guam I don't need to do that because I can face the reality that I have been dispossessed from my lands for military purposes. . . . You don't need to go to foreign wars [when injustices and inequality already] exist in a place called America" (2002).

One might assume that given Nasion Chamoru's familiarity with the US military, their views might have been taken seriously. The organization's activism was certainly instrumental in "winning a court case about the implementation of the public law on the Chamorro Land Trust Act" (Stade 1998, 196). This law enabled the local government to distribute or lease federal or "excess military" lands to Chamorro landowners. Despite such accomplishments, Nasion Chamoru was not popularly received. Due to members' vocal protests, as well as their radical, even threatening, physical appearances, some Chamorros shunned their tactics as disrespectful and shameful. The stereotypical image of Nasion Chamoru was of a group of bald or long-haired men wearing combat fatigues and sporting tattoos. Chamorro elders, a key target audience for the organization, sometimes spoke out privately or publicly against Nasion Chamoru. In particular, the older wartime generation did not appreciate these activists, almost all of whom were born after the war, telling them how to interpret their war memories.

Indeed, from Agueda Johnston to Rev Joaquin Sablan, Chamorros of the wartime generation dictated, in large part, how the war should be remembered locally. Frequently, the older wartime generation publicly stated their feelings about the meaning of the war in general and of Liberation Day in particular. They also showed no significant interest in debating how the war should be remembered nationally in Japan or the United States. On the other hand, Nasion Chamoru hoped that the Chamorro elders would listen to them, and perhaps change their way of thinking about the war, America, and ultimately their loyalties to the United States. The organization's members did not anticipate a refusal on the part of the *manamko'* to listen to their views. Nor did they foresee the elders challenging their overall premise and authority to speak about the war and the island's involvement in it.

The *manamko'* commonly responded to Nasion Chamoru by saying, "You weren't there, boy. You did not live during the war. That is why you cannot understand the war. And that is why you should not voice your views. Furthermore, the Americans liberated us! They did not liberate you!" (Benavente 2002). In short, the elders first reminded the organization's members that they were "boys," part of the younger postwar generation's lower rank in terms of familial hierarchies. The elders also scolded the organization's members for having the audacity to speak about a war they never experienced and, in effect, told them to "shut their mouths." In the elders' minds, they were the ones "liberated," not those of the postwar generations.

Consequently, those in Nasion Chamoru listened to the elders and revised their forms of protest, from public demonstrations to mainly written statements. As Benavente noted, "We really softened our attempt to continue protesting Liberation Day.... Out of respect for the *manamko'*, we chose that the next protests we [would] do in terms of our battles [would be on] paper, in editorials, letters to the editors" (2002). Over a few years, the elders successfully conveyed and reinforced their interpretation of Liberation Day's significance to Nasion Chamoru. During the fiftieth anniversary of World War II in 1994, called "Golden Salute," Nasion Chamoru offered a new look in terms of its contestation of Liberation Day. Out of respect for the older wartime generations, as well as in deference to returning war veterans, the organization "put protesting Liberation Day in the back burner for now" (Benavente 2002). The activists realized, with the aid of their elders, that the American veterans were not directly responsible "for the problems caused by the federal government" (Runquist 1994). As Angel Santos remarked, "These [American] veterans deserve the highest respect and honor for their unselfish sacrifice in saving our lives during the war" (Runquist 1994).

Although its approaches changed slightly, Nasion Chamoru's purpose continued. On the occasion of the fiftieth anniversary, activists "passed out fliers to the veterans on Liberation Day asking for their support in Guam's quest for self-determination" (Eclavea 1994). Amid the commemorative activities of welcoming parties, dinners, island tours, and fireworks, the issue of Chamorro self-determination was raised among the veterans. Public meetings and even family barbecues were held for the veterans, hoping that they would support Chamorro political decolonization. While it remained unclear what the veterans generally felt about decolonization efforts in Guam, a few listened openly to members of Nasion Chamoru. For example, Edward O'Bryan said that he hoped that "you guys get your land back" (Eclavea 1994). William Putney, another veteran, stated, "I think your goal here is right. I understand your impatience. We didn't liberate Guam to be a second-class group of people" (S Limtiaco 1994). Reflecting on why he came to Guam in the first place, Joe Benak commented, "As a very young soldier landing near Agat beach, my personal vision was to help retake the island, free the imprisoned Chamoru people, and go home to farm-living from where I came. . . . To my personal amazement, little did I know that the people of Guam were not given back their land after the war. Liberation? Put yourself in my shoes. When you come here willing to give your life, you come to free people that have been imprisoned. . . . You don't come here to take their soil" (Ray 1994b).

It is apparent from these remarks that some American veterans expressed concern about the injustices committed in Guam. They perceived their roles as "liberators" of an oppressed people, yet failed to realize that America's expansion into the Pacific was not premised on liberation. In any event, the veterans did not change the island's political status. Nor could they, or anyone else, tarnish their image as "heroes." Already, for half a century, many American veterans had enjoyed the privilege of being called "liberators." The collective memory of Chamorros as a "liberated" people helped to perpetuate this image of American soldiers and sailors. Liberation Day likewise mediated the memories and histories of the war, particularly as expressed by Chamorros of the war and postwar periods. Narratives of colonial triumph and indigenous loyalty have dominated, both in the collective memory of Chamorros and in the annual, local commemoration of the war in Guam. How colonial and indigenous memories of the war are commemorated in the Northern Mariana Islands is the subject of the next chapter.

Chapter 5
The Land without Heroes

In the Northern Mariana Islands, war commemorations also dictate in large part the ways in which people remember and understand the war, then and now. In particular, the island of Saipan sets the terms for commemorative activities in the Northern Mariana Islands. Civic ceremonies, national memorial projects, and pilgrimages of mourning represent some of the publicly recognized commemorations in these islands. The central war commemoration, also called Liberation Day, celebrates not the invasion of American military forces on 15 June 1944, but the release of civilians from Camp Susupe on 4 July 1946. Unlike celebrations of American liberation in Guam, most reminders of the war in the Northern Mariana Islands invoke feelings of apathy and loss. In this chapter I explore the origins and historical development of Liberation Day in the northern islands, as well as the various commemorations created by Americans and Japanese, in a place more aptly called the land without heroes.

The "Liberation" of Camp Susupe

In Camp Susupe, Saipan, Chamorro and Refaluwasch families lived under the rules of the American military government. They were granted time to farm and fish during the day, but they had to return to the camp in the evening. Under the supervision of military officers, indigenous police guarded the perimeter of the campground to ensure that the rules of the internment camp were met. Military officials argued that the restrictions protected Chamorros and Refaluwasch from the dangers of war, specifically unexploded ordnance and sniper fire from Japanese stragglers. The regulations also attempted to deter sexual relations between the large number of American soldiers and the small number of indigenous women. The relatively safe environment of the camp provided opportunities for families enrolled in classes to gain fluency in the English language, as well as familiarity with the military's portrayal of American political and social life. While some Chamorros appreciated the much-needed food and medical aid, the internment camp still subjected them to US military segregationist policies and procedures. Further, life inside the campgrounds rarely matched life outside. Many looked forward to the day when they would be allowed to return to their family lands.

Finally, on 4 July 1946, after two years of internment, the military government released civilians from the camp. Gathered around the village bandstand, military officials, with the aid of Chamorro translators, addressed the eager and excited crowd. Naval Commander L G Findley reiterated some of the achievements of the American rehabilitation project. "As you know," he said, "my duty here has been working with you—your problems have been mine and your gains have been a feeling of accomplishment to me." Proud of the work of the US military government, Findley stated, "We have covered a good piece on the right road during this period." He spoke in particular of "highlights," such as the construction of new homes, the demolition of Susupe's fences, the increase in wages paid to postwar employees, and the repatriation of Asian settlers. "Best of all," Findley claimed, "every one is free to engage in any sort of legitimate business or work." In closing, he praised the people and administration for striving to make Saipan a "model American island" (Findley 1947, 2). Two years of US military rule, he implied, had not only raised "native acceptance of American customs," but had also succeeded in eradicating all forms of loyalty to and identification with Japan (USTTPI [1947?], 15).

The closing of Camp Susupe would not have occurred without the assurance that Chamorros were becoming more loyal and supportive of the American military rehabilitation project. Additional factors contributing to the discharge of civilians included the surrender of Japan a year earlier and the conviction that the island was secure. Not surprisingly, Chamorros and Refaluwasch were joyful on returning to their lands. In an interview, Tun Manuel Celes described how his heart was set free on leaving the camp (Celes 2002). His "heart," he exclaimed, no longer felt *"mafñot,"* or "tight." Gesturing excitedly to his chest, Tun Manuel said his "heart opened up." A free heart, he said, allowed one to breathe comfortably. In his own poetic way, Tun Manuel depicted the removal of Susupe's fences as emancipation from the violence of war. Although the occasion provided reason to celebrate, other considerations tempered Chamorros' feelings of happiness with sadness, given the various problems that had yet to be addressed. Numerous Saipanese regarded 4 July 1946 as the day "to reconstruct that which had been destroyed"; in addition to rebuilding homes and ranches, some of the unfortunate ones had the "pitiful tasks of locating the sites where their loved ones fell victims to the war" (*District Panorama* 1966). Nevertheless, as the editors of the Saipan newspaper *Pregonero* observed, the dismantling of the fence around the camp "marked the beginning of freedom for the People of Saipan"; they realized that "this day was their day of Liberation" (*Pregonero* 1947).

Chamorros in Rota, Saipan, and Tinian may have shared similar spiritual views of perseverance and survival with their cousins in Guam. But the cultural, political, and religious import of American liberation and loyalty that reflected the general Chamorro war experience in Guam found no early meaning or relevance in the northern islands. As military officials had previously noted of their invasion and rehabilitation campaigns in the Northern Mariana Islands, Chamorro loyalties appeared predominantly, if ambivalently, "pro-Japanese." In naming 4 July 1946 Liberation Day, the civil administrators of the time knowingly invoked the American holiday called Independence Day. They hoped to positively influence indigenous perceptions of Americans in the islands. The inaugural Liberation Day introduced Chamorros, initially in Saipan and later in Rota and Tinian, to the tradition of American commemorations in general and to the significance of American loyalty in particular. However, it lacked local traditions of commemoration such as special masses and processions. Various villages also failed to host elaborate feasts and parades in honor of the Americans, practices already familiar to those in Guam.

Based on the dearth of commemorative activities, it appeared that Liberation Day was an idea with little resonance among the Chamorros of the Northern Mariana Islands. Instead, many Chamorros directed their energies to returning to their homes rather than participating in a celebration that represented the peculiarly American principles of freedom and liberation. In certain respects, Chamorros in Saipan appreciated the newly granted freedom to resume their daily lives. Yet the concepts of freedom, liberation, and even loyalty, as articulated and promulgated by the American military government, were novel to the Chamorros of the northern islands. These terms needed to be instilled and adapted to preexisting and previously Japanized notions of national loyalty and collective identity among Chamorros. During the American project of rehabilitating the Northern Mariana Islands, military officials publicized, with some success, an image of a generous America. The distribution of food and medical supplies reinforced the image of a compassionate America and, in turn, Chamorros were greatly impressed by the culture of the Americans. In 1947, a year after the release of civilians from Camp Susupe, Liberation Day activities continued.

The military organizers hoped that the annual commemoration would perpetuate American political and social ideals originally introduced by the American rehabilitation project. They desired that Liberation Day would help to release Chamorros from their Japanese past and introduce them to an American future. Chosen for his familiarity with American commemorative activities, Adrian Sanchez, a Chamorro veteran from Guam, coordinated the second Liberation Day on 4 July 1947. Because of the activities held, this date has often been mistaken as the origin of the commemoration. Unlike the previous year, when speeches on the significance of freedom and the American rehabilitation project were the principal focus, the second commemoration offered the public opportunities to participate in the festivities. In a competitive spirit, people caught greased pigs, climbed poles, danced, ran relay races, and wrestled. The events were accompanied by the tunes of the navy band during the day and later at night. Food booths and exhibits of indigenous arts and crafts also caught the appetites and attention of passing visitors and guests. With the addition of these social activities, Saipan's Liberation Day barely resembled its counterpart in Guam. Sanchez's approach to the commemoration of Liberation Day in Saipan was more civic-centered.

Prior to Sanchez's tour of duty in Saipan, from 1944 to 1948, he worked as an enlisted steward in the United States Navy. He was a war veteran and, in some respects, a "liberator" among his people. On Saipan, the military government designated him a school administrator to assist in the teaching of English. As a military man, raised in American-occupied Guam, Sanchez knew he was dealing with a different population of Chamorros who rarely identified with the Americans. In crafting the second commemoration of Liberation Day, he viewed the celebration as a venue to strengthen social relations between Chamorros and Americans, as well as a place to instill pride in Chamorro culture. As one military report indicated, the commemoration "was planned . . . to revive native traditions and contests, neglected during the war years, and to acquaint island American personnel with native methods of living and working."[1]

Although the celebration was deemed an achievement in terms of public participation, events did not go as planned. For example, Sanchez later learned that the local priests discouraged public dancing. "Being from Guam," he explained, "a party without dancing was unheard of, but in Saipan, this was actually not the right thing to do" (A Sanchez 1990, 20). Sanchez did not elaborate on the reasons for the local clergy's opposition to public dancing. Perhaps they disapproved of the explicitly civic dimensions of the commemoration, as some of the elders and priests had argued in respect to Guam's Liberation Day in the 1950s. Or perhaps the priests had moral reservations about the sexual attractions and desires the dancing might have evoked.

At any rate, Saipan's Liberation Day would not be celebrated again until 1958, placating anyone who might have been offended by its initial form and meaning. As a result of people's indifference to the commemoration, it lapsed for nine years. However, its absence did not signal the demise of other ceremonies and fiestas. Catholic religious rituals resumed with the reconstruction of churches. People celebrated the coming of life in the form of baptisms with the same spiritual devotion and care they took to lament the passing of loved ones. The brief elimination of Liberation Day did not suggest that colonial and indigenous memories of the war had faded into obscurity. Rather, Chamorros increasingly began to share their memories of the war whenever important opportunities arose, but they did so privately. Generally reserved about their war memories, most Chamorros of the wartime generations rarely disclosed their stories to those outside the extended family, let alone to those in public spaces. In part because their memories of death and strife were so emotionally charged, many preferred to stay silent. Moreover, they saw no need to share their stories of the war with Americans, whom they had once believed to be their enemies.

In the early 1950s, several Chamorro leaders in Saipan challenged the prevailing notion that "America" held no meaningful place among Chamorro memories of the war. Certainly, Americans garnered Chamorro appreciation for food, shelter, and medicine during the postwar era of rehabilitation. But Americans had yet to instill among Chamorros of the Northern Mariana Islands their self-proclaimed image as "liberators." That objective was soon to be fulfilled, at least for some Chamorro leaders of the period. At a farewell party for naval personnel in 1951, Chief Commissioner Elias P Sablan and Mayor Ignacio Benavente spoke to the departing military officials with the kind of compassion directed to well-respected people. In raising the importance of the Americans during the war, Chief Sablan proclaimed, "My people prayed, and waited for the day when the Americans would come. They had faith in the American people. They had faith in the American principles of freedom and liberty. . . . Many of my people had never before seen an American. But on that unforgettable day, when from the hills and hiding places we watched the heroic Marines, Sailors and Soldiers streaming to our shores, God told us that we were safe, the Americans had come. Men from the other side of the world had come to free my home and my people."[2]

Mayor Ignacio Benavente repeated many of Sablan's pious descriptions of the Americans, though he openly regretted the "blind or hard-hearted" behaviors Chamorros often exhibited toward Americans in the immediate postwar era. Thus his manner, in addressing the crowd of navy officials, was apologetic. Moreover, he assured them that negative attitudes toward Americans had largely diminished—attitudes that had been shaped by the mixed experiences at Camp Susupe and by the histories of Japanization in the northern islands. With an increasing sense of appreciation for American economic and philanthropic aid, Benavente further argued, Chamorros now cooperated more openly and easily with Americans. In particular he praised the benefits of education, the contributions of doctors, and the improved political representation granted to Chamorros. On behalf of the Chamorros of Saipan, and the entire Northern Mariana Islands for that matter, Benavente humbly asked military officials "for forgiveness of all our disobediences and negligence to your orders, for our lack of respect and gratitude towards you." Ever appreciative of American generosity, Benavente pledged the island's "allegiance to the flag of the United States of America. . . . You will be gone from our Island, but your memories will continue to live in our hearts for many years to come." With these closing words, Benavente attempted to refashion Chamorro memories of Americans, from "wartime barbarians" to "peacetime humanitarians."[3]

In their speeches to departing military officials on Saipan, Sablan and Benavente said more than farewell. Rather, they reinterpreted Chamorro wartime experiences and memories in ways that complemented the celebratory narratives of the American war effort and rehabilitation project. A decade earlier, most Chamorros in the Northern Mariana Islands had viewed Americans as enemies of the Japanese empire and as suspicious persons. Families prayed for the war to end, but it was highly unlikely that Chamorros prayed for the arrival of "heroic" Americans, as Sablan claimed. What characterized Chamorro spiritual views during the war was ambivalence, as neither Japan nor the United States captured the full religious attention of Chamorros. For example, Cristino Sablan Dela Cruz remarked, "We prayed the good nation would win the war, and luckily our prayers were heard" (Roxas 1989). Likewise, Herbert Del Rosario noted in an interview, "Maybe it was God's blessing that the Americans came to save the Chamorros" (Del Rosario 2002).[4] Despite the uncertainty surrounding Chamorro spiritual and social views of Americans, Sablan and Benavente argued that Americans were fundamentally good people. If anything, they implied, Chamorros should be ashamed of themselves for their histories of "disobedience" toward Americans.

The efforts to erase negative Chamorro memories of Americans indicated a change in indigenous perceptions of the war. At the center of these cultural and historical interpretations rested conflicting and shifting notions of loyalty. As Chamorros in the Northern Mariana Islands gradually humanized Americans, a process that started during the rehabilitation period, they began to appreciate them as a people. Formerly accustomed to working under Japanese laws and regulations, Chamorros now adjusted to the American political system of governance. Before long, Chamorros, in particular the political elite, grasped the significance of the language of loyalty in the American context. By the early 1950s, Chamorro leaders understood the political power of the United States and the perceived economic, medical, and social benefits attributed to it. Guam to the south served as the primary, though idealized, example of economic progress and prosperity, which some Chamorros in the north desired to replicate. The island's acquisition of American citizenship in 1950, as well as the celebrated history of Americanization there, inspired some Chamorros of the Northern Mariana Islands to strengthen their political relationship with the United States.

On 17 April 1950, several prominent Chamorro leaders, many of whom were educated under the former Japanese mandate and the recent American rehabilitation project, petitioned the United Nations for political integration with the United States. They included Ignacio Benavente, Antonio R Guerrero, V D L Guerrero, Jose S Pangelinan, and Elias P Sablan. Of the three political statuses for decolonization offered by the United Nations, these leaders chose to "incorporate" into, rather than become "independent" from, the United States.[5] At the time, the Northern Mariana Islands were part of the Trust Territory of the Pacific Islands (TTPI). Based on their petition, these Chamorro leaders wanted to secede from the trust territory and to initiate the decolonization process. "It is our fervent hope," they wrote, "that all of the islands of the Northern Marianas be incorporated into the United States of America either as a possession or as a territory." They desired that "someday these islands may be considered a part of the United States and its people attain American citizenship."[6]

Although the exact conditions and terms of this political process would not be worked out until the 1960s, during the political status negotiations between the Northern Mariana Islands and the United States, Chamorro leaders of the immediate postwar era felt that "their goals of freedom and democracy could be best achieved in a relationship with the United States" (Willens and Siemer 2002, 9). The glorification of Guam as an American territory, as well as an increasing acceptance of American political and social values, prompted Chamorro leaders in the Northern Marianas to explore the question of sovereignty under the United States. As Olympio T Borja explained, "Our relationship with Guam isn't just the fact that we have relatives there. . . . It is much more than this. We grew up in close proximity to American style of living. Our beliefs are much the same as the Americans" (*Micronesian Star* 1971).

They Came for the Dead

In an era of economic and political upheaval, several Chamorros from Saipan strove to impart a sense of cohesiveness and certainty in terms of indigenous perceptions of war, memory, and history. Among American military officials, some Chamorro leaders fashioned an image of an indigenous population appreciative of the American presence, in times of both war and peace. The influence of nearly thirty years of Japanese colonialism, along with the history of indigenous loyalties to Japan, seemed to have disappeared altogether in the 1950s. Liberation Day, a commemoration that ended as quickly as it began, primarily represented American memories of military triumph and "rehabilitative" achievement. Not until 1958, after ten years of suspension, did Liberation Day festivities resume. Some Chamorros now demonstrated their newfound loyalties to the United States. After all, as a few attested, Chamorro beliefs were "much the same" as those of Americans.

While some struggled to represent all Chamorros as loyal subjects of the United States, Don Farrell asserted, "It is important to note that there was not complete cultural and political unity among the islands of the Marianas" (1991a, 481). The emerging rhetoric of American loyalty glossed over the diversity in views about Japan, the Mariana Islands, and the United States. But the poor visibility of Liberation Day as a key commemoration of American valor, as well as the general lack of public support for sovereignty under the United States, ensured that attempts to express Chamorro loyalty to America remained marginal at best. In the early years of its appearance, Saipan's Liberation Day failed to carve a niche among the larger tradition of religious commemorations, such as the fiesta. As a commemoration of the war, Liberation Day existed in relative obscurity because it failed to exhibit war memories and histories of the Northern Marianas that resonated with the Chamorros' experience there. Compared to Guam's Liberation Day, Saipan's version showed little by way of historical representation and interpretation of the war.

Falling short as an instrumental marker and maker of history, Saipan's Liberation Day quietly receded in the wake of increasing war commemorations emanating from Japan, Korea, and Okinawa. These new commemorations, primarily Japanese peace memorials and bone-collecting missions, spoke more directly to the politics of war remembrance and war commemoration in the Mariana Islands. As in Guam, the removal of the Naval Security Clearance in 1962 allowed the government of Japan, as well as private organizations, to travel to the Northern Mariana Islands and begin the process of memorialization. The opening of travel routes between Asia and the Mariana Islands permitted numerous families, formerly sugarcane laborers or relatives of deceased soldiers, to return to the islands in a collective effort to memorialize the dead. Part of the wider peace movement in Japan, these bone-collecting missions and peace ceremonies would never have occurred without the official endorsement of the Japanese government. With Japan's rapid economic recovery and increased political pressure from the Japan Bereaved Family Association, the Japanese government made it "publicly acceptable" to hold memorial services for those who had died in the war (Orr 2001, 138). Private agencies and religious groups quickly took advantage of opportunities to memorialize the war dead at home and abroad. In the 1960s and 1970s, Asian war memorials surfaced without being publicly challenged. During this period, the memorials in the Northern Mariana Islands escaped scrutiny from some American veterans. Japanese, Korean, and Okinawan commemorative practices continued fairly uninterrupted (figure 10).

In the Northern Mariana Islands, bone-collecting missions, cremation rituals, memorial projects, and pilgrimages were well under way, and with a greater sense of commitment and fervor. Of the numerous factors involved in the spread of these religious and commemorative projects, two stood out. First, the government of Japan sponsored a larger number of affiliated and nonaffiliated bone-collecting missions, returning war veterans, and visiting members of bereaved associations in the Northern Mariana Islands

FIGURE 10. Japanese peace memorial, Tinian, 17 December 2005. *(Keith Camacho)*

than in Guam. Many returned to Rota, Saipan, and Tinian as ex-sugarcane laborers or as families of deceased soldiers. They came back to the islands "to reminisce about shared experiences, to see what has changed on the island and in their lives, to right old wrongs" (Poyer, Falgout, and Carucci 2001, 340). Eiichi Takashima regularly revisited Rota as a member of Rota Kai, or the Rota Remembrance and Friendship Association. The group, originally formed on 20 August 1978, "has continued to make an annual pilgrimage to the island of Rota to venerate the souls of lost family members and reconnect with the Rotanese community" (Ombrello 2003).[7] "Rota is an island . . . where my memories of good times as well as hard times are deeply engraved" (Takashima 1981).

Second, innumerable remains were scattered over the islands, such that "it wasn't uncommon to find untouched bones just a few feet off the side of Saipan's northern roads" (Kiener 1978, 35). Because the American military's wartime practice was to leave soldiers of the Japanese Army untouched, buried in mass graves, or sealed in caves, a vast number of exposed and concealed skeletons littered the islands of Tinian and Saipan. According to American military records, 37,829 "Japanese" died in Tinian and Saipan, more than double the number of 18,377 "Japanese" deaths in Guam (Farrell 1991a, 287; Rogers 1995, 194).[8] The status of the Northern Mariana Islands as a former Japanese colony, as well as the larger number of

unrecorded deaths there, encouraged the proliferation of Asian war commemorations. "The Japanese, Okinawans, and Koreans occasionally return
to honor their dead and remember their years" in the Northern Mariana
Islands (Farrell 1989, 66).

Memorial planners such as Tokuichi Kuribayashi, a prominent indus-
trialist from Japan, understood the purpose and meaning of returning to
the islands. For almost half a century, Japanese entrepreneurs and laborers
had settled in the Northern Mariana Islands and made their homes there.
As the former supervisor of Saipan's sugar manufacturing company, Nanyō
Kōhatsu Kaisha, Kuribayashi intended his memorial to be "all embracing."[9]
Although he clearly lamented the passing of the sugar company's employees, he wanted a memorial that commemorated everyone, regardless of
their ethnicity, who suffered during the war. "Through the erection of the
Peace Memorial Statue," he wrote, "the memories of the people who once
contributed to the development and cultural advancement of the Pacific
Islands, including those who died as a result of the last Pacific War, irrespec-
tive of nationalities, age and creed, will be forever enshrined."[10] On 22 January 1972, Kuribayashi, like many before and after him, saw the memorial
through to a relatively peaceful completion.

The idea for many commemorations originated in the direction and
work of bone-collecting missions. As early as 1968, the government of Japan
began sending bone-collecting missions to the trust territory. At that time,
Japan's Ministry of Health and the Welfare Graves Mission to Micronesia
were collecting the remains of the "military dead." Unwilling to identify
the remains, a process officially viewed as "impractical," the Japanese government "declared all who died during World War II as being 'military,'
regardless of whether they were actually military or civilian."[11] Therefore,
archaeological measures and methods were seldom used in the salvaging of
remains. In many cases, the bone-collecting missions sent the unidentified
cremated remains to the Chidorigafuchi Shrine, Japan's National Tomb for
Deceased Soldiers, in Tokyo. If a body was identified—itself a rare occur-
rence—the mission sent the remains to the family. By 1976, these missions
had collected remains of approximately twenty-eight thousand persons
from the islands of Saipan and Tinian (Hall 1976, 50).

The rationale behind the refusal to distinguish between individual
remains reflected more than a deficiency in archaeological resources, a
lack of monetary funds, or a policy of practicality. At root in the decision
to cremate the remains immediately was the ardent desire, on the part of
many volunteers and veterans, to reunite the deceased with the spiritual
worlds of their families. The missions believed that the dead had for years
already been deprived of a proper burial, and that any delay would only
further aggravate them. Unfortunately, this rather loosely organized policy
of locating and cremating human remains gave rise to a number of problems. As Scott Russell noted in an interview, "the Japanese bone-collecting

effort is kind of strange. Everything is done very unscientifically" (Russell 2002).

As a result of not scientifically categorizing the remains, the missions indiscriminately gathered the bones of Koreans and Okinawans. In part, Japan's official policy of treating all remains as presumably belonging to the Japanese military, as well as the predominant concern to cremate the remains at once, contributed to the missions' inability to identify bones. In a sense, these missions replicated the colonial hierarchies of Japan's empire in Asia and the Pacific Islands, subsuming all of Japan's wartime subjects into one homogenous, Japanized mass. In appropriating all of the war dead as "Japanese," the Japanese government ultimately denied Koreans and Okinawans—once considered Japanese nationals—the opportunity to identify and mourn those lost during the war in the Northern Mariana Islands.

Consequently, the missions failed to document the number of "non-Japanese" remains collected and cremated, creating unsettled tension among groups such as the Koreans, who may never know what happened to their conscripted soldiers and laborers during the war. Further, the missions compounded the problem of identifying human remains by collecting ancient Chamorro skeletons in areas perceived to be Japanese wartime graves, such as shoreline caves. In Tinian, Russell stated, one mission, using a bulldozer, "ripped up" a *latte* site, an ancient Chamorro village area, in search of Japanese bones.[12] "It didn't matter if they were four thousand years old, [the remains] were Japanese bones in their eyes" (Russell 2002). Local archaeologists intervened to prevent the mission from destroying the *latte* site and from inadvertently retrieving the remains of Chamorros. Since that event in the late 1970s, local historic preservation offices have required that every bone-collecting mission enlist the aid of an archaeologist to oversee digs.

Apart from such instances of infringing on Chamorro burial sites, as well as the unresolved issue of properly identifying war remains, the relationship between Japanese missions and local authorities remained cordial. For instance, in his assessment of the missions in 1971, District Administrator Francisco C Ada remarked, "The conduct and cooperativeness of the Japanese Governmental Mission, the Student Group and the Memorial Associations were of a very high level, and beyond reproach."[13] A few Chamorros, such as the late Juan Sanchez and Antonio Benavente, the former chief of police, assisted a variety of missions in locating human remains from the war period (*Commonwealth Examiner* 1979a). On Benavente's death in the summer of 1979, a Japanese mission even offered a "moment of silent prayer" to acknowledge their respect and reverence for the man (*Commonwealth Examiner* 1979b). The cremation ceremony that recognized his passing, as well as that of thousands of the Asian war dead, was held in the Marpi area on the northern coast of Saipan. By the early 1970s, most cremation rituals took place in this general vicinity. The favored areas included Banzai

Cliff and Suicide Cliff, places in Marpi where a small number of Asians had committed *gyokusai,* or "honorable deaths," during the war (see map 3).

The missions cremated many remains in Marpi in large part because of the historical and spiritual significance of the area. Once again, as in the time of war, veterans and families of the deceased "faced north," in prayer, not only to Japan, but to their respective homelands like Korea and Okinawa. In time, with the aid of their governments and private organizations, these missions developed numerous memorials throughout the Marpi landscape. As Francisco Ada observed, "In the future, we are hoping that the entire area, encompassing the Peace Memorial, the Okinawa Memorial and the Last Command Post, can be fully developed into a public Peace Memorial Park."[14] Aware of the controversy surrounding the construction of the Yigo Peace Memorial Park in Guam, local administrators in Saipan hoped that nothing similar would arise there.[15] To reassure Japanese veteran and bereaved associations, Francisco Ada informed them, "The Marianas District Administration is very sympathetic with the worthy mission of the Government of Japan to recover the remains of the Japanese War Dead from the Marianas, and generally speaking, with the erection of appropriate memorials."[16] By "appropriate," authorities meant memorials that abided by local laws, respected local customs, and cooperated directly with the governments of Japan and the trust territory.

Although the guidelines appeared straightforward, some local officials were apprehensive about Marpi's future image, given the proliferation of memorials. They speculated that the memorials might create the impression that Marpi symbolically represented Japan. Their unease was further heightened when Japanese memorial planners referred to Marpi as Japan's "Nippon Park" of the Pacific. Accordingly, the trust territory government reminded the Japanese and others that Marpi should not "be referred to as the 'Nippon Park of Marpi,' as the intention of this area is a general public park for the people of the Marianas (and visitors), and not an exclusive 'Nippon' park, even if the Okinawa and Japan memorials are eventually located there."[17] On the other hand, some local entrepreneurs and leaders in Saipan believed that the memorials in Marpi had economic value as possible tourist sites. With the introduction of a tourist economy in the 1960s, including the completion of Saipan's Royal Taga Hotel in 1967, concerns for a viable economy soon superseded anxieties about the image of Marpi. Though the park remained a public venue, some advocated that it be seen more as a tourist location.

Specifically, a few local leaders proposed to treat memorials and missions located at Marpi not only as religious sites, but as advertisements for travel to the Northern Mariana Islands. "It is felt that such a Park development would become a major tourist and historical attraction for Saipan. Government of Japan officials have indicated a great deal of enthusiasm as to this concept, and . . . local authorities . . . have displayed equal enthusiasm and pleasure."[18] Like Guam's political elite, leaders in Saipan, such as Governor Carlos Camacho, argued that tourism "will permit increased revenues to provide the necessary infra-structure and needed government services. . . . Japanese people can spend their holidays in a relaxed and friendly atmosphere" (*Commonwealth Newsletter* 1981). Targeting a Japanese audience, local authorities in Saipan aggressively represented the Northern Mariana Islands as a promising tourist destination. Within a short period, increasing numbers of Japanese tourists began revisiting "Suicide and Banzai Cliffs to hold religious ceremonies and reminisce [about] the past" (Sakamoto 1971, 13). The economic appeal of Asian war memorials also drew Chamorros closer to a foreign economy predominantly managed by a familiar people. For instance, Concepcion Mangloña observed that the areas Japanese hold dear in their memories of wartime Tinian should be beautified "so the Japanese will realize that we care about their ancestors" (1986).

Even before Asian war memorials were recognized as tourist sites, Chamorros from the Northern Mariana Islands occasionally assisted the Japanese and others in accomplishing their commemorative endeavors. It was quite common for Chamorros to welcome Japanese, Korean, and Okinawan organizations back to the islands, showing respect and sympathy for their families and friends lost in the war. For example, in addressing a group of Okinawan mourners in 1986, Tinian Mayor Ignacio Quichocho said that Chamorros "share all the sorrows for which you had endured all throughout the long years since the war" (*Marianas Variety News and Views* 1986c). During Liberation Day festivities in 1980, Saipan Mayor Francisco M Diaz, "clothed in a Japanese coat and handed a wooden sledgehammer," participated in a sake ceremony of friendship (Dickhudt 1980). At another event, Rota Mayor Benjamin T Manglóña stated, "Here, in this hallowed ground, are buried the ashes of some of our Asian friends and neighbors, our Asian brothers and sisters who did not go home. . . . They made the ultimate sacrifice for their country, [dedicating their lives to] the great struggle. . . . We, too, love them, [as] they are part of our Island's history" (2001, 2–3). As these statements illustrate, the introduction of tourism and the renewed image of the Japanese as "tourists" did not alarm Chamorros in the north. In Guam, however, Chamorros of the wartime generation did not fully appreciate the development of a tourist industry that catered to the Japanese. In contrast, demands for sensitive representations of and relations with the Japanese rarely disturbed Chamorros in the Northern Mariana Islands.

Such expressions of affection for the Japanese demonstrated that Chamorros from Rota, Saipan, and Tinian respected the Asian survivors and veterans of the war. Despite memories of the economic, political, and racial hierarchies of the Japanese government, the Chamorros of the Northern Mariana Islands chose to remember the peoples of Japan's empire in personal terms of friendship. In contrast to Guam's dominant wartime impression of the Japanese as "victimizers," Chamorros in the Northern Mariana Islands viewed them in complementary and contradictory ways. Though the Japanese military forced a "change in attitude" among Chamorros of the northern islands during the war, numerous Chamorros still remained loyal to a Japan whose image extended through the very fabric of Chamorro society. Loyalty to Japan meant more than identifying with Japanese imperialism. It suggested a deep and real connection, however ambivalent and uncertain that might be, to the peoples and politics of that vast empire.

Chamorro involvement in the spread of Asian bone-collecting missions and war commemorations indicated that loyalties to Japan had never been entirely repressed. Postwar loyalties to Japan in the Northern Mariana Islands rarely, if ever, reflected militarist dispositions of greatness and victory. Rather, they can be described, in part, as local variations of *higaisha ishiki,* or "victim consciousness." This idea of victim consciousness stems from the social processes through which Japanese have come to remember the war, principally as "victims" of wartime propaganda and nuclear devastation in Hiroshima and Nagasaki (Dower 1996, 64). In their shared sense of nostalgia, respect, and sympathy for the war dead, some wartime generations of Chamorros, Japanese, Koreans, and Okinawans recalled the war in terms of *higaisha ishiki.* Their representation of themselves as "victims" stemmed in part from a general negation of Japan's wartime militarism, a focus on bereavement and mourning, and a common identification with Japan proper. For some Chamorros of the wartime generations, these issues of conciliation and commemoration illustrated what postwar loyalty to Japan meant in a time when loyalty was increasingly shifting to the United States.

American Patriots Unbecoming

As illustrated by the spread of missions and memorials in Saipan, war commemorations continued to serve as sites of cultural and historical representation. In developing these commemorations, people remembered the war, renewed social relations, and identified with a familiar colonial power. Japanese religious and commemorative activities particularly drew the attention of Chamorros in ways that Liberation Day could not. The commemoration of Camp Susupe's release of civilians on 4 July 1946 had yet to function as an important platform for indigenous views of the past and present. At best, some described Liberation Day as "subtly merging into the traditional American July Fourth activities" (*Commonwealth Newsletter* 1980). Beauty queen contests, dances, feasts, parades, and sporting events all demonstrated the American aspects of the commemoration. Perhaps its largest achievement, then and now, lay in its support for education. For several decades, from the 1970s to the 1990s, Liberation Day organizers raised monies for various local scholarships that benefited not only students but also local churches and various community projects.

At worst, the commemoration has been characterized as "dull" and as unappealing to the general public (*Marianas Variety News and Views* 1976). Referring to the commemoration of Liberation Day in 1973, Joaquin I Pangelinan asserted, "This year ended with less candidates [for Liberation Day Queen], fewer floats and less money. . . . I don't think that the people are celebrating Liberation Day for its real meaning. Today the meaning of Liberation is fading away, and for the young generations it has no meaning, no value" (*Marianas Variety News and Views* 1973). Pangelinan accurately assessed the overall direction and significance of Liberation Day in the decades that followed the war; it remained simply another day for Chamorros to rest, work, or recreate. Further, the holiday had begun to lose its "explicit historical content, and young people may be unaware" of its origin and purpose (Poyer, Falgout, and Carucci 2001, 338). The commemoration lacked social, political, and emotional meaning, "because the people who survived the liberation didn't really talk much about it. It wasn't a big deal . . . being liberated from the Japanese at the end of the war" (McPhetres 2002).[19]

Though Liberation Day specifically celebrated the war experiences of Chamorros and Refaluwasch, and was a holiday made in their honor, it was not an important day of remembrance and reflection. Prior to the fiftieth anniversary of World War II, Liberation Day remained a holiday for the officials and not for the people of the Northern Mariana Islands.

Some American war veterans wanted to change public perceptions of such commemorations. Revisiting the islands on 15 June, the anniversary of the US invasion of Saipan, some American war veterans desired respect and recognition for their involvement in the war. They particularly aspired to see their military achievements etched into the commemorative landscape of the Northern Mariana Islands. However, other veterans cared little about commemorations made in their honor, and a smaller number maintained contact with Chamorro families (*Commonwealth Examiner* 1979c).

Still, the concern shared by some Americans veterans that their military "sacrifices" should be commemorated persisted, as did the idea that signs should be displayed in Saipan as physical reminders of the war they left behind (eg, American tanks, buildings, and battlefields). Given the abundance of American war sites in Saipan and neighboring islands in the Pacific, some American veterans argued, "It would be foolish to wait another twenty years before acknowledging the significance of these properties" (Apple and Rogers 1976, 34). Veteran Sam Weintraub noted, "More Americans are returning to the islands where they spent their youth in uniform, and they want monuments and memorials and museums built in tribute to them"

(Hook 1983, 10). By the late 1970s, when Japanese missions and memorial projects were waning in number, some American war veterans arrived in the islands to find their lofty expectations unfulfilled.

Of approximately thirty war memorials and monuments on Saipan in 1983, many of them dedicated by Japanese, Koreans, and Okinawans, just three commemorated the American war effort (Hook 1983, 8).[20] Some American veterans did not find this unequal distribution of war memorials amusing. Navy veteran Charles Mathis surmised that the general absence of American war memorials stemmed from Saipan's "deliberate" attempt to appease Japanese tourists. Americans "did a lot here," he argued, and their military achievements should be remembered over those of the Japanese (Sylvester 1983, 12). Veteran Len Maffioli noticed that Saipan "had memorials to the Japanese, lots of 'em, and even to Korean laborers but not to my division" (*Marianas Variety News and Views* 1986a).

Taking the initiative, and with the assistance of local contractors and veteran associations, in the summer of 1986 Maffioli erected a monument in honor of the Fourth Marine Division. Speaking at the unveiling ceremony for the monument, Marine Colonel Karl Miller remarked, "Saipan is part of the Marines and the Marines are part of Saipan. A Marine may not know where New York City is or Rome is but he does know about Saipan" (*Marianas Variety News and Views* 1986b). Attempting to inform if not intimidate others about the Marines' military involvement in Saipan, some veterans even posted an American flag on Suicide Cliff in Marpi. The cliff rose above an area called the Last Japanese Command Post, where Japanese, Korean, and Okinawan peace missions frequently gathered to pray for the dead. An unidentified person "rappelled down that cliff and tacked the biggest American flag they could find right to the cliff . . . about in the late '80s. . . . Their idea was, 'By God, we are going to let those Japanese tourists know who really won the war,' because by looking at all these monuments you have no idea who won the war" (McPhetres 2002).

Despite the relative success of such impromptu efforts to promote American valor and loyalty, some American veterans continued to criticize Chamorros for their failure to develop comparable projects. The level of frustration among them and their supporters increased to the point of attracting national media coverage in 1984. Clyde Haberman, a writer for the *New York Times*, said that the fortieth anniversary of war in the Northern Mariana Islands "came and went" without the grandeur of Normandy's commemoration. "Here, no government leaders talked about liberty and sacrifice. No crowds gathered. No big guns boomed in salute, no honor guard paraded, no anthems sounded. Yet the events here four decades ago were as critical to the ultimate Allied success as the landings in northern France" (Haberman 1984).

In reporting the scarcity of commemorative activities dedicated to the United States, some American journalists and veterans focused on the absence of indigenous loyalty to America in the islands. They argued that tourism, an industry that catered to a Japanese audience, diverted Chamorros and the local government from celebrating the role of the United States in World War II. Some veterans remembered the war in terms of their collective understanding of themselves as "liberators." Others regularly expressed "themes of patriotic orthodoxy" couched in the rhetoric of loyalty, that is, "war as holy crusade, bringing new life to the nation and the warrior as a culture hero and savior, often likened to Christ" (Linenthal 1993, 4). Some of them asserted that Chamorros should be grateful, given the American "liberation" of the Northern Mariana Islands, as well as the islands' recent political affiliation with the United States.

From the signing of the covenant on 15 February 1975 to the establishment of a United States Commonwealth on 9 January 1978, the people of the Northern Mariana Islands chose democratically to be a part of what they often called the "American political family."[21] This political process culminated in the granting of American citizenship to the people of the Commonwealth of the Northern Mariana Islands (CNMI) on 3 November 1986. Yet for some American war veterans, the Chamorros of the Northern Mariana Islands, supposedly Americans, were an anomaly. Some of them clearly expressed their loyalty to the United States, a key component in the political status talks of the time, while others remained indifferent, uncertain, or anti-American. As Weintraub noted, the Northern Mariana Islands "are an American territory taken for military purposes, but they are not pro-American" (Hook 1983, 8).

As these American veterans soon realized, Chamorros of the Northern Mariana Islands did not exhibit any "pro-American" characteristics. Based on their assessment of Liberation Day and Japanese peace memorials, most American veterans believed that Chamorros were not patriotic. Given the polemical nature of some Chamorro criticisms of the United States, one did not have to turn to commemorations to appraise the contested nature of Chamorro loyalties. Referring to the Americans as capitalists, Daniel T Castro, a writer for the *Micronesian Star,* asserted that Americans serve only one goal: to exploit the monies and labor of the Northern Mariana Islands (1971, 5). Another author noted that Americans were "imperialists" intent on controlling the islands (*Free Press* 1974). Such critiques of Americans as imperialists, as well as the absence of American patriotic commemorative activities, suggested that Chamorros were anti-American.

But collectively, the Chamorros of the Northern Mariana Islands were neither anti- nor pro-American. What some American veterans failed to grasp or recall was that the ambivalent nature of loyalties stemmed from the recent histories of American and Japanese colonization. That Chamorros remembered the war in local terms, and not in terms restricted exclusively to the narrative of American liberation, eluded some American veterans. Chamorros remembered the war according to their experiences under both Japanese and American colonial rule. In the first few decades after the war, from the 1940s to the 1980s, the meaning of war commemorations varied. Neither victimization nor liberation narratives totally dominated indigenous memories of the war. And no matter how successfully American veterans promoted their own memories of the war, particularly their image of themselves as "liberators," they could not alter indigenous collective memories of the war.

Nor could these Americans see themselves as conquerors of lands and peoples. In presenting the story of American liberation, some American veterans in Saipan, as well as in Guam, rarely saw their role in that light. Yet, as others would attest, Americans arrived in the western Pacific as both "liberators" and "conquerors." For instance, Lazarus E Salii, later president of the Republic of Palau, once wrote, "If the Americans came as liberators, they were surely also conquerors." Challenging the notion that Americans "sacrificed" their lives for the liberation of Micronesia, Salii stated that the islands "were not and are not for sale for blood or money; that the blood which was spilled 'coming over the reef' . . . was not spilled at the request, or for the benefit" of the peoples of Micronesia (1972, 37).

Except for Guam Chamorros, Pacific Islanders throughout Micronesia—including Chamorros of the Northern Mariana Islands—did not view the Americans as "liberators." As Senator Joseph S Inos observed, "I doubt that 'Liberation' in its traditional meaning was in the minds of most of our people, nor on their lips when the [American] guns opened up on that fateful 15 June 1944." Rather, the idea of American liberation seemed to appeal more "to our Guamanian relatives" (Inos 1991, 4). Some American war veterans, not widely accepted as wartime "liberators" in the Northern Mariana Islands, left the islands disappointed by the actions of "ungrateful" Chamorros.

The Making of American Memorial Park

The cold reception of some American war veterans in the Northern Mariana Islands did not impede their return to the islands. Fast approaching their senior years, American veterans continued to visit the islands to show family members where they had fought during the Pacific War. Seeking closure to an emotionally charged part of their past, some of them demanded local recognition of their efforts. When they realized that the Chamorros of the Northern Mariana Islands did not regard them as "heroes," some veterans expressed shock, anger, and disbelief. In an attempt to ease the discomfort shared by these veterans, local government officials informed them that Chamorros did memorialize the American war effort, citing the commemoration of Liberation Day as one example. But American veterans may or may not have understood that Saipan's Liberation Day celebrated the release from Camp Susupe, rather than the arrival of American military forces. The lack of appropriate commemoration disappointed them.

To counter some of the veterans' failed expectations of Liberation Day, local officials "pointed out that the CNMI has always taken the position that American Memorial Park in Garapan is to serve as a living memorial to the US forces involved in the battle for Saipan" (*Marianas Variety News and Views* 1986b). Conceived in 1975 by federal and local officials, as part of the Covenant to Establish the Commonwealth of the Northern Mariana Islands, the park included 133 acres of beach and coastal wetlands.[22] In its initial years of existence, the park encompassed a plant nursery and a few picnic tables. Its lone, "hard-to-find," granite monument made it difficult for visitors to understand the area's significance in American military history (*Marianas Variety News and Views* 1983). The entire area bore little resemblance to an American national park; at times, trash littered the place (*Marianas Variety News and Views* 1980). Veterans came across a park with neither the splendor nor symbolism indicative of the American "liberation" of the Northern Mariana Islands.

The unappealing appearance of the American Memorial Park insulted the veterans' expectations for a place "sacred" in their minds. Although American military forces actually landed at Chalan Kanoa, a village south of Garapan, veterans nonetheless regarded the park as an American battlefield. In the ensuing decades, to the surprise and satisfaction of some American veterans, the image of the American Memorial Park would change according to the narrative of liberation. Like American battlefields elsewhere, from Gettysburg to the Alamo to Pearl Harbor, American Memorial Park served as a place where "the struggle for ownership, . . . the right to alter a story, is a vibrant part of the site's cultural history" (Linenthal 1993, 215). But in order to generate the site's value as an American battlefield, planners of the park first had to convince its stewards, the Chamorros, of its utilitarian import. As Gordon Joyce explained, park rangers aimed to persuade the peoples of the Northern Mariana Islands "that it's their park" as much as it is a park for American veterans (*Marianas Variety News and Views* 1980). In this manner, founders of the park avoided plans that might instill "a morbid or heavy feeling to the park" (Sayon 2002).[23] Instead they wanted a "living memorial" composed of "a pavilion, a visitor center, a museum, various recreational facilities, and pedestrian and vehicle circulation and parking" (Arroyo 1992). The living aspect of the memorial would encourage the public to use the park's facilities, as well as invite visitors to reflect on histories of the war.

However, the question of funding prevented the rapid implementation of the plans. A few years after its opening, some inquired, "Will the U.S. Congress appropriate funds to develop this unique park?" (*Commonwealth Newsletter* 1979). As with early postwar Liberation Day festivities, plans for the development of American Memorial Park waned for several years. Neither the local nor the federal government aggressively sought monies for the projected cost of the park, which was not considered an essential project. As some American veterans argued, it appeared there was no place for American commemorative activities in the Northern Mariana Islands. Additionally, the park was surrounded by natural swamp habitats, with designated endangered species (NPS 1989, 9). Environmental considerations also hampered the construction of recreational and commemorative facilities. As the fiftieth anniversary of the end of World War II approached, the future of both Liberation Day and the American Memorial Park seemed less promising.

By the early 1990s, however, support for the American Memorial Park had increased. Chamorro leaders publicly acknowledged the significance of the park, not in terms of its utility as a recreational site, but in terms of its value as an American war memorial. In the past, some Chamorros had periodically praised the United States for its generosity in helping them survive during the immediate postwar era. At times, an even fewer, marginal number of Chamorros had called the American soldiers "heroes" in their memories of the war. The ambivalent character of indigenous loyalties to Japan and the United States ensured that no singular, dominant memory of the war existed for several decades. But with the passage of time and the passing of the war generations, more Chamorros embraced the narrative of American liberation.

Nearly half a century after the war, Chamorros such as Governor Lorenzo I Guerrero urged the public to preserve the memory of the American "liberation" of the Northern Mariana Islands by supporting the American Memorial Park (*Marianas Variety News and Views* 1993b). Seeking financial and moral assistance for the park, Representative Juan N Babauta stated that Saipan expected many American men "who fought on our beaches to return next June. We had hoped that they would find a fitting tribute to their courage and patriotism at the American Memorial Park" (*Marianas Variety News and Views* 1993a). If the park failed to receive proper funding for its completion, Babauta implied, American veterans "won't see much in the way of a US memorial, just the rather impressive monuments established by the Japanese, Koreans, and Okinawans to honor their fallen" (*Marianas Variety News and Views* 1992). Criticizing the United States Congress for delaying the obligatory funding of the park, Benjamin Manglona asserted that it would be "a shame for our fellow Americans to continue to ignore this memorial to all those who gave their lives in the defense of our freedom and liberty" (Arroyo 1993). Formerly criticized by American veterans for being anti-American, some Chamorro leaders of the 1990s attempted to change that image by arguing for the completion of the American Memorial Park.

Faced with the approaching fiftieth anniversary and international commemoration of World War II, some Chamorros wanted the world to know their place in American history and America's place in Northern Mariana Islands history.[24] Of all the war stories available to them, many chose the story of American liberation. The fact that the Northern Mariana Islands were now a commonwealth of the United States also contributed to the inclusion of the narrative of liberation; yet, the desire for a commonwealth did not necessarily resolve or suppress the ambivalent loyalties some Chamorros felt toward Japan and the United States.

Nevertheless, the push to complete the American Memorial Park demonstrated a significant shift in Chamorro memories about the war. As Senator Joseph Inos noted, the American Memorial Park "will for all times stand for the sacrifices of thousands of young men from an alien people who came to our shores and set us free. . . . [These American soldiers] never heard of us and our islands, but nevertheless, they died for us. When they came ashore on 15 June 1944, charging through a man-made hell beyond description and imagination, it marked the beginning of a new era" (Rebusio 1992). Invoking the once unfamiliar narratives of liberation and salvation, made popular and prevalent by the American military and the Guam war experience, Chamorros in Saipan gradually reshaped their memories of the war. The Chamorro commendation of the American war effort, as well as their prodding of the federal government, eventually proved successful. After several years of debate, on 3 March 1994 the US Department of Interior granted the commonwealth the three million dollars needed to see through the final architectural and construction phases of the park (*Marianas Variety News and Views* 1994a).[25]

With the major parts of the American Memorial Park slated to be ready by the summer of 1994, in time for the fiftieth anniversary of World War II, excitement and praise filled the air. Calling it the "Golden Tribute—Year of Friendship," the organizers of the fiftieth Liberation Day sought to "stress the need for peace and harmony between all nations and, particularly, between the United States and Japan" (Tenorio 1994, 1). Despite this stated aim, the celebration primarily honored American war veterans from near and far, among whom was a small group of Navajo Indians who served as Code Talkers during the war. In front of the Navajo Nation Inn, Window Rock, Arizona, Navajo veterans, family members, and representatives of the Northern Marianas gathered to commemorate the war (Graves 1994). The ceremony was held in Arizona because many could not afford to travel to the islands. Those fortunate enough to make the journey encountered a population eager to treat them as "heroes." During his trip to Saipan with his brother Norman, a veteran, Vern Steyer recorded a friendly conversation in his diary. "A man came out of the store, walked across the parking lot and came on our bus. He said that he had just found out who we were, so he wanted to personally come to thank us for coming back to Saipan and for what the Americans did to give them their freedom." Pleasantly surprised, Steyer continued, "After his little speech he left the bus, walked over to his car and drove away. Again the genuine appreciation shown to us by the native people was a highlight of our Saipan experience."[26]

Impressed by the hospitality and appreciation of Chamorros, American war veterans collectively felt comfortable returning to the islands, perhaps for the first time. Ed Olson, a Marine veteran, said that the fiftieth anniversary "couldn't have been better. Not only were the people at the hotels and at the events friendly and considerate, everyone else we met was great as well" (Scanlan 1994d, 3). "Everywhere we went," added veteran Barney Brewer, "things were just perfect. The ceremonies were superb with the greatest degree of dignity. But the old guys really enjoyed the hospitality we were shown by Saipan's people. There wasn't one person who didn't offer us cold drinks, food or anything else they could do for us" (Scanlan 1994d, 3). Another veteran, Cliff Farris, "never felt greater warmth and kinship" than with the peoples of the commonwealth, whose "outpouring of generosity is unparalleled and makes the sacrifices we made on this island fifty years ago all the more worthwhile" (Scanlan 1994b, 4). Equally enthusiastic about the return of the American veterans, Chamorros and the wider public of Saipan also expressed their gratitude for being "liberated" by the Americans.

John Angey, a corporal in the Marine Corps, remembered, "I'm really grateful to them. The stories I heard about them as a child here on Saipan made me want to join the corps. . . . I respect those men with all my heart. They're really my heroes" (Scanlan 1994a, 2). Venerated as symbols of American democracy and freedom, the veterans were also praised for introducing the ideas needed for Chamorros to create a local government. As Governor Froilan C Tenorio said, American "action on 15 June 1944, brought with it the seeds of this commonwealth's ultimate political union with the United States of America" (Scanlan 1994c, 4). Lieutenant Governor Jesus C Borja observed that "these ideas" of democracy and freedom specifically "took root" in Camp Susupe (de la Torre 1995). The sacrifices of American soldiers and the political ideas introduced by them, remarked Congressman Juan Babauta, had led to the "gratitude and recognition of a Pacific community that has since become a loyal member of the American family" (*Marianas Variety News and Views* 1994b).

As the fiftieth anniversary of the war continued, the language of American loyalty appeared to be widespread. Local leaders even pressed the American Armed Services for official recognition of approximately sixty-four Chamorro and Refaluwasch men who served, as scouts, under US military forces during the war. Later, these men obtained the privileges and prestige of being considered "heroes" of the US military.[27] The atmosphere of the "Golden Tribute" suggested that the narrative of American liberation and the language of American loyalty suppressed competing memories and histories of the war. The fiftieth anniversary represented the largest expression of American loyalty yet. But, as Genevieve Cabrera asserted, Liberation

Day "still causes a bit of confusion" (2001, 3). In their attempts to narrate a cohesive history of the war that emphasized American goodwill and generosity, many compromised the ambivalence and complexity of Chamorro war memories and loyalties. Although the narrative of American liberation has come to dominate contemporary memories of the war, Liberation Day continues to "express the special sensitivity and unique viewpoint" of the people of the Northern Mariana Islands (Tenorio 1994, 1).

Recent endeavors to develop a dominant narrative of the war risk the alteration, exaggeration, or loss of many wartime memories. Camp Susupe is a case in point. Some Chamorros perceive their rehabilitative internment as simply part of surviving the war. Others believe they were unjustly separated from their farmlands, as well as from their extended families elsewhere. Shortly after the war, some also expressed happiness at being freed from the campgrounds. Others later praised Americans for introducing them to the political concepts of democracy and freedom. Yet, over time, the camp has come to connote images of extreme hardship and deprivation, analogous to "the infamous German concentration camps in Europe" (Meller 1999, ix). For the younger wartime generation, Camp Susupe represented freedom denied to their elders, whereas others saw the camp as representing freedom itself. These conflicting memories of the past emerged as a direct result of the ascendance of the narrative of American liberation. Similarly, American veterans participated in presenting a so-called objective history of the war. By forgetting or repressing their past disappointments with Chamorros, they reinforced the rising notion that the narrative of liberation always existed uncontested in the Northern Mariana Islands.

But, given that many Chamorro war memories did not embrace the narrative of American liberation, resistance to celebratory understandings of the war resurfaced a year later, during the commemoration on Tinian. Initially, Tinian's role in the American bombing of Japan in 1945 did not figure prominently in Chamorro memories of the war. But with the postwar settlement of Chamorro families on the island, Tinian's participation was recalled. Since the early 1990s, some criticism has emerged concerning the commemoration of Liberation Day on the island. Rather than promote the island as a site of American nuclear warfare, Taotao I Redondo, a peace activist group, chose to remember the war on Tinian in ways that supported peace and reconciliation at the local and global levels.

Comprising educators and peace activists, Taotao I Redondo developed films, workshops, and peace gatherings to inform others about the harmful effects of war in general and nuclearism in particular. As Jesus C Borja announced, "The point of the ceremonies we have proposed is to defuse confrontation and offer an opportunity for persons of diverse beliefs regarding this anniversary to come together in a solemn, respectful atmosphere. . . . The opportunity to feel differently is essential to the process of healing and conflict resolution is what the committee wishes to offer in the proposed ceremonies" (Arroyo 1995, 3). While the group could commemorate anywhere on Tinian, they specifically chose to hold a peace gathering at the island's "exclusive military use" zone, otherwise known as the EMU. Located in North Field, the original location of the atomic bomb pits and airplane runways, the EMU fell under the control of the United States Navy. When Taotao I Redondo requested permission to hold peace ceremonies on 6 August 1995, the date of the American bombing of Hiroshima, the navy responded with an emphatic no.

As Rear Admiral D L Brewer III explained, the navy discouraged any commemorative activity at North Field because "military support of such activities may cultivate" unfavorable criticism (Dumat-Ol 1995c, 3). Although the National Park Service had declared Tinian's North Field a "national historic landmark" in 1985, the Department of Interior granted the navy management and use of the area. Therefore, the "U.S. Navy's official position regarding its long-term strategic needs for North Field is to continue its use for military training. And . . . this use precludes considering North Field as a national historic park administered by the National Park Service" (NPS 2001, 1). Jerry Facey, chairperson for the fiftieth commemoration, noted that although Tinian would be recalled worldwide, "people will not be honored, people will not be recognized" (Dumat-Ol 1995b, 4). Despite calls for a peaceful demonstration, the navy refused to grant Taotao I Redondo access to the atomic bomb pits (figure 11). Fearing interna-

FIGURE 11. Atomic bomb pit, Tinian, 17 December 2005. *(Keith Camacho)*

tional and national criticism, as illustrated in the controversy around the Smithsonian's exhibit of the *Enola Gay*, the navy declined to support the group's efforts.

Taotao I Redondo wanted to promote peaceful, cooperative understandings of the war reminiscent of Japanese peace missions, rather than to perpetuate accounts of military triumphs and victories. Regarding the role of the Japanese in the war, Senator David Cing asked, "Are we afraid that we are going to offend the Japanese? I was born and raised [in Tinian] and I am not really happy to let the world know that I came from a place where the atomic bombs that destroyed Hiroshima and Nagasaki came from, but that is history. . . . Are we doing justice to people who want to listen to history?" (Dumat-Ol 1995b, 4). Strongly disappointed, Cinta Matagolai Kaipat replied, "As an indigenous person I can see the Navy's decision as an attempt to deny us our right to participate in the healing process. . . . It is an insult to my family and the people of the Marianas to deny them the right to acknowledge their pain and their attempt to heal their pain" (Dumat-Ol 1995a, 3). Despite these outcries, the navy maintained its position to deny the organization access to the bomb pits. The CNMI government, dependent on the Japanese tourist economy, did not aggressively defend Taotao I Redondo's goals.

Neither appeals for historical justice nor indigenous healing moved naval officials. Undaunted by these responses, Taotao I Redondo continued with its educational and commemorative activities in the Marianas and elsewhere in Japan. At the close of the fiftieth anniversary of World War II in the Northern Mariana Islands, organizations such as Taotao I Redondo strove to impart a more comprehensive and sensitive understanding of the war. But no person or organization, engulfed by the now imposing narrative of American liberation and the rising appeal of loyalty to the United States, could offer effective critical insight into the wider historical implications of the war.

Over just a few years, the commemoration of Liberation Day in the Northern Mariana Islands became a celebration of American triumphalism in ways reflective of Guam's Liberation Day tradition. The Northern Mariana Islands was transformed from a "land without heroes" into a "land with heroes." Many praised the generosity of American soldiers, as well as the military service of Chamorro and Refaluwasch men in the war. Liberation Day came to connote pride and loyalty to America in ways it could not in the past. But if the American veterans represented the island's "liberators," from what, then, had they "liberated" the Chamorros? Chamorros have posed this question since the war began on 15 June 1944, when American military forces arrived in Saipan. In part, the changes in indigenous loyalties have influenced the ways in which Chamorros have come to remember, commemorate, and ultimately understand not only the notion of liberation, but the entire war period and the diverse people involved in it.

Given the relative absence of Japanese participation in the fiftieth anniversary, it appeared that Chamorros, especially those of the postwar generations, had come to represent the period of Japanese colonization as an anomaly in the island's history. Contemporary commemorations of Liberation Day seldom describe the role of Japan and the Japanese. It is as if the Japanese, as well as other Asian cultural groups, conveniently disappeared from a narrative of war that emphasizes American liberation. With the local government's dependence on tourism, it seems reasonable to avoid offending the Japanese in any way (Fujitani, White, and Yoneyama 2001, 22). But postwar relations among Chamorros and Japanese remained largely amiable, and continue to do so among the aging war generations.

What has occurred in the Northern Mariana Islands is a change in indigenous perceptions of the American commemoration. During the immediate postwar era, Chamorros rarely embraced Liberation Day as a holiday they could call their own. Throughout the following decades, Chamorros created no war commemorations, let alone memorials for Japan or the United States. Not until the early 1990s did Chamorros use war commemorations to present their war histories to America and to the world. Recognizing the significance of commemorative sites, such as Liberation Day and the American Memorial Park, Chamorros became active participants in the making and remaking of their own histories. In doing so, they wrestled among themselves over what memories of the war should be portrayed, altered, or suppressed. Like their relatives to the south, Chamorros in the Northern Mariana Islands intend to make a tradition around commemorative activities. And like their southern sisters and brothers, they, too, have suppressed controversial and compelling memories of the war.

Chapter 6
On the Margins of Memory and History

Since the first commemoration of World War II in 1945, there has been a concerted effort to remember the war in the Mariana Islands. Of all the commemorations, Liberation Day has emerged as the pivotal celebration in both the Northern Marianas and Guam. It is a significant occasion for the interpretation, mediation, and representation of a diversity of war memories. But it is also unique for what its organizers fail to remember. From its early years in the late 1940s to its fiftieth anniversary in 1994, the planners for Liberation Day commemorations have made no attempt to remember the controversial events and figures of the war. Committees for the commemoration of Liberation Day in both Guam and the Northern Mariana Islands have rarely celebrated the roles of Chamorros working for Japan's police and sex operations in wartime Guam. There has been a collective endeavor to forget the indigenous "collaborators" of Japan's military occupation of Guam, that is, Chamorro police assistants, Chamorro interpreters, and Chamorro sexual slaves.

The reasons behind the attempt to erase these agents of war from collective memory and public scrutiny are varied and complex. That these Chamorro women and men were called "collaborators" is one of the primary reasons for their marginalization in this context. Implicit in any contemporary discussion of collaboration is the notion of "disloyalty" to one's ethnic group, the very concept that brings into public view the divergence in Chamorro loyalties to Japan and the United States. At stake in the remembering of these women and men are not so much their individual behaviors and attitudes, but what their "disloyal" actions collectively mean within the wider American narratives of loyalty and liberation.

In this chapter I explore the histories of what might be understood as collaboration in the Mariana Islands by examining the wartime roles of Chamorro interpreters, police, and *i famalaoan guerra siha* from the Northern Mariana Islands working with the Japanese colonial administration in Guam. The Chamorro phrase *i famalaoan guerra siha* translates into English as "the women of war." I use this phrase to counter the Japanese colonial and sexist term "comfort woman," and as an inclusive category of representation for indigenous female agency. As noted in the introduction, the terms "military sexual slavery," "sexual slavery," and "sex slave" are also used when referring to the Japanese institutionalization of brothels and other "sex houses" in the Mariana Islands and the wider Micronesian region. While confusion sometimes arises in distinguishing between brothels and comfort stations, as the lines between privately owned and military-sanctioned sex enterprises were often blurred, it is important to underscore the shared forms of gendered violence promoted by these institutions (McClintock 1995, 7). And although the degrees of agency granted to and exerted by the women varied from one sexualized setting to another, one cannot overstate the profoundly violent nature of these transactions across the board.

In this chapter, although other terms are used to describe colonial and indigenous female agency, the phrase *i famalaoan guerra siha* applies directly to all forms of Chamorro female agency during the war. Guam is chosen as a reference point because the greatest wartime contact between "Americanized" and "Japanized" Chamorro women and men occurred there. Through the intracultural exchange fostered among these groups, the idea of collaboration as betrayal of the American nation and of the survival of Guam Chamorros emerges. The degree to which collaboration generated wartime violence and betrayal, as well as postwar amnesia and malaise, is my larger concern in this chapter.

The Japanese Police System in the Northern Marianas

Wartime collaboration, as a synonym for cooperation, existed in a variety of forms throughout the Japanese-occupied Mariana Islands, from the start of World War II in 1941 to its final days in 1945. Chamorros under Japanese colonial rule served in a number of roles, including rice farmers, teacher aides, construction workers, cooks, housemaids, and nurse assistants. Reflecting the racial hierarchy imposed by the Japanese, many Chamorros received low incomes in comparison to the Japanese, Koreans, or Okinawans. Yet a substantial number of Chamorros earned more money than did Palauans and Yapese, whom the Japanese considered lower in cognitive abilities and social status. Other Chamorros, especially during the height of the war in 1944, received no monetary compensation at all and found themselves forced into mandatory labor camps. All these types of employment—voluntary, compensated, or forced—indicated that Chamorros labored to varying degrees to maintain the Japanese colonial empire in the Mariana Islands and elsewhere in neighboring islands. However, no wartime roles garnered the stigma of collaboration more than those of the indigenous police and the women of war. The indigenous police especially set "Chamorros against each other in a way that has had longstanding repercussions in the relations" among them (Poyer, Falgout, and Carucci 2001, 39).

The intracultural "repercussions" that would later be associated with wartime collaboration in Guam in general and the indigenous police in particular were not direct products of the war period. The infrastructure of an indigenous police service had already existed in Micronesia for a couple of decades prior to 1941. The Japanese police began with the establishment of the Nanyō-chō in 1922. This police organization, composed of indigenous attendants and Japanese supervisors, was patterned after the police system first established in Taiwan in 1895. The Japanese police system in Taiwan "became the model that the Japanese transferred and applied to their other colonies" (Chen 1984, 220).[1] Given the different administrative politics of Japan's colonial empire in Korea, Kantō (southern Manchuria), and Nanyō (South Seas), no true uniformity existed among its various police systems. Yet Taiwan's practice of consolidating a police hierarchy, employing indigenous people, and exploiting traditional leadership led to a structure of authority and surveillance that organized succeeding police systems in Japan's colonial empire (Chen 1984, 224–227). The police force of the Japanese mandated islands of Micronesia was no exception.

As in Taiwan, the Japanese police hierarchy of the Nanyō constituted "at the top . . . a police section, *keimuka,* headed by a superintendent, *keishi,* under whom served police inspectors, *keibu,* and assistant inspectors, *keibujō,* and still farther down, policemen, *junsa.*" The Japanese recruited *junkei,* or "native constables," to perform an array of duties, some of which included collecting taxes, investigating misdemeanors, and supervising construction (Peattie 1988, 74). The *junkei* typically ranged in age from the twenties to the early thirties, but a few recruits were even younger. The Japanese trained these young men for three months, outfitted them in white uniforms, and paid them a monthly salary of twenty-five to thirty yen (Hezel 1995, 167).

These police assistants served as liaisons and interpreters for both the Japanese colonial administration and their respective island communities. By 1937, approximately 170 men made up the police force of the Nanyō-chō, with a ratio of 1.2 Japanese patrolmen to one *junkei* (Chen 1984, 224, 235). The Japanese government built police stations in each of its administrative capitals, such as Koror, Palau, and substations beyond the capitals and in neighboring villages as well. The Japanese designated roughly five to eight *junkei* per island district. Supported by the *sosonchō,* or appointed Micronesian leaders, the indigenous police enforced Japanese civil, legal, and public health regulations (Poyer, Falgout, and Carucci 2001, 18). Given these significant responsibilities, the indigenous police possessed a level of authority unmatched by their elders and village chiefs. In Japan's colonies, and the Nanyō was no exception, the police force was the "backbone of the local administration" (Peattie 1988, 73–74).

In the Northern Mariana Islands, the indigenous police system followed the general patterns first created in Taiwan and eventually adapted in the mandated islands of Micronesia in 1922. As early as 1915, however, Chamorros began working as "patrolmen" for the Japanese naval government of Saipan.[2] The Japanese specifically chose Chamorros because of their so-called racial superiority over the Refaluwasch. The Japanese "always tended to favor the Chamorros of the Marianas as the most advanced and adaptable of the Micronesian peoples" (Peattie 1988, 112). Therefore, the majority of Refaluwasch "furnished the bulk of the labor for the pick-and-shovel work, yet received the lowest wages and the smallest food ration" (Peattie 1988, 100). It was unlikely that Refaluwasch collectively pursued or were given the opportunity to work as patrolmen. The Chamorros recruited by the temporary Japanese naval government received better salaries than those working in menial labor and, as a result, markedly improved their social and economic status.

Foremost among the various objectives of the Chamorro patrolmen was to assist the Japanese Navy in enforcing sanitation regulations and punishing criminal offenders. The perceived state of sanitation and health among Chamorros and Refaluwasch attracted the attention of Japanese officials, whose goal was to locate and eradicate such diseases as yaws and dengue. The patrolmen devoted an equal portion of their time to detaining those found guilty of committing crimes. Some of the "criminal offenses" included gambling, homicide, defamation, consumption of liquor, forgery of documents, and theft. Given the segregated structure of Japanese colonial society in the Northern Mariana Islands, the "crimes" tended to be culture specific. No Chamorros and Refaluwasch, for instance, were charged for "forging documents" in 1934. How could they? Only a select few were engaged in administrative service. But, in that same year, the police arrested ninety-six natives for drinking liquor, presumably *tuba,* a fermented sap from the stems of the coconut tree.[3]

After the abolition of naval rule in 1922, the duties of the patrolmen ended in favor of the newly established Japanese colonial police, who performed similar duties and charged people for similar crimes. Under a civil administration and a centralized police hierarchy, the Japanese police created a main branch office in Saipan, with an outlying station in each of Tinian and Rota. A staff totaling 17 employees occupied these stations, each including its own inspectors, indigenous assistants, and police officers. By 1939, the now large police force consisted of 5 lieutenants, 4 assistant lieutenants, 49 Japanese police officers, and 11 indigenous assistants. In the same year, there were "four police stations on Saipan, three on Tinian and two on Rota" (USDN 1944, x).

Given a lack of data, the total number of Chamorros who served as patrolmen and police assistants cannot be accurately ascertained. But the memories people have of the Japanese police officers and their Chamorro assistants remain clear. Fear of the police was particularly strong. For example, Tun Manuel T Sablan vividly recalled his experience as a messenger for the police in Saipan during the early 1940s. Describing evening police duty in Garapan, he said, "We had only two police officers on night duty at any one time. One stayed in the office, and one walked his beat in the whole Garapan area. That is how disciplined the people were before the war. People were afraid to commit any crimes" (2002, 35). Tun Manuel also witnessed firsthand why people feared the police. "Working at the police station," he observed, "people were arrested and brought in. Many of them were Koreans who were rounded up at night. I don't know why they were arrested, but the police would beat them up or sometimes just slap them" (2002, 35). Tun Manuel wanted to know why the police punished these Koreans, but he never dared to question police motives or actions. "You see, there is one thing about Japanese times—you don't know and you don't ask" (M Sablan 2002, 35). As former police officer Tun Benigno Sablan put it, the "Japanese policemen were really crazy. They would hit you if you were bad" (1981, 33).

Unable to request information on alleged criminal cases, the public remained ignorant of what the Japanese deemed good or bad behavior, innocent or guilty parties. For some Chamorros a sense of vulnerability compounded their more general fear of the Japanese police system. People "were presumed guilty on arrest and examinations of suspects took place in secret; the conception of habeas corpus (the individual's right to have his or her case tried before a court) was not recognized, and the use of torture to extract confessions of guilt was the rule of thumb" (Lamont-Brown 1998, 18–19). However, the fear associated with the police during times of peace would pale in comparison to the confusion and terror that characterized the time of war.

Indigenous Police and Interpreters in Wartime Guam

In the years leading to the Japanese military invasion of Guam in 1941, the police system in the Northern Mariana Islands had become increasingly militaristic. Faced with new militarist objectives, the police system was preparing for war with the United States and its allies. Established in secrecy, the Kempeitai (military police) was an empire-wide force that aided the civilian police in arresting those determined to be spies or traitors to the emperor. By the late 1930s, the Kempeitai had gained a reputation for interfering in the control of "speech, meetings and labour disputes, justifying intervention by the need to control anti-military and anti-war movements" (Tipton 1990, 120). Although addressing the issue of espionage remained an important agenda for both the civilian and military police, the initial aim of the Kempeitai was to train indigenous interpreters for the invasion of Guam.

The interpreters were chosen based on their strong understanding of the Chamorro and Japanese languages, as well as familiarity with administrative responsibilities. The proposed agencies for the Japanese occupation of Guam demanded that interpreters be "familiar with a similar agency on Rota, Saipan, or Tinian" (Farrell 1991b, 223). While some Japanese understood the local vernacular of Chamorro, official government policy discouraged them from learning indigenous languages, let alone the English language of American-controlled Guam. Further, the Kempeitai considered English "to be an 'enemy' language in Japan; thus, Kempei students were hardly ever encouraged by their mentors to learn foreign languages. Interpreters were, therefore, employed by the Kempei in Japanese-occupied territory" (Syjuco 1988, 7).

Knowing that these indigenous interpreters would be used in the war was enough reason for Chamorro families in the Northern Mariana Islands to feel further alarmed and confused. Tun David Sablan, a young man at that time, remembered when his father, Tun Elias Parong Sablan, departed for war with the Japanese. "I will never forget," he said, "we were all crying because Dad was leaving to go to war" (D Sablan 2002, 41). Others, like Tun Henry S Pangelinan, himself an interpreter, recalled that he "was not very much interested" in going to war. But "there was a rumor that if you refused to go the Japanese would kill your whole family" (2002, 80). This rumor may not have been far from the truth considering that the Japanese police system openly sanctioned the threat and use of punishment. The Japanese policy of forcefully conscripting interpreters without advanced notification and, in some cases, without monetary compensation heightened the state of crisis for Chamorros (De Leon Guerrero 1984).

Tun Vicente T Camacho clearly recalled the day when the local police and the Kempeitai came to his mother's home. He was then in his early teens. Two Chamorro police assistants and a member of the Kempeitai directed him to work for the secret military police. Concerned about her son's future, Vicente's mother "became very worried, wondering what was wrong. She began to cry and was very scared." In response, the two Chamorro police assistants reassured her that "there was nothing to worry about." They told her that he would work at Guam for a period of six months, alternating with another Chamorro interpreter from Saipan. In a rare challenge to their instructions, Vicente's mother said "no to the Kempeitai" (V Camacho 1992, 24).

According to Tun Vicente, his mother reminded the police that her husband "had already been conscripted to work for the military at the 'X' unit, and no one else was left to support the family. Only me, since my younger brothers were still too young. So she cried and cried—she put on a real fuss, so that I wouldn't have to go to Guam." The Kempeitai "took pity" and allowed Vicente to remain on Saipan. However, he still had to work for the Kempeitai on Saipan, a job he considered very dangerous and secret because of the reputation the police had among Chamorros. He indicated that he, along with others, never worked more than one month on a Kempeitai mission. Nor did he receive any information about future plans and orders. "Even though I worked there, I didn't know about all the things the Kempeitai were doing" (V Camacho 1992, 24–25).

While Vicente's mother was able to prevent him from traveling to Guam to work for the Japanese, the majority of Chamorros recruited for duty as interpreters had no choice but to comply. A total of seven groups of Chamorros left the Northern Marianas for civil and military duty in Guam. From December 1941 to January 1942, the Japanese sent approximately seventy-five Chamorro men and three women from the islands of Rota and Saipan to serve as "staff assistants, police investigators, interpreters" (Rogers 1995, 172). All of these Chamorros worked in a variety of positions, yet each one assumed responsibility as interpreter for their Japanese employers when the need to work in the Chamorro vernacular arose. As Tun Antonio R De Leon Guerrero, a Saipanese Chamorro, explained, "I had to interpret for the [South Seas Development Company], and then the police and the school teachers—all of them. Interpreting is really hard work" (De Leon Guerrero 1993, 33).

Tun Antonio noted that interpreters fulfilled a number of roles, including acting as assistants to the Japanese police. They sometimes became implicated in the duties and responsibilities of the civil and military police in Guam. Chamorros from the Northern Mariana Islands, particularly the indigenous police, sometimes volunteered or unwillingly participated in the intimidation and persecution of their brothers and sisters in Guam. Shortly after the arrival of military forces in Guam, the Japanese civilian police established their office and prison in the capital village of Hagåtña. Police substations—all under the Minseibu (civil administration)—were subsequently placed in every village of the island. An unidentified number of northern Chamorros worked for the civilian police and at least four of them fell under the direct authority of the Kempeitai: Antonio R Camacho, Felipe C Mendiola, Francisco T Palacios, and Henry C Pangelinan. These Kempeitai employees performed work similar to their civilian counterparts and were part of a labor force of approximately eighty-nine Kempeitai stationed throughout the Nanyō (Lamont-Brown 1998, 35). In addition, there were a few Guam Chamorros whose efforts lent support to the administrative and investigative activities of the police force.

However, much of the work of the civil and military police forces fell on the shoulders of the interpreters and their Japanese supervisors. In general, the police forces in wartime Guam aimed to assimilate Chamorros to Japanese ways of thinking. They also intended to deter any form of espionage and to eliminate any pro-American sentiment. As Tun Henry S Pangelinan recalled, the Japanese attempted to "convert" Guam Chamorros to the Japanese system, but the process proved difficult given that Guam Chamorros were "real believers in America" (2002, 80). Consequently, numerous Chamorros suffered various forms of punishment, most notably resulting from the failure or refusal to bow to Japanese buildings and officials. Other offenses included "stealing, assault and battery, gambling, intoxication and crimes involving sex" (P Sanchez 1979, 92). "So many people on Guam did nothing, but being a suspect in Japanese custody was the same as being guilty" (Pangelinan 2002, 80). In short, every day Chamorros faced numerous hardships, simply because of their prior affiliation and persistent loyalties to the United States.

Lino and Regina Chargualaf referred to the Saipanese interpreter Nicolas Diaz as one of the men who openly delighted in humiliating and intimidating Chamorros in Guam. They recalled that "physical punishment was hard" working under the supervision of such men as Diaz, who "severely punished the one person who brought him *tuba*. And he hit the man just because he was late with the *tuba*" (Owings 1981, 143). Another Chamorro from Guam, Jesus Crisostomo, agreed, stating that Diaz, a supervisor among a crew of cave diggers, "made us work like animals" (Owings 1981, 180). In addition to his harsh physical demands, Diaz also required others to entertain him.

Quite often, Nicolas Diaz forced his crew to provide him with food, *tuba*, music, and dance. He even compelled one subordinate to shower him at a nearby river. As Crisostomo noted, Diaz "was the interpreter for the Japanese, so all the things he did, all the things he wanted to be done, we were supposed to obey him. If he said that we were going to sing, and no one wanted to sing, they had to sing anyway because if we didn't sing, he was going to give us a slap to the face. . . . It would have been better, the treatment of one Japanese that was very cruel, than that particular man from Saipan. . . . Really, we would have liked better the worst Japanese, the cruelest Japanese, than that Chamorro from Saipan. . . . [Diaz] didn't see that Guam Chamorros were his equals, his peers. He didn't look at the Guam Chamorros as Christians just like him. His system was a very bad system" (Owings 1981, 181).

Nicolas Diaz typified the negative demeanor of several indigenous police and interpreters. Some Chamorros from the Northern Mariana Islands, like Diaz, might have personally enjoyed inflicting trauma among others. But many more Chamorros, it can be argued, fulfilled their roles as interpreters and police as a matter of duty and obligation to the Japanese colonial government. Under the direct supervision of Japanese civil and military administrators, Chamorros from the Northern Mariana Islands had no choice but to enforce the laws and demands of the colonial government. Wherever they worked, from rice fields to mining operations to construction sites, the interpreters and police exerted a threatening authority. As Tun Henry S Pangelinan stated, "We were tied down with the rules of the Japanese Empire. . . . Physical contact was not by will, but by constant pressure from superiors." He also said that interpreters generally had "sympathetic" feelings to their extended families in Guam, but often felt restrained from helping them with their daily wants and needs (K Phillips 1984, 16).

Despite the existence of interisland kin relationships, interpreters and police could not publicly sympathize with the "Americanized" Chamorros. Wartime conditions dictated that Guam Chamorros be identified, in principle, as ambivalent subjects of Japan's Greater East Asian Co-Prosperity Sphere. But, in reality, Chamorro interpreters were "enemies" to those in Guam in ways that Guam Chamorros were "enemies" to the interpreters. Tun Antonio R De Leon Guerrero explained, "We had been given Japanese education, and then been drafted by the Japanese, right? So even though we were the same Chamorro people, we were enemies, since we had come at the orders of the Japanese" (1993, 35). Additionally, Kan'ichi Ogawa, former director of the General Affairs Department of the Minseibu, said, "In times of peace, interpreters can be used to facilitate and gauge mutual understanding.... [However], during an occupation, the occupied become your enemy.... Saipanese Chamorros had to maintain the attitude of an occupying force even in times when they met members of their own clan or relatives who lived on Guam" (Higuchi 2001b, 25).

Unlike the majority of Guam Chamorros, the interpreters and especially the indigenous police possessed tremendous authority and social mobility. "Although they were of no particular high rank, employment by the military alone provided them with a sense of superiority" (Higuchi 2001b, 61). Their comprehension of the Japanese language and the expectations of their superiors enabled the interpreters to attain positions of power over their Chamorro counterparts in Guam. In understanding the views of the occupying force, they clearly held an advantage over other Chamorros. At times, some interpreters exploited this inequitable relationship for social, economic, and political advantage. Yet, in the racial hierarchy of Japanese colonial governance, the Chamorro interpreters always remained subordinate to the Japanese. In the words of one Japanese administrator, the Japanese often perceived the indigenous police as *"tora no i wo kariru kitsune"* (a fox wearing a lion's coat) (Higuchi 2001b, 25). This condescending view of the indigenous police reflected but one aspect of Japanese colonial governance overseas. These types of views also showed the limits of authority granted to the interpreters. Nevertheless, the image of authority assigned to and perpetuated by Chamorro interpreters led to the deterioration of social relationships among Chamorros.

Without a doubt, the emergence of intracultural conflicts in Guam negatively affected the maintenance of indigenous kin and familial relationships, as Tan Marikita Palacios Crisostomo, the wife of an interpreter, remembered. Reaching the island in 1943 accompanied by her husband Luis, Tan Marikita noted, "It was a bad situation there. [Guam Chamorros] would come to the chief of police and say that other Chamorros were hiding weapons or they were doing this or they were doing that. Sometimes they lied. Maybe they were jealous of somebody, or they were enemies for this reason or that" (Crisostomo 2002, 84). In her recollection of life on

Guam, Tan Marikita avoided mentioning particular people and events. She purposely spoke in general terms, careful not to offend anybody who might have been implicated in these events. Defending her husband's wartime role in the occupation, she stated that his work "never had a bad effect" on her extended family in Guam (Crisostomo 2002, 84).

As Tan Marikita observed, local affairs in wartime Guam were in disrepair. Problems arose not only because of the imposition of Japanese assimilation and wartime policies, but also because the agents involved in implementing those policies were Chamorro interpreters, police, and others from the Northern Mariana Islands. Recalling the problem of employing Chamorros from the islands of Rota and Saipan, Kan'ichi Ogawa told how Chamorros from Guam "entered the Minseibu office and suddenly came over to me to make an appeal. The Guam Chamorros did not like to enlist the interpretive services of the Saipanese Chamorros to communicate. [They] particularly resented the Chamorro civilian patrolmen." In response to concerns of the Guam Chamorros, Ogawa stated, "My role as a bridge between the Japanese and Chamorro sides could only go so far. When a person told me that he/she had been struck by a Saipanese patrolman, all I could say was, 'You just have to bear with it'" (Higuchi 2001b, 24).

The Japanese "Comfort Stations"

Due to the colonial administration's failure to resolve the problem of interpretive work, many Chamorros just had to "bear" with the wartime circumstances they faced. The colonial administration knowingly perpetuated those circumstances in which Chamorros sometimes found themselves fighting rather than peacefully negotiating with each other and the Japanese. The enlistment of Chamorro interpreters and police from Rota and Saipan did not lessen the growing sense of discontent and uneasiness on the part of Guam Chamorros. Nor did the establishment of "comfort stations," or brothels for Japanese military personnel, minimize the increasing anxiety, confusion, and violence among everyone on the island. Contrary to the term's connotations, the introduction of *ianjo* (comfort stations) simply underscored the imperialist, gendered, and violent dimensions of Japan's wartime empire.

To some degree, Japan's military sexual slavery originated along with the development of its army and police systems at the turn of the twentieth century. The rise in military brothels accompanied the rise in military and police activities in the Asian and Pacific regions. For example, the Kempeitai administered the systems of sexual slavery in Korea and Manchuria (Lamont-Brown 1998, 44). As part of a longer tradition of Japanese sexual slavery at home and abroad, the economic, logistical, and social dimensions of the comfort stations paralleled and imitated the Japanese sex industry. Yuki Tanaka has argued that after the Meiji Restoration, or the creation of the modern Japanese nation-state, the number of Japanese brothels proliferated overseas. The women were called *karayuki-san,* literally "a person traveling to China. . . . Originally coined by the people of northern Kyushu, the term came to be applied specifically to the impoverished rural women sold into prostitution far from home" (Tanaka 2002, 167).

By way of underground labor networks, the *karayuki-san* served Japan's military and police organizations, as well as civilian populations as far away as Australia, Hawai'i, and South Africa (Tanaka 2002, 167). The Japanese army employed the services of brothels as early as 1905 (Chung 1997, 222). The Japanese government's provision of sex slaves for its overseas military, police, and even administrative personnel occurred at a later time. "It was not until late 1937 that the Japanese government created an official brothel policy and began to systematically establish brothels in areas where soldiers were stationed" (Chung 1997, 222).

At an international level, the Japanese government intended to avoid criticism regarding the manner in which the military personnel, particularly army soldiers, interacted with women abroad. Alerted by incidents of mass rape in Shanghai in 1932, the Japanese government and the Ministry of War attempted to suppress all criticism by developing "comfort stations" for the military. "As a result of its experiences in China, the establishment of military brothels in occupied areas was part of its plans. . . . Brothels were . . . created in Malaysia, Singapore, Indonesia, and the Philippines, as well as in China" (Chung 1997, 224). The purpose was twofold. The first goal was to prevent the spread of venereal disease among the Japanese soldiers. As part of the military's policy to control the biological exchange of such diseases, Japanese doctors encouraged the use of contraceptive devices, lectured on hygiene, and required regular "health" checkups for the women (Hicks 1996, 319). The second objective was to deter soldiers from "raping" women—yet, of course, the entire process was a form of institutional rape and sexual slavery.

Theoretically, the aim was to reduce military forms of aggression toward women in particular and civilians in general. In the military's estimation, providing soldiers with the opportunity to engage in sexual relations also boosted their morale and, it was believed, protected them from injury and death (Oh 2001, 9). Through the military's seemingly benign position on "comfort stations," Japan attempted, again, to promote itself as a "liberator" from Western colonial rule in Asia and the Pacific. By projecting the image of an organized sex industry in the Greater East Asia Co-Prosperity Sphere, the Japanese government and its military aspired to create an idealized environment of cooperation, mutual respect, and tolerance in its colonies. Nothing could be further from the truth, as Japan's two provisions for "comfort women did not function as an effective measure for either problem, and in particular for the problem of random sexual violence against civilians in occupied territories" (Tanaka 2002, 32).

By 1942, approximately four hundred "comfort stations" existed throughout Japan's wartime empire, with ten reportedly functioning in the Nanyō (Chung 1997, 224; Tanaka 2002, 27). Further, anywhere from eighty thousand to two hundred thousand women were exploited, in some sexual or social capacity, as *ianfu* (comfort women) (Schmidt 2000, 13; Tanaka 2002, 31). Initially involving Japanese women, the military sexual slavery system soon employed or forced Korean and Taiwanese women to work as sexual slaves and domestic laborers for the Japanese military. Very soon after the military organized its sexual slavery system, the Japanese government discouraged the use of Japanese women, arguing that they should "bear and bring up good Japanese children, who would grow up to be loyal subjects of the Emperor rather than being the means for men to satisfy their sexual urges" (Tanaka 2002, 32). As a result, vast numbers of women from Korea and Taiwan, many of whom came from poor economic backgrounds, served the demands of the military sexual slavery system. The Japanese military also enlisted the sexual services of women from its colonies in Asia and the Pacific, frequently by means of deceit, intimidation, and violence, along with the kidnapping of young girls and women (Tanaka 2002, 29).

While the term *ianfu* belies the exploitive nature of Japan's military sex industry, it was not the only euphemistic term that replaced its predecessor, *karayuki-san*. Given the large mobilization of Korean women for the "comfort stations," the term *teishintai* (volunteer corps) came into use. Although *ianfu* may have been the accepted and official term, other terms included "barmaid *(shakufu)*, women in the drinking business *(shūgyōfu)*, courtesan *(gijo)*, or other professional women *(tokushu fujo)*, all of which refer to prostitutes" (Chung 1997, 221). Much of this vocabulary regarding sex slaves came from the *ianfu* themselves, many of whom provided the most vivid and detailed depictions of themselves and the industry that exploited them. However, the histories of Japanese military sexual slavery remain unwritten, as speculation and conjecture dominate much of the extant documentation. The wider economic, political, and social motives and consequences of the military sexual slavery have yet to receive much critical examination. The lack of knowledge about sexual slavery stems partly from the shame that causes some survivors to remain silent. "Shame associated with the sexual enslavement induced silence. In the conservative and Confucian societies of East Asia the silence was dominant. Women who returned home spoke rarely if at all of their past experiences" (Schmidt 2000, 16). Officially treated as top secret, the materials on military sexual slavery and the *ianfu* exist in limited quantities or do not exist at all as a result of being destroyed by military officials toward the end of the war (Schmidt 2000, 15). While the "comfort stations" clearly publicized Japan's positions on sex, venereal disease, and rape, the particular details of military sexual slavery remain largely unknown.

From the time of their establishment in 1937 to the last stages of the war, the logistical and managerial operations of military sexual slavery took place in relative secrecy. Apart from the military's visible, public, and voluntary use of military sexual slavery, not much is known about the agents involved in its rise and decline in the Nanyō. That the Nanyō-chō used police officers to supervise the operation of comfort stations clearly reveals the interdependent relationship between the police and the brothels. It was not uncommon for some indigenous police, island elites, and Japanese men to drink alcohol, smoke, or visit "geisha houses," another synonym for "comfort stations" (Poyer, Falgout, and Carucci 2001, 64). Before 1922, though, when the Japanese naval government ruled Micronesia, geisha houses and other forms of prostitution were outlawed. With the increase of Asian immigration to Micronesia in the 1920s and 1930s, prostitution became "an inevitable accompaniment" (Peattie 1988, 209). Around this time, various bars, restaurants, and geisha houses—all sites of prostitution—surfaced to cater to the sexual and social desires of Japanese and Okinawan men. From Tinian to Palau, "every Japanese town in Micronesia had its *hana machi* 'flower quarters'—rather shabby little buildings with incongruously poetic names where men could eat, drink, and enjoy the company of women for an evening" (Peattie 1988, 209).

Clearly, not all brothels were restaurants, and not all restaurants could be considered brothels. Yet, it is estimated that as many as eighty brothels existed throughout Micronesia, not counting the ten official "comfort stations" that served the Japanese military there and elsewhere in the Pacific. Reportedly, some comfort women earned an average annual salary of one thousand yen, or approximately $2,850 (Peattie 1988, 338n35). While the sex industry in the Nanyō evidently thrived, complementing other forms of social entertainment and festivities, not much is known about its impact on the island societies. Based on the histories of military sexual slavery elsewhere in Japan's empire, it is likely that the "comfort stations" primarily catered to male immigrant laborers, military and police personnel, island elites, and Japanese administrative officials.

The wider indigenous male populations most likely would have been excluded from the "comfort stations" or brothels. What can be said with certainty is that the Japanese male military and the male police played a major role in the administration of the sexual slavery in times of peace and war. In the Northern Mariana Islands, no extensive research has been done that would indicate the level of indigenous political, sexual, and economic engagement in the "comfort stations." The secrecy surrounding the Japanese sex industry, the dearth of written materials on the subject of "comfort stations," and the shame associated with prostitution all make it difficult to assess and understand the entangled relationships involving sex, empire, and collaboration.

The Women of War in Guam

In wartime Guam, the introduction of what Chamorros call *i guma ka'ku* (the house of sex) reveals some insights into issues of empire, collaboration, and sex. Of course, brothels existed in the northern islands of Rota, Saipan, and Tinian. The issue of when the Japanese military and police specifically introduced sexual slavery there during the war (1941–1944) has yet to be addressed. To the south, in Guam, the establishment of "comfort stations" came on the heels of the arrival of the Japanese military and police. In terms of their exact origin, Tony Palomo stated that the Japanese created them "as early as a month after capturing" the island. He speculated that a total of five homes were built to serve as "comfort stations," with three situated in Hagåtña and the remaining two in Anigua and Piti (Palomo 1984, 79). Anywhere from thirty to fifty women worked in these stations. Most of them were Koreans, but there were also Chamorros, Japanese, and Okinawans.

Some contend that Chamorros contributed the greatest number of women to the *guma ka'ku* of Hagåtña. A Chamorro elder with familial ties to Hagåtña, Tan Concepcion M Tolentino, recalled that "mostly Chamorros" worked in the "comfort stations" of this village (2005).[4] She added that "there were also Koreans . . . and Palauans and Saipanese," drawing attention to the possibility that Micronesian women worked there as well. Although not much information is available about the introduction of women from Palau and Saipan, it is known that not many Japanese women worked in the "comfort stations" of Guam. Only a few Japanese women worked in the sex industry, and those who did served Japanese military officers exclusively. The building named Akashino doubled as "a first-class Japanese restaurant" and "comfort station" only for naval officers (Higuchi 1999, 6).[5]

Other "comfort stations," usually located along the Hagåtña River, were reserved for enlisted soldiers and sailors. The central organization that supervised military sexual services was the Nanyō Kōhatsu Kaisha (South Seas Development Company). This private company specialized in the production of sugar and in the mining of phosphate, among other economic ventures. In addition to these economic activities, the company maintained an intimate relationship with the Japanese military, particularly the navy. From the time of its inception in 1921, the Nanyō Kōhatsu "advanced into the occupied territories in the South Seas under the command of the military" (Higuchi 1999, 10). Not only did the company work with the military, it also abided by the military's orders and objectives, taking on the managerial responsibilities for the provision of sexual services to the Japanese military in Guam. Some of those responsibilities included the recruitment of women, the payment of their wages, and the organization of their medical checkups—all efforts to produce the image of a local prostitution economy while simultaneously attempting to disguise the violent conditions under which it existed.

Still, as in many cases regarding the management of military sexual slavery, the financial structure of each "comfort station" in Guam remains a mystery. Although certain administrators of the Nanyō Kōhatsu can be identified, it remains difficult to pinpoint the economic relationships between the company, the military, the "comfort stations," and the police. These relationships are "uncertain"; the "financial implications of Nanyō Kōhatsu for Korean or old Japanese owners of *ianjo* remain equivocal" (Higuchi 1999, 9). Even Kan'ichi Ogawa, a Japanese administrative official, knew about a "secret fund" that circulated among those in charge of the "comfort stations" (Higuchi 2001b, 28). Yet, he could not recall where the monies originated, nor could he determine their exact purpose. Perhaps the confusion served a particular objective—to ensure that no single individual would be held accountable for what was essentially the management of sexual slavery in Guam. Despite the uncertainty surrounding the financial aspects, other factors regarding the operation of "comfort stations" can be determined with greater clarity and conviction.

On the topic of recruitment, the Japanese military stationed on Guam "demanded to take mixed blood Chamorros of European ancestry, who were mostly from the upper-class, to become *ianfu* for the soldiers. [The civil administration] strongly opposed this idea because they thought that it would raise a riot among the people of Guam" (Higuchi 1999, 13). A former Japanese witness and employee of Nanyō Kōhatsu, Toraji Tanaka, agreed. He recalled that since "many high-class Chamorro women" had already developed relationships with some military personnel, there was no need to recruit them (Higuchi 2001b, 70). Instead, the military hired women "who formerly had sexual relationships" with Americans during the early 1900s, when the US Navy occupied Guam (Higuchi 1999, 13). That the military eventually decided to recruit Chamorro women from a group of prostitutes reflects a common fear expressed by Japanese officials in general. The majority of women recruited had to come from poor parts of their respective societies because Japanese officials feared that the public humiliation of "island elites" might result in social unrest (Chung 1997, 228). Toraji Tanaka himself, among other Japanese in Guam, expressed the fear that abuse directed at island elites might generate public outcry and protest. Approximately fifteen Chamorro women, then, supplemented the estimated forty-two Asian sexual slaves, some of whom originally worked in Saipan (Higuchi 1999, 11; Palomo 1984, 79). These women were called

"Monday ladies" *(famalaoan lunes siha)* since under the administration of the American navy they received medical checkups on Mondays.

As Monday women, they had earned a negative reputation for frequenting the American saloons of Hagåtña prior to the war (Rogers 1995, 134). Specifically, their reputation as "prostitutes" stood in stark contrast to an environment of American naval discipline and Chamorro Catholic spiritualism. Referring to the Monday women of Hagåtña, American anthropologist Laura Thompson determined that the "few prostitutes on the island are not licensed. They are watched to some extent by the police, confined as vagrants and treated in the naval hospital" (1941, 172). Some young men turned to "the 'wild' girls of the town—the prostitutes, bar girls and a few women with illegitimate children" (L Thompson 1941, 219). The reasoning behind such activity, Thompson argued, lay in the notion that the "older unattached women provide a sexual outlet for the bachelors, who occasionally keep a concubine and her illegitimate children in another part of town" (1941, 219). Thus, the Monday women emerged as the first group of Chamorro women conscripted to serve Japanese male sexual needs. "By the middle of 1942, a number of local women were living with Japanese officers, including the Governor and the Chief of Police. These were generally the same women who hob-nobbed with American officials before the outbreak of war" (Palomo 1984, 80). To say that the Monday women "hob-nobbed" with the Japanese implies that some Monday women volunteered their sexual services or pursued meaningful relationships with the Japanese.

Tony Palomo wrote about one such incident, recounting a conversation in which the wife of an American prisoner once accused a Monday woman of "lowering herself" by residing with a Japanese military officer. The Monday woman responded by asking, "Why is it that when a woman has an affair with a Japanese, she is lowering herself, but when she has an affair with a Chamorro or an American, she isn't. . . . When God proclaimed the Ten Commandments, and demanded that 'thou shalt not commit adultery,' He did not say that adultery would be sinful only if one of the parties is a Japanese." Defending her position, the woman reiterated that Chamorro women who married Japanese prior to the war did not lose their status. Besides, she said, "the Japanese are winning the war . . . so, how can you say they are lower than other men?" (Palomo 1984, 80). Palomo concluded that this particular Monday woman would not only maintain relations with the Japanese, but would also resume relations with the Americans should they win the war.

This example illustrates that some Monday women willingly became sexual partners of the Japanese. But others did not. The motives of those who worked as sex slaves remain unclear. One can surmise that they might have acquired a very limited and often unstable level of economic, political, and social power. As with sex slaves located elsewhere in Japan's empire, it is quite plausible that the Monday women provided sexual services "in return for food, cigarettes, medicines and the safety of their children" (Lamont-Brown 1998, 44). In their individual acts of defiance to preconceived norms of Chamorro womanhood, some Monday women also resisted Guam Chamorro notions of loyalty to America. Some of them clearly demonstrated that they were not simply objects of Japanese male desire and lust. They actively and consciously chose what they believed were appropriate paths for their lives.

On the other hand, the Japanese military and police forcefully or manipulatively coerced Chamorro women to work in the "pleasure quarters" of Guam. Based on the available evidence, the Japanese military enlisted the services of local "collaborators" to recruit women. Like the recruitment methods of the Japanese military in Indonesia and the Philippines, women in Guam were sometimes "duped into prostitution or abducted for sexual purposes by collaborators (including civil police) within their own ethnic groups" (Lamont-Brown 1998, 44). Some allege that Samuel T Shinohara, with the assistance of several Monday women, recruited Chamorro women for the "comfort stations." Prior to the outbreak of war in 1941, Shinohara married into a Chamorro family and became president of the island's Japanese association. Given his strong grasp of the English, Chamorro, and Japanese languages, as well as his public allegiance to Japan, he was the person most likely to have recruited local women (Higuchi 1999, 18). Some believe that he forced an unidentified number of Chamorro women to serve the needs of Japanese military officers and enlisted personnel. Recollecting Shinohara's role during the war in a manuscript titled "Chamorrita," Agueda Johnston and Clyde Cramlet stated that he was "regarded as a spy and despised by the loyal natives for his willingness to do the dirty work for the Japanese." In borrowing various domestic items like bedspreads and sewing machines from local families, they presumed that he "led native girls, who feared to refuse, to work as 'maids' for the Japanese officers" (Johnston and Cramlet [1965?], 237). Hisashi Hirose, a former Japanese navy sailor stationed in Guam, confirmed the role Shinohara played in the recruitment of *ianfu:* "Shinohara gathered Chamorro women in dire straits, . . . all of the officers had their own exclusive Chamorro girlfriends" (Higuchi 2001b, 63).

It is highly doubtful that Guam Chamorro women collectively courted Japanese military personnel. Although some Chamorro women worked as "maids," performing various domestic duties, it can be argued that they were also subjected to forms of sexual exploitation and violence. Once a Chamorro woman worked for the Japanese, in capacities such as teacher assistants or rice paddy workers, she sometimes became vulnerable to sexual harassment by her male employers. Beautiful looking women were especially worried. As Tan Concepcion M Tolentino remembered in an interview with her daughter, the Japanese targeted "families with lots of pretty girls in their homes" (2005). The fears Chamorro women associated with working for the Japanese soon became widespread. In another interview, Anthony J Ramirez, a Chamorro genealogy expert, recalled asking his grandfather, "What does a father do when you know that here's the Japanese and the word is going around that atrocities are being committed against women?" "Well," the grandfather replied, "he rounded up all his family. Went up north and hid all his daughters from the Japanese men because they pleasure in women" (Ramirez 2004). Although Ramirez did not explain what happened to his aunts, he stressed that many young women went to great lengths to avoid *i guma ka'ku.* Women, he said, purposely took few showers, wore dirty clothes, and spread rumors that they were infected with various diseases.

If recruited, women feared most the possibility of being disgraced among their families. The shame placed on the women, assuming they were single, made it difficult for them to find suitable marriage partners. "If a woman is disgraced," Ramirez remarked, "it is very hard for that particular woman to marry." Deviation from the expected gendered norms generated much concern on the part of both the women themselves and their families. As Ramirez observed, the sexual conditions for Chamorro women of that time were "really restrictive." Many perceived male behavior in terms of *checho lahi,* literally meaning "male work," but more precisely meaning the general attitudes and actions of men. In this regard, Chamorro cultural norms tolerated aggressive and promiscuous male sexual behavior with women. However, in respect to *checho palauan* (female work), cultural norms demanded that women guard and protect themselves from sexual activities with men outside of marriage. This attitude partly explains why the introduction of "comfort stations" in the context of colonial rule greatly affected the women involved. To a certain degree, it did not matter how Chamorro women perceived themselves in their relationships with the Japanese. The issue involved something much larger than individual attitudes and actions. As Ramirez effectively argued, "Whatever you do by behavior reflects your family" (2004). That is why the women experienced disgrace, shame, and tragedy on a profound level. Their behavior—individually motivated or not—often shamed their entire families and clans.

The women of war in Guam, *i famalaoan guerra siha,* have consequently been categorized into what Higuchi called "three types of women." They include "those women who were local wives of Japanese servicemen; those who prostituted themselves; and those who were forced to accept sexual relations" (Higuchi 1999, 1). These categories describe the general structure of Chamorro female relations with the Japanese and vice versa; yet each woman lived her own dynamic story of adaptation, resistance, or submission. As well, some Chamorro women were girlfriends or lovers of Japanese military personnel, complicating further the range of social and sexual relations between Chamorro women and Japanese men. Even the label "Monday women" does not adequately address their behaviors and attitudes. As Ramirez stated, Monday women "freely choose to be in association with a lot of men," implying that not all Monday women worked as sex slaves (2004). Some Monday women certainly volunteered their services, and perhaps many more were forced to work as the so-called comfort women. Despite the daily threat of Japanese sexual violence, women in general persevered through adverse conditions. As many Chamorros understand, women played very important roles in helping their families survive through the war. "Chamorro women, from teenagers to grandmothers, cared for children and elderly family members. They ensured the families' survival by providing food through bartering, farming, and fishing at a time when food was scarce" (Manibusan 1993).

Tempering stories of survival and domesticity were stories of defiance and tragedy. A few months prior to the American land invasion of Guam on 21 July 1944, Japanese violence and atrocities toward Chamorros rapidly increased. For example, Dolores Mesa, a young Chamorro woman, resisted the requests of a Japanese naval officer. Because of her unwillingness to succumb to his demands, "she was tied to a coconut tree in the hot sun for a full day without food or water, and while there, threatened with stabbing or decapitation with a bayonet" (*Guam News* 1948). She survived the ordeal, though her mother and others were not so fortunate. The Japanese rounded them into a hole and threw in grenades, killing approximately twenty-nine Chamorros. Dolores Mesa did not instigate these violent incidents. Many of them stemmed from Japanese military brutality directed at innocent civilians throughout the island. Another group of Chamorro men and women died on 18 July 1944. Tan Beatrice Emsley, who was fourteen years old at the time, survived the massacre. According to her, the Japanese bayoneted the men first, all of whom cried out to Yu'us and their mothers as they were being executed. Presumably the Japanese also raped the women, though Emsley did not openly admit or deny such an incident.

On the same day, in the jungle area of Hagåtña, unknown Japanese military personnel brutalized the women. One officer "ripped off" the dress of one of them and "began to cut her breast with the saber. [Her sister then] rushed forward to save her, [but the] Japanese guards stopped her and bayoneted both sisters before throwing their corpses into the crater" (Wiseman 1984, 19). The Japanese bayoneted the remaining women, including Beatrice Emsley, who recalled feeling nothing of her "execution." She only remembered what felt like a splash of water as she fell, dazed, into the ditch of moaning women. When the Japanese left the scene, she surfaced, holding her wounded neck, and went to seek food, refuge, and medicine. Dolores Mesa and Beatrice Emsley were two among a small group of people to survive such massacres in Guam.

It is misleading to suggest, though, that sexual violence occurred only between Chamorro women and Japanese men. Although histories of women conscripted for Japanese sexual slavery definitely warrant historical attention, scholars should also be aware of other local and intracultural sources of violence. Military sexual slavery took place in a violent environment and inflicted shame and disgrace on the women, clearly illustrating the oppressive and gendered dimensions of the Japanese wartime empire. But wartime violence against Chamorro women extended beyond the exploitive conditions of the "comfort stations." *I famalaoan guerra siha* were not the only women who ran the risk of being shamed, disgraced, and ostracized by their own families. Intracultural sexual relations among Chamorros, in particular, provided an equally complicated picture of sex, empire, and loyalty in Guam. Specifically, Guam Chamorros generally looked down on Chamorro women who pursued, willingly or through coercion, sexual relations with Chamorro men from the Northern Mariana Islands. Some labeled these women outcasts, disloyal to the assumed norms of the American nation and Chamorro culture.

Although oral histories of these events are scarce, some materials are available for comment and reflection. For example, letters written around the 1940s shed light on the issue of intracultural relations among Chamorros in Guam. In a letter dated 12 October 1944,[6] Carmen O Herrero wrote to her brother, E R J Ojida, in New York, telling him about several women, among them his "girlfriend," who had married men from Saipan. Though brief, her letter revealed the climate of anxiety, confusion, and shame that surrounded some of these women. Directly addressing her brother, she asked first, "Have you heard that the Dinga girls . . . are married to pro Japs, fellows from Saipan?[7] Now I want you not to feel bad, because your girl friend is also married to one from Saipan." Consoling her brother, she continued, "If she is that type, I won't feel bad about it." Herrero then told her brother about the woman's family, and how they had responded to her marrying a Saipanese. She wrote, "Her family are against it very much but I guess she got fooled by all the Jap propaganda . . . because, you see, the Saipan guys were thought to be big shots, as they thought they were. . . . However, [the Saipan Chamorros] only fooled the foolish."

On the surface, Herrero's letter demonstrates that women from Guam may have married men from Saipan for political and economic gain. After all, they married "big shots." But in marrying Japanese men or Chamorro interpreters, the women jeopardized their social standing among their Guam Chamorro counterparts. A variety of motives, other than individual desires for material gain and higher status, may also have existed. Some families voluntarily offered their daughters to men from Rota and Saipan. These families may have seen such intracultural marriages as lesser forms of social degradation, especially when compared to the stigma surrounding Chamorro "Monday women." Also, by marrying an interpreter a woman might be able to protect her family from physical harm by the Japanese military. Each case of intracultural marriage surely varied, as did the motives and consequences. Nevertheless, no matter what those motives might have been, the consequence of shaming one's family simply perpetuated the intracultural conflicts among Chamorros. Not even the sacred sacrament of matrimony could overcome the social stigma attached to these marriages.

In another letter, dated 25 September 1944, Jesus L G Cruz reflected on the complicated nature of intracultural marriages.[8] Writing to his brother Joseph L G Cruz, Jesus talked about the reconciliation, if any, between loyalty and love. "Brother, you don't know what is going on. Our sis Flora she also had a bad luck." Recalling the Japanese wartime occupation, a period still vivid in his mind, he said that their sister "happen to be in love with a man from Saipan." Demonstrating the family's genuine love for their sister, he stated, "brother we don't blame her for being in love with the man. . . . But when she thought of marrying, we advise her to wait until the war is over." Referring to their sister's fierce sense of independence, Cruz noted regretfully, "She will never listen to any one of us. Even the Priest advise but she won't listen. Teachers of scools [sic] talk to her and also her best friends. But still she will never pay attention. . . . Brother, she really shame us all. . . . But we can't do anything, for on that moment I have found that love is blind."

In his letter, Jesus Cruz recognized that sometimes "love" takes precedence over even the most entrenched notions of cultural and familial obligation. Apparently, Flora Cruz not only refused to listen to her peers and family members but also to her teachers and a priest, an act considered highly disrespectful. By remaining committed to the unidentified man from Saipan, she resisted the collective beliefs of her particular island society. She opposed the ideas, implicit in the letter, that Guam Chamorros should remain loyal to the United States and should avoid "collaborative" contact with Chamorros from Rota and Saipan. It is not known if she changed her loyalty to Japan, or if she considered such an idea in the first place. Flora Cruz's actions defied the perceived cultural, gendered, and political norms of her time, and thus "shamed" her family. Like her, the women of war in Guam have had to bear the burden of shame, then and now. Why have the stories of *i famalaoan guerra siha* remained marginalized in histories of war? Why have the women, from the actual survivors to their descendants, not actively participated in war commemorations? What do their stories say, ultimately, about the making of history in the Mariana Islands?

Collaboration and Commemoration

Given the scope of these questions, one might think that the women of war lived separate lives and performed separate tasks under the Japanese colonial administration in Guam. That they sometimes found themselves in the dimly lit rooms of so-called "comfort stations," by force or personal choice, does not suggest they were isolated from the issues and events of the time.

The women of war played very important roles in the everyday happenings of the island. Historians have yet to examine, understand, and truly appreciate those roles. This argument can also be applied to the non-Chamorro sex slaves—women whose lives scholars truly know little about. As for the men who raped or engaged in sexual relations with the women, evidence reveals more about their official motivations than about their personal emotions and thoughts. Some Japanese military officials saw the establishment of the "comfort stations" in Guam as a normal and essential military procedure. Yet they failed to grasp that the institutionalization of sexual services and sexual slavery was anything but normal for others. The introduction of military sexual slavery profoundly affected colonial and indigenous notions of sex and love, lust and rape. In the context of wartime collaboration, the establishment of the "comfort stations" further complicated and constrained intracultural relations among all Chamorros. The introduction of Chamorro police assistants and interpreters from the Northern Mariana Islands also contributed to the rise in intracultural conflict.

In the name of wartime assimilation policies, the Japanese colonial government did not intentionally create these intracultural divisions among the indigenous population. Nevertheless, they knowingly contributed to the severing of social relations in Guam among the interpreters, the women of war, and the wider Chamorro population. This process resulted in the surfacing of alternative meanings for "collaboration," a term originally associated with cooperation. In this respect, the idea of collaboration as a form of betrayal and disloyalty emerged with greater force, meaning, and consequence. As demonstrated elsewhere in the military regimes of France, Italy, and Nazi Germany, the term "collaboration" generally signified disloyalty to one's own social group (see, eg, Paxton 1972). In other words, the rise in fascist warring states and the local "collaborators" who supported them gave shape to the meaning of collaboration as "an uneven distribution of power, an uneven partnership in which one party operates under duress or, even worse, betrays the interest of its own group" (Gross 1991, 71). Jan Thomas Gross described collaborators as those "who would make the occupier the beneficiary of the trust vested in them by the population that had elected them to positions of authority, or those who are ready to accept posts that are traditionally vested with authority in a given community" and in service to the occupiers (1991, 72).

Much of the broadening of the term "collaboration" also stemmed from its legal usage during war. In late August 1944, only a month after the invasions of Saipan, Tinian, and Guam, the United States military conducted a series of investigations of those accused of collaborating with the Japanese in Guam. The military intelligence officers concluded that Japanese and "half-Japanese" civilians, Chamorro interpreters, Japanese military personnel, "comfort women," and others who worked directly with the Japanese colonial administration were collaborators. But in the war crime trials that followed these investigations, from 1945 to 1949, those charged with per-petuating atrocities toward Americans and civilians primarily came under the scrutiny of the US naval court system.[9] Among the various cases tried, the military court found several Chamorro interpreters guilty of murder and attempted murder by torture. Most of the Chamorros "found guilty in the collaboration trials were deported to Saipan or received short terms of hard labor in Guam" (Maga 2001, 110). Although some Chamorro women were implicated in these cases, none received any court sentence. On the other hand, some Japanese officers received death sentences; they were held responsible for promoting war crimes, especially those committed against civilians and American prisoners of war.

The legal ramifications of collaboration in Guam demand further study, but what is particularly disturbing is not so much the sentencing of alleged collaborators, as the wider, ongoing impact of collaboration with the Japa-nese. Among the wartime and immediate postwar generations of Chamor-ros, a collective, though suppressed, postwar malaise has emerged. This malaise manifests itself especially in memories of the violence done to *i famalaoan guerra siha* and the violence of the interpreters. Rick Castro, whose extended family resides in the village of Chalan Pago, Guam, recalled this feeling among his elders during a 2004 interview: "You couldn't talk [about *i famalaoan guerra siha*, because the elders could not] express the kind of horror of that defacement, physical, spiritual defacement to the women. . . . Looking back now, it's just a whole entire blanket for the most part, you know, a collective, mental, emotional malaise that was never dealt with" (R Castro 2004).

This collective malaise has also been observed in the Philippines. The "quarantine of silence around collaboration is at least a partial contributor to the disturbing symptoms of social malaise in contemporary Philippine life" (Steinberg 1967, 165). Comparing collaboration to a disease, David Steinberg wrote, "As with a cancer that is secretly feared but consciously ignored in the hope that it might vanish by itself, Filipinos have gone to some great lengths to avoid examining the consequences of collaboration" (1967, 164–165). Steinberg's assertion that memories of collaboration in the Philippines function like cancer illustrates the severity of the issue. Even though nobody in the Mariana Islands has likened collaboration with the Japanese to a disease, the relative silence on the issue is widespread among Chamorros.

In the Northern Mariana Islands, memories of collaboration with the Japanese are rarely mentioned among Chamorros. Having experienced the war in terms of loyalty to Japan, Chamorros there did not develop entrenched notions of betrayal in the way that Chamorros in Guam did. In this respect, Chamorros *cooperated* with the Japanese, rather than "collabo-rated" with them. This is not to say that Chamorros in the Northern Mariana Islands have not been affected by the idea of collaboration as betrayal. On the contrary, some Chamorros recognize that the interpreters sent to Guam during World War II have created an uncomfortable legacy very much felt in contemporary times in the Northern Mariana Islands. Herbert S Del Rosario, a Chamorro archivist from Saipan, said in an interview that the memories of these men "hurt the northern Marianas very much. . . . I've heard that several of the Saipanese police were recruited and went down to Guam and they beat up a lot of people from Guam. . . . As a result, [a] bitterness" developed on the part of Guam Chamorros that "never went away" (Del Rosario 2002). Samuel McPhetres, an educator in Saipan, asserted in an interview that even Chamorros of the Northern Mariana Islands have been affected by the histories of interpreters and police in Guam. "For the most part they are so ashamed" that nobody has come forward to talk about their roles as interpreters or police officers. The histories of interpreters have created a "tremendous amount of hostility that is very deep, and that still exists" (McPhetres 2002).

Tun Henry S Pangelinan, one of the few interpreters who sometimes talks openly about his memories, agreed that he contributed to the emergence of intracultural conflicts among Chamorros. Now elderly, he said, "I cannot remember everything from those days" in Guam. "The little things I can forget easily. [However,] those crimes against humanity I can never forget" (Pangelinan 2002, 81). Ashamed of his wartime role as an interpreter, Pangelinan now looks back at the violent actions committed against those in Guam as "crimes against humanity," rather than as his moral duty to the emperor of Japan. Although he clearly shows remorse for what he did in Guam, Pangelinan is "not interested in seeing any of the ones" he knew on the island. Wanting to forget these aspects of the war, Pangelinan stated, "I am eighty years old now. I am subject to go any time. I am just glad that this is behind me" (2002, 82).

Scattered memories of interpreters have surfaced from time to time as topics of discussion, yet the roles of *i famalaoan guerra siha* continue to elude public reflection and debate. The women have kept quiet, despite the recent visibility generated by increasing numbers of former sex slaves seeking apologies from the Japanese government. For example, some Korean sex slaves "testify about their experiences of exploitation and violence in terms of the larger socioeconomic, cultural, and political issues—the difficult circumstances that they and their families faced under [Japanese] colonialism. . . . Women survivors speak out by asserting their multivocal identities: they state that they are elders, women, poor, and subjects who were subordinated by both imperial/colonial and national governments because of their gender and ethnicity" (H Kim 1997, 74). Unlike some Korean sex slaves who have aggressively sought international representation and economic compensation from the Japanese government, no Chamorro elder has come forth publicly in the Mariana Islands to voice her views. "Not a single woman has stepped forward to participate in the war claims pres-

ently being made elsewhere in Asia. . . . These marginalized stories of life
have the potential to disrupt the dominant paradigms but don't because
the social and political costs are tremendous and the returns have yet to
present themselves" (Diaz 2001, 159).

As Vicente M Diaz suggested, the "costs" involved in the publicizing of
such memories are too great. While it is possible, as he noted, that these
memories "circulate in private circuits," they may not enter the public
sphere because of their highly charged emotional, social, and political content (Diaz 2001, 159). It is already evident that the women of war, as well as
interpreters, have been labeled as guilty of shameful acts. Up to the recent
fiftieth commemoration of Liberation Day in the Mariana Islands, they
have received no mention in the islands' official narrative of war. As Diaz
implied, any effort to commemorate these survivors of war might serve only
to create further shame and disgrace for them and their families.

Thus, these women and men, their descendants, and well-meaning
people, might not commemorate their experiences for fear of re-inflicting
undue pain and suffering. Nor have the commemorations of World War
II in the Mariana Islands attempted to chart the memories and histories
of these significant people. To do so would mean talking about wartime
collaboration and the origins of disloyalty and intracultural conflicts in the
islands. It would be an effort to contest the concepts of American loyalty
and liberation in the Marianas—concepts that also represent, suppress, and
alter the indigenous and colonial memories of the war in these islands.
What would such contestations produce in terms of war commemorative
activities? Under what premise would they occur? To what extent would
such efforts cause additional shame or much-needed reconciliation among
Chamorros? These kinds of questions illustrate the dual process of "making
history" in the Mariana Islands—a process that is as much about forgetting
as it is about remembering. As Marita Sturken has pointed out, "remembering is in itself a form of forgetting" (1997, 82). The future of World
War II commemorations in the Mariana Islands, and indeed the future of
understanding the past, also depends on this process of remembering and
forgetting.

Chapter 7

On the Life and Death of Father Dueñas

This book opened with a discussion of Chris Perez Howard's novel *Mariquita,* a story about the tragic death of the author's mother, Mariquita, during the Japanese wartime invasion and occupation of Guam. I then examined the social construction of colonial and indigenous memories of World War II in the Mariana Islands. Employing an interdisciplinary approach, in various chapters I explored the construction of these public memories through the entangled historical development of loyalty and liberation, colonial expansionist and occupational policies, indigenous cultural politics, rehabilitation programs, and, lastly, commemorative activities. I have also endeavored to replicate the novel's treatment of Japan, the Mariana Islands, and the United States. Few novels, let alone histories of the war, focus on the poetics and politics of the local and the global, the colonial and the indigenous, and the Pacific's "place" in the East-West dichotomy.

It is only fitting, then, that this book should commemorate the novel and its agents of war and survival, rather than simply end with a summary conclusion. As this project has demonstrated, commemoration does not imply merely celebration, lamentation, or closure. Commemoration also suggests, more pointedly, an active contestation and deliberation of the past by peoples of different cultural, economic, and political traditions in the present. In this chapter I revisit these issues of war, memory, and history as expressed in one central, though underdeveloped, historical figure in the novel, Father Jesus Baza Dueñas (figure 12). On 12 July 1944, "Father Dueñas was one of several people beheaded in Tå'i by the Kaikuntai after suffering weeks of torture. Many others were beaten, tortured and killed elsewhere—some were herded into caves and killed with grenades. In the midst of this inferno, Mariquita and the other girls awaited their fate" (Howard 1986, 78).[1] Through an understanding of the life and death of Father Dueñas, as well as those around him, scholars may reflect further, not just on the "fate" of war victims and, conversely, the "glory" of war victors. That is the stuff of war histories. Instead, I propose Father Dueñas as an ethnographic and mnemonic figure of the war as a way to help scholars think about the possibilities of and limitations on advancing indigenous studies on World War II.

FIGURE 12. Father Jesus Baza
Dueñas, Guam, early 1900s.
*(Manuscript Collection, RFT Mi-
cronesian Area Research Center)*

On the Life and Death of Father Dueñas

In the Pacific Islands, some war commemorations focus on important figures of local and even transnational significance. Some of them are commemorated precisely because they "fit neatly into war narratives with their
scripts of loyalty and liberation" (White 1995, 542). These individuals are
local figures in that they speak to various indigenous experiences of the
war, yet they are transnational figures in that they also represent competing national narratives of victory and defeat, tragedy and triumph. Jacob
Vouza of the Solomon Islands is one example. In a fiftieth anniversary commemoration of major Pacific battles in 1992, he was hailed as a "war hero"
because "his story could be assimilated so well into the dominant narratives
of liberation in which local actors play the part of loyal native, ratifying the
Allied epic of war" (White 1995, 546). American veterans' associations have
praised Vouza for being a courageous wartime aide, and numerous books
and memorabilia about the war continue to portray him as a war hero. A
civic statue was built in his honor in 1990, the only one of an indigenous
person "erected in Solomon Islands public space," and second to the previously constructed statue of Christ at the Anglican cathedral in the capital,
Honiara (White 1995, 542).

Yet Vouza also participated as one of the leaders in the anti-British Maa-
sina Rule movement in the Solomon Islands during the 1940s, challenging
British colonial authority and demanding local autonomy (White 1995, 552).
Although British colonial officials arrested him in 1947, he was released and

not charged with any criminal activity because of his status as a war hero. The memorialization of Vouza suggests, in part, that the indigenous actor in these memories of the war is "not portrayed as passively loyal but as a deft manipulator of the signs of dominance and submission" (White 1995, 552). Vouza appropriated whatever roles he believed could have advanced his various interests, demonstrating that discourses of loyalty and disloyalty can be shaped and altered on both local and transnational levels.

While the narratives of US liberation gain the most publicity in commemorations of the war in the Solomons, less widely known memories of the war are not insignificant. Transnational remembrances of the war often draw from monolithic narratives of victory or defeat, yet marginal views of the past continue to contend for increased visibility, legitimization, and reflection. Similarly, the commemoration of World War II in the Mariana Islands draws from narratives of loyalty and liberation, revealing that colonial and indigenous remembrances of the war compete for public reflection and representation. For example, the story of the life and death of Father Dueñas raises questions about the future of war commemorations in the Mariana Islands, as well as the very theoretical and methodological grounds for studying them.

On 19 March 1911, Jesus Baza Dueñas was born to Josefa Baza and Luis Paulino Dueñas. In 1938, at the age of twenty-seven, he became the second priest of Chamorro ancestry to be ordained in the Philippines (PSECC 1995, 179).[2] Returning shortly thereafter to Guam, Father Dueñas shared with another priest, Father Oscar Lujan Calvo, the duties of attending to the religious affairs of the island's Catholic population. From 1941 to 1944, Father Dueñas managed the spiritual needs of the southern half of Guam, with Father Calvo taking care of the northern villages. Under Japanese wartime rule, the island became a site of conflicting cultural, political, and religious interests, with Dueñas sometimes at the center of events. Unlike the more diplomatic Calvo, who yielded to the demands of the occupational forces, Dueñas had little reserve in the way he conducted affairs with the Japanese. Calvo believed that Dueñas lacked tact, but called him a "very brave man," not openly fearful of cultural embarrassment, physical pain, or political persecution (Calvo 1994).[3]

But the war had created a new set of colonial conditions and circumstances in Guam, as it had throughout the Mariana Islands and neighboring regions. Despite or because of the threat of violence, Dueñas sometimes defied the orders of the Japanese colonial government, seeking shelter in his faith in Yu'us and risking his life in the process. Indeed, he may have sought a form of martyrdom premised on resistance, rather than one based on sixteenth-century Christian notions of conquest and conversion in the New World. Or, quite simply, Dueñas probably saw the Japanese, like other "children of God," as his peers, neither lower nor higher in socioeconomic rank and status. Perhaps his education for the priesthood, combined with a critical indigenous perspective, enabled him to interpret the war in local and global terms. As an actor in the theater of the Pacific War, perhaps Dueñas welcomed all forms of opposition for, in his mind, no one could threaten his belief in God's spiritual protection and intervention. Or perhaps people have come to remember him in such terms.

When asked by Catholic Japanese priests to encourage village parishioners to attend Japanese-language masses, Dueñas openly refused their requests, stating in effect that Christian missionaries speak the Word of God and not the word of foreign lands and propaganda (Sullivan 1957, 164). He also "read American magazines in public when they were outlawed, burned candles in his church when he wasn't supposed to, and continued to speak out against the invaders" (*Pacific Daily News* 1973). Knowing that Dueñas was a "poor collaborator," Japanese colonial authorities contemplated deporting him to the Northern Mariana islands of Rota or Tinian (Sullivan 1957, 163). This never happened because it was believed that exiling Dueñas might incite the Chamorro population, whose loyalties to Japan were already questionable. In the view of the Japanese colonial government, Dueñas did not bow properly to its demands. He consistently suffered from a "stiff neck."[4]

Furthermore, in his diary,[5] Dueñas privately reflected on the contradictions of Japan's "liberation" rhetoric of "Asia for Asians" and an Asia-Pacific region without Western colonial rule. He often indicted Japanese colonialism as intrusive and violent, writing that the Japanese civilian and military populations on the island had "the freedom to slap, to kick . . . even to kill." Dueñas wrote that the Japanese called Chamorros "thieves," yet it was the Japanese who forcefully displaced Chamorro families in the southern village of Sumay and indiscriminately expropriated locally farmed vegetables and livestock. In a section of his diary titled "Justice and Equality," Dueñas described how an unidentified, presumably Chamorro, pregnant woman was forced to surrender her seat on a bus to a Japanese police officer. Evidently drawing from his Christian faith, as well as from American principles of democracy and egalitarianism, Dueñas penned a series of brief ethnographic sketches of life under Japanese wartime rule.

He criticized almost everyone around him, especially the "privileged" Chamorros of Guam.[6] Dueñas mentioned that the island's elite, many of whom had ties to the previous US Naval Government, received "special" bus passes and rations from the Japanese colonial government. He also expressed disappointment and disgust at the attitudes and behavior of some Chamorros from the Northern Mariana Islands. But rather than focus on their loyalties to Japan, Dueñas scrutinized their loyalty to Yu'us. "Saipan people," he wrote, "boast of their Catholicity, yet they whipped, lashed, kicked, injured and even killed innocent people. . . . Out of 40 or 60, only 6 go to Church and 3 or 4 received the Sacraments. . . . They marry in the civil courts with women of bad reputation." He concluded, sarcastically, that "they are good Catholics because they claimed to be so."

Given his incomplete account of Chamorro inter- and intracultural relations in Guam, it is not clear whether Dueñas felt "betrayed" by the privileged or violent practices of other Chamorros. He did not say much about
the state of colonial affairs in the Northern Mariana Islands, nor did he
explicitly contrast American and Japanese forms of colonialism. At the same
time, he did not speak in terms considered "loyal" to either nation-state. In
many instances, Dueñas clearly judged others on the basis of a strict moral
code, as revealed in the beliefs and customs of Chamorro Catholicism.
One wonders, though, why he made no explicit reference in his personal
diary to the American navy sailor George R Tweed. Along with five other
Americans, Tweed fled from the Japanese military authorities and, with the
unselfish assistance of Chamorro families, tried to elude capture by scout
groups led by the Japanese police. Of the six, only Tweed survived to see
the end of the war. The other five Americans were captured and perished
by either Japanese bayonet or gun.

"I'd have liked to be absolutely alone, but I had to trust at least one
other person in order to obtain food" (Tweed 1994, 129). Though suffering
because of limited resources, numerous Chamorro families aided Tweed
because he symbolized the United States. They even gave him the best
food, like cakes, chickens, corned beef, eggs, turkey, and whiskey—items
that were already scarce. As Tun Joaquin Limtiaco remembered, "Tweed
was a symbol of the United States which was fighting in the war. . . . We
were determined to fight, too, in our own way" (*Guam Daily News* 1960).
Throughout the entire war period, Chamorro families from various parts
of the island assisted him in one way or another. Tweed "began to obligate"
Chamorros to provide resources for his survival.

Chamorro notions of respect, assistance, and reciprocity "captured in the
phrase *inafa'maolek,* demand that when one is approached with a request
by a stranger, and especially one who has some authority behind him or
one in need, one must try as far as possible to fulfill that request" (Flores
2002, 322–323). Tweed may have understood the custom of *inafa'maolek,*
taking advantage of Chamorro generosity. Thanks to the widespread help
of Chamorros, as loyal and even culturally obligated colonial subjects,
Tweed lived in at least eleven locations in the central and northern parts of
Guam, often moving through the jungle to find refuge. By helping him, the
Chamorro families risked their lives, knowing that anyone caught helping
Tweed would be severely punished or executed by the Japanese colonial
authorities. Dueñas knew this too.

Based on the diary alone, itself an incomplete narrative with missing
pages and passages, it is unclear whether Dueñas extensively contemplated
Tweed's impact on the island and on the Japanese colonial government.
Still, they knew each other and the kind of political and social capital each
possessed. Dueñas remained a spiritual caregiver of the people as much
as Tweed remained a symbol of America's possible return to the island.

Both resisted Japanese colonial governance, with Dueñas sometimes openly defying Japanese authority and with Tweed carefully avoiding it. They also understood, as many realized, that the life and death of Dueñas was very much intertwined with the circumstances of Tweed's life. In 1943, a year before the American invasion of the Mariana Islands, the stakes in the survival of these two men increased, as did questions about Chamorro loyalties to Japan and the United States.

Tweed clearly knew that a strong, collective expression of Chamorro loyalty to the United States would guarantee his survival. Reflecting on his thirty-one months of hiding in Guam's jungles, he wrote, "I could not have survived one week if it had not been for the loyalty of the Chamorros" (Tweed 1944, 19). Yet his perceptions of Chamorro loyalty remained inconsistent and contradictory, neither totally accepting nor rejecting the notion of Chamorro loyalty to the United States. In his memory of 1942, which marked a year into his hiding in Guam's jungles, Tweed noted that he "did not know how loyal the natives were" (1944, 20). On numerous occasions, he wrote that "Chamorro gossip" nearly revealed his whereabouts to the Japanese military and police forces.

Tweed observed that Chamorros "would die to save me, but in their simple, primitive way they could not resist telling others that they had seen me or helped me" (1944, 20). He even began to equate Chamorro acts of gossiping with betrayal and disloyalty. In various caves and makeshift shelters, Tweed wrote, the "constant fear of betrayal marred my happiness" (1944, 104). "But, again, like all those noble and innocent people, they talked too much. It seemed impossible to stop them. Once I counted . . . 26 persons who had heard where I was or had been there to see me" (Tweed 1944, 108). "I warned them again and again, but still they talked" (Tweed 1944, 20). But how could the Chamorros of Guam not talk about "Joaquin Cruz" (Tweed's "underground name"), let alone the surrounding and impending perils of the war? (Tweed 1994, 100). How could they not have reflected critically on their cultural symbols of survival? How could they not have engaged in what they knew were deep cultural practices of obligation, historical events of profound implication, and political acts of everyday resistance? How could they not have embraced their roles as, in the words of Michel-Rolph Trouillot (1995, 150), the "actors and narrators" of historicity?

Many Chamorros in Guam knew that their lives were interwoven with the lives of Tweed and Dueñas. Local stories about Tweed—whether big or small, false or true—helped Chamorros to interpret the local and global consequences of the war. If they failed in assisting Tweed, then Tweed failed in aiding them, and so too would the United States fail to return to the island. But Tweed also tried not to "fail" the Chamorros of Guam. As he noted in retrospect, in a letter to the *Pacific Daily News* in 1977, long after the war had ended, "During the entire ordeal I realized that if I antagonized just one Chamorro who knew where I was hiding I would be finished very quickly; . . . Therefore, I took every precaution to remain on friendly terms with the people."[7] Tweed's friendliness may not have extended beyond the late Antonio Artero, the Chamorro farmer who sheltered him for twenty-one months, the longest time he stayed in any one place. As an indication of their friendship, Artero likened Tweed to his "brother" (Leeke 1977, 2). And like other Chamorros, Artero helped him because of his lack of food and shelter, as well as because he symbolized the United States. But Tweed probably liked Artero less for his offerings of food, labor, and shelter than for his ability to remain quiet. As Artero proudly claimed, "Not even the finger of the Japanese come over to my body. . . . But you know why?" Referring to the power of silence, Artero stated, "I took the needle and the thread and sew my mouth" (Leeke 1977, 3).

Although Artero voluntarily "sewed his mouth," lessening the chances of revealing the whereabouts of Tweed, the idea of maintaining silence did not apply to all Chamorros, let alone the "gossip" network that crisscrossed the island. As much as Tweed proclaimed his gratitude and appreciation for Chamorro assistance, he still discouraged anyone from talking about him—conversations, it is alleged, that later led to the death of Dueñas. On 31 August 1943, almost a year before the Japanese execution of Dueñas and the subsequent American invasion of Guam, Tweed wrote a letter to Agueda Johnston (the educator who would later create the island's first Chamorro-centered commemoration of the war, Liberation Day) signed "J C, " as in Joaquin Cruz, and addressed to "J" as in Johnston (figure 13).[8]

FIGURE 13. Navy sailor George Tweed with Marian Johnston Taitano (left), Agueda Johnston (right), and Eloise Johnston Sanchez (back). *(Emilie G Johnston, reproduced with permission)*

Tweed often secretly corresponded, or "gossiped," with Johnston. They shared news about the American military activities in the Pacific region, increasing Tweed's visibility and risk of capture, especially since messages and articles like magazines and food often traveled through their hands into the hands of others. Tweed even produced several editions of a typed, one-page, newspaper called the *Guam Eagle*, which he circulated only briefly for four months in 1942 because he soon realized that it posed a risk (Tweed 1944, 104). Further, he had a girlfriend, "Tonie," whom he saw frequently until the final months of the war (Tweed 1994, 96). And Tweed wondered why many Chamorros talked about him? And yet he continued to write letters to others?

Josefa, Antonio Artero's wife, eventually delivered Tweed's letter to Johnston at her residence in Hagåtña. The letter expressed Tweed's deep consternation over what he believed were Chamorros disloyal to the United States. By this time in the war, the Japanese police had begun to interrogate and physically punish Chamorros disloyal to Japan, specifically those suspected of harboring Tweed (Rogers 1995, 178). As Japanese navy sailor Hisashi Hirose explained, investigations of suspected Chamorros were done in "secrecy. . . . If we received information concerning [Tweed's] whereabouts, we set up blinds on nearby hills to those locations mentioned" (Higuchi 2001b, 62). Thus, suspected "pro-American" Chamorros like Tun B J Bordallo and Tun Joaquin Limtiaco, among numerous others, experienced various beatings by the Japanese. In a humorous but serious manner, Tun Joaquin recalled that it "seemed that whenever the Japanese felt like clobbering someone, they'd pick me up at my ranch. Each time they got a tip as to the whereabouts of Tweed, in they come and back to the calaboose I go" (*Guam Daily News* 1960). In his letter, Tweed intimidated Johnston by threatening violence comparable to that endured by those persecuted by the Japanese, but at the hands of the Americans.

Warning Johnston to remain silent on matters pertaining to him, Tweed wrote, "consider what will happen when the Americans come, as they will in a short time now. Instead of being jubilant and celebrating with the rest of us, you would have a far more serious position to face. . . . I can name at least three men," he continued, perhaps referring to Chamorro "collaborators" for the Japanese, "who will face a firing squad when they [the US military] arrive." Referring not only to her perceived connection to disloyal Chamorros, but also to her gender, Tweed emphatically asked, "Do you want to place yourself alongside of them? In wartime, the U.S. Army officials have no compunction against shooting a lady, for a military offense." As if that threat did not suffice, he claimed, "Even if you were fortunate enough to escape such a tragic end, it would mean long years in prison for you. Your own self-respect would be gone, also the love and respect of those whom you love and who love you." Finally, Tweed proclaimed, "The Japs would not even know I am in Guam if the people had not talked so much."

More words of distrust, rage, and terror filled the pages of the letter, which then concluded, rather cordially, "with sincere sympathy and admiration, your true friend, J.C."

When asked in 1977 to recall her interactions with Tweed during the war, Johnston did not mention the letter and its contents. She simply remarked that if Tweed "were any kind of hero, he would have turned himself in" (Fichter 1977b, 2). Johnston, herself interrogated and beaten by the Japanese police, said that she would never have revealed anything about Tweed to the Japanese. "The Japanese could have killed me three or four times," she said firmly, yet "I would not have given them the satisfaction of giving them information about Tweed" (Fichter 1977, 2). Johnston might personally have despised Tweed, but she could not deny his symbolism. He still represented the hope that America, or another "liberating" force, would save the Chamorros of Guam from Japanese wartime rule.

After the war, Tweed was also silent about the letter he had written to Johnston. After all, its contents would have tarnished his reputation as a "war hero," or as one correspondent put it, as a "man who survives against all odds, against time and despair, against the thousand, small, cruel indignities of war" (Brown 1966, 19). Moreover, the letter would not have portrayed Tweed as an American symbol of wartime hope, trust, and survival. During the war, Tweed sometimes tried to distance himself from Chamorros, the same people offering him relatively safe refuge. He specifically refused to "go native," attempting to uphold his image as a "civilized" being.

Discussing how he felt when hiding in a cave, Tweed wrote, "I was tired of squatting in front of the fire like a savage, at mealtime, reaching into my kettle or frying pan for food." Missing the furnishings of a Western home, such as a chair and table, he desperately wanted "to sit and read in a civilized and comfortable position, rather than cross-legged on my mat or with my back against the rock cliff, legs stretched out like ramrods in front of me." He also shaved his beard once a week, or whenever he planned to meet somebody, so he could "feel civilized" (Tweed 1994, 164). Did Tweed, then, not want to be like Chamorros? Or did he see himself becoming like them, but refused to identify locally with their indigenous culture? And did he envision Chamorros as like Americans or as unlike Americans?

One wonders if the American sailor George Tweed truly appreciated Chamorro forms of assistance and if he saw Chamorro loyalties to the United States as meaningful and relevant forms of resistance to Japanese colonial rule. The attitudes and behaviors of Tweed, as well as Guam Chamorro understandings of him, illustrated the various and complex power relationships embedded in the everyday survival of people on the island. In attempting to understand the life and death of Father Dueñas, it is important to consider the various circumstances surrounding the wartime survival of Tweed and the Chamorros of Guam. Important issues of historical representation and erasure come to the fore in trying to explore the role

Tweed played in the death of Dueñas. In the final days before the death of Dueñas on 12 July 1944, the politics of American and Japanese colonialisms and indigenous Chamorro cultural agency forcefully converged on the priest and those who wished to see him live or die.

Some claimed that Tweed killed Dueñas, even though the two probably never met face-to-face. Others said the Japanese police, the Kempeitai, murdered Dueñas. Or maybe the "talkative" nature of Chamorro gossip silenced the priest. A few might even have argued that Dueñas was already dead, perhaps "reborn," as the divine will of God had predetermined his life and death at an earlier time. Whatever the case, Dueñas knew about Tweed and about his risking the lives of Chamorro families. Some recalled that at one point in the war Dueñas traveled to the northern village of Yigo, where Tweed was hiding, to "tell the people that if Tweed kept on acting badly to tie him up" (*Pacific Daily News* 1973). Overall, though, Dueñas cared little about the man, unless, of course, Tweed was endangering others. And whenever the Japanese police questioned Dueñas about the whereabouts of Tweed, he simply informed the Japanese that he, too, knew few details about the American. Tweed likewise initially had no interest in forging a relationship with Dueñas.

Of all the diverse actors and narrators of the war, it was a "woman of bad reputation" who eventually merged the stories of Tweed's life and Dueñas's death. In the village of Inalåhan, where Dueñas conducted many of his Catholic services at Saint Joseph's Church, a "woman in his parish . . . was not leading an exemplary life."[9] She was Nettie Durham, a Chamorro woman who "became friendly" with a Japanese official named Churima (Josephy 1946, 85). Churima worked for the Japanese Minseibu office in Inalåhan. Dueñas disapproved of their relationship, partly because Durham had already been married twice before the war, both times to American sailors (Josephy 1946, 85). But Dueñas appeared particularly disturbed by Durham because "everything she wanted, Churima had done for her" (Josephy 1946, 85). Through the relationship she wielded tremendous power, rivaling and perhaps even surpassing the power of priests like Dueñas. Rather than help members of her village community, she used her power to fulfill her own personal needs. For example, people from the village worked for her, providing her with chickens and produce, and, if they protested, the Japanese threatened them with arrest (Josephy 1946, 85).

Eventually, Dueñas fielded complaints from the Chamorros of Inalåhan and took them to the main office of the Minseibu in Hagåtña. At the office, it is rumored, one of Churima's colleagues overheard the reason for Dueñas's visit (Josephy 1946). What began as a complaint filed by Dueñas regarding Durham's abuse of local resources and labor soon spiraled into a series of accusations against the priest. The charges that Dueñas disobeyed Japanese orders were not new. For example, some believed that Dueñas upset a Japanese police officer for not returning to Inalåhan before sunset, because he spent time at a baptism in a nearby village. Another charge stated that Dueñas harassed a Japanese official to return his horse saddle. That Durham helped to arouse suspicion of Dueñas also attracted the attention of Japanese officials. But the allegation that Dueñas publicly met the American sailor George Tweed immediately sparked the interest of Japanese police officials and set in motion their interrogation of Dueñas and others deemed guilty with him (Josephy 1946, 86).

The Japanese police sent an unnamed Chamorro interpreter from Rota or Saipan to tell Dueñas, ignorant of the charges directed against him, to go to the Minseibu office in Inalåhan. Dueñas complied, only to find that his nephew and local attorney Eddie Dueñas had been arrested. On 8 July 1944, Father Dueñas was taken into custody, as was Juan Pangelinan, who was suspected of harboring Tweed. Within hours, the men were beaten by the Japanese. Repeatedly, the Japanese asked them if they knew where Tweed hid. Eddie Dueñas informed the Japanese that his uncle knew how to get to Tweed. The priest then replied that his nephew, already disoriented from the torture, spoke nonsense.

Later that evening, the Japanese police transferred the men to a Japanese police station at Tutuhan, a small mountain overlooking the village of Hagåtña. There, in a shack, the beatings resumed. Francisco G Lujan, a neighbor who lived nearby, "heard everything that went on." Lujan stated, "Every time the priest denied that he knew the whereabouts of Tweed he was hit with a club." The Japanese made Dueñas "kneel on the floor, and they placed a club in the joints of his legs and they jumped on it." A few Chamorro interpreters, such as Antonio Camacho, participated in the interrogation of the three men. The "Japanese were hollering at [Dueñas] and yelling at the interpreters, and the interpreters were shouting at Father Duenas" (Lujan and Limtiaco 1965, 10).

After several hours of torture on the day of their arrest, the Japanese tied the men to wooden posts outside the shack. They remained in seated positions until they were moved to Tå'i on the evening of 12 July. Earlier that afternoon, Juan Flores and Joaquin Limtiaco, men from Guam hired by the Japanese police to apprehend suspects, had returned to the Tutuhan police station. They saw the poor condition of Dueñas and the other men. Without delay, Flores and Limtiaco asked Dueñas if he wanted to escape from the Japanese. They offered to untie the men and help them flee. In response, Dueñas is reported to have said, "The Japanese know they can't prove their charges against me. I appreciate your offer, but we must also think of our own families. You must know what would happen to them if we escaped. I'm positive the Japanese will retaliate against them." Firmly, the priest instructed the men, "Go and look after your families." Already weak from days of dehydration and physical abuse, the priest absolved the young men of their concern for him and the other two prisoners. Finally, he said, "God will look after me. I have done no wrong" (J Limtiaco 1960, 8).

Moving beyond War Histories and Histories of War

On the morning of 13 July 1944, news traveled quickly that Father Jesus Baza Dueñas, along with his nephew Eddie and fellow prisoner Juan Pangelinan, had been executed by the Japanese police at Tå'i. Notice of the deaths of these men came from a Saipanese interpreter by the name of Joaquin Dueñas. At the Manenggon camp in the village of Yo'ña, Joaquin Dueñas, a possible relative of Father Dueñas, told other Chamorro families that he had witnessed the murder of Father Dueñas. He stated that the Japanese had transferred the priest and the other two men to Tå'i, where the Japanese agricultural unit was stationed. The motives for transferring the men to another site were not clear, as numerous executions and massacres took place in different sites and for a variety of reasons in the summer of 1944.

A few days later, on 18 July 1944, Mariquita Perez Howard, the mother of Chris Perez Howard and the subject of the novel *Mariquita*, disappeared in the same area. That she perished in the same village as Dueñas illustrates that many people shared a collective war story of life and death, triumph and tragedy. In this respect, memories of the war in the Mariana Islands can be described collectively, in that they refer to a common war past. Americans, Chamorros, and Japanese, all of varying generations, now share a collective memory of the war. To put it another way, the war has provided an important local and global reference point through which the colonizer and the colonized can come to terms with their diverse interpretations of the past.

The life of Father Jesus Baza Dueñas reveals that the politics of colonialism, indigenous cultural agency, and commemoration continue to inform the meaning and direction of public memories. For example, religious followers have described Father Dueñas as a "revolutionary, extremely dedicated to American democracy and ideals" (*Umatuna Si Yu'us* 1954a). Others claimed that he was a "simple, but aggressive priest" (*Pacific Daily News* 1970). A college preparatory school and seminary for Catholic priests, named Father Dueñas Memorial High School, was built in his memory in 1949. Located in Tå'i, the school boasts a life-size statue of the priest, who stands upright, with his arms and palms facing forward. The peaceful gesture welcomes visitors and students alike to the place of his wartime death and postwar memorialization.

In contrast, the American sailor George Tweed has not been given a central place in the commemoration of the war in Guam. Although many Chamorros interpreted him as a symbol of America during the war, not even the postwar commemoration of Americans as "liberators" could have "saved" Tweed from Guam Chamorro criticisms of him as a "betrayer" and a "coward." Another reason for some Chamorros' refusal to celebrate Tweed as a "hero" is that they felt he had not adequately demonstrated his appreciation to them. In other words, he failed to *ina'fa'maolek,* that is, to reciprocate food, labor, or cash to the Chamorros who fed, clothed, and sheltered him. For example, Tweed petitioned the Chevrolet Motor Company to purchase and ship a car to Antonio Artero in Guam for his assistance in keeping him alive during the war. The company gladly obliged, sending Artero a vehicle in 1946. Some Chamorros may have misinterpreted the car as Tweed's "gift" to Artero, but in fact it was the Chevrolet Motor Company that paid all of the expenses. Some Chamorros felt that their wartime generosity had been taken for granted and so refused to recognize the sailor as a celebrated figure (see Flores 2002). By highlighting Tweed's selfish behavior, many Chamorros also saw him as a symbol of American colonial greed, individualism, and invasiveness.[10] In the Chamorro vernacular, these Chamorros may have described Tweed as *taimamalao,* a person without shame, because of his failure to reciprocate food, labor, or cash to those who assisted him during the war.

After the war, many Guam Chamorros believed that had Tweed surrendered to the Japanese police nobody would have been unnecessarily persecuted and tortured. Because Tweed failed to give himself up—an act many Chamorros at the time had discouraged him from—several Chamorro families suffered Japanese police cruelty. As Tun B J Bordallo recalled, "I was hoping . . . that Tweed would appear before the Japanese officials and say, 'I'm the one you want; these people [Chamorros] are innocent; do not punish them anymore'" (Fichter 1977a, 3).

In the Northern Mariana Islands, few Chamorros are aware of the life and death of George Tweed. As Juan C Camacho explained in a 2004 interview, Tweed represents "the history of Guam and not the history of the CNMI and that is why we in the CNMI don't know him." The case is different for Father Jesus Baza Dueñas. Camacho stated that Chamorros in the Northern Mariana Islands still refer to him as "the one who was killed in Guam during the Japanese occupation." The people remember the priest, he said, because of the shared Catholic tradition among Chamorros. Yet the older generations often hesitate to "elaborate" on why the Japanese executed Dueñas. Perhaps the story of the life and death of Dueñas does not correlate with Chamorro narratives of loyalty to Japan in the Northern Mariana Islands. Or perhaps the story of Dueñas, cast in the light of a "victimized" Chamorro Catholic, disturbs Chamorro notions of intracultural sameness and difference in the Northern Mariana Islands. As Camacho noted, a "silent feeling" emerges when topics like Father Dueñas, interpreters, and police assistants are remembered and discussed among friends and family (J Camacho 2004).

These silences resonate not only in memory, but in history. For example, the reasons why Joaquin Dueñas, the Chamorro interpreter from Saipan, chose to describe the death of Dueñas in the climax of the war remain elusive. One wonders what happened to him afterwards. Did members of the camp embrace or assault him? Did his extended families in Guam and the Northern Mariana Islands call him loyal or disloyal? And did he later choose to remember or suppress these memories of the war? Unfortunately, little is publicly known about this man or about Nettie Durham, the Chamorro woman who ran the Minseibu office in the southern village of Inalåhan and who helped to ensure the arrest of Father Dueñas. Not much is known about her life and death, or about her rise to power at a time when women, let alone indigenous women, held no place in Japan's wartime empire. What did other Chamorros and Japanese think about this particular woman? Regrettably, their stories remain untold. Conversely, one might ask why these histories have been suppressed, and what these silences from the past reveal about the production and transmission of knowledge in the Mariana Islands. Ultimately, how might these perilous memories of the war challenge and unsettle historical common sense? (Fujitani, White, and Yoneyama 2001, 21).

Like their interpreter, police assistant, and sex slave counterparts, Joaquin Dueñas and Nettie Durham have been framed in the context of wartime "collaboration" with the Japanese. To understand the motivations and consequences of Chamorro cooperation with the Japanese military and police forces in Guam, one must question the sometimes taken-for-granted moral and political connotations of collaboration. Scholars "must legitimately ask how the moral subject that collaboration presupposes was fashioned, not retroactively judge that subject's acts. [This perspective] helps to turn collaboration into a problem to be investigated, not a moral failure to be tagged or condemned. This is not to say that moral considerations have no place in the study of collaboration, but it is to advise that we look more closely at the conditions within which individuals made choices" (Brook 2005, 5). By doing so, one can come to terms with the ways in which American and Japanese colonialisms, as well as indigenous adaptations to colonial rule, fostered divergent loyalties and intracultural divisions among Chamorros. Then "stasis and change, tradition and innovation become not oppositional but dynamically interconnected" in the context of cross-cultural and intracultural relations in the Mariana Islands (Diaz 1992, 16).

One of my goals in this book has been to assert that culture is a process of local and global identification and differentiation. By examining the various relationships among colonized and colonizer in the Mariana Islands, I have shown that cultures are shaped by adaptation and resistance to external forces and by internal struggles with continuity and change, and that cultures also shape the very local and global structures that sometimes govern them. These considerations must be taken seriously and critically, as most histories of the war in the Pacific rarely acknowledge the politics of indigenous cultural agency, let alone the various exchanges and encounters among colonial and indigenous societies there. In addressing representations of Pacific Islanders in the historical record, I have demonstrated that Pacific Islanders are not a singular, cultural "type." They are not the "noble savages" or "ignoble savages" of American imaginations, much as they are not the non-Asian "Others" of Japanese imaginations.

These arguments are not new. But, in many ways, they demand attention because histories and historiographies of the war continue to portray Pacific Islander cultural agency in terms of the agent-victim binary. To this end, it is important and necessary to foreground the socially fluid and historically specific dynamics of culture. Challenging long-held assumptions about cultural identity in the Pacific, for example, David Gegeo stated, "We often think of our identity as having been shaped primarily in remote times by our traditional cultures and secondarily by missionization. Yet, World War II was the most important turning point in the recent history of our islands and of ourselves. This is because the war greatly increased contact with the First World in a dramatic and even violent way" (1988, 8). The creation of "modern identities" has resulted from this increased contact among diverse peoples, new technologies, and various ideas in the Pacific (Fujitani, White, and Yoneyama 2001, 10). Pacific Islanders' cultural constructions of themselves "depend in great part on local understanding of what makes people alike and different, of 'who we are,' but [they have] also been shaped by Spanish, German, and especially Japanese and American ideas" about what Pacific Islanders are or should be (Poyer, Falgout, and Carucci 2004, 316). In addition to Pacific Islander notions of land, community, and kinship, Pacific Islander cultures have been "shaped in response to what colonial powers have told them about themselves, and in response to the structures that these foreign administrations have established to rule them" (Poyer, Falgout, and Carucci 2004, 316).

Therefore, the conflicting and divergent loyalties expressed by Chamorros of the Mariana Islands reflect the different colonial histories of American and Japanese colonial governance in times of peace and war. Moreover, the fragmented loyalties among Chamorros demonstrate that "Chamorro culture" has been constructed by local and global forces, as well as by internal and external processes. On the one hand, the varying degrees of Chamorro notions of identification and differentiation illustrate a much longer history of cultural change and instability among this indigenous population, stretching farther back than the establishment of Spanish colonial sovereignty in the seventeenth century. Tremendous diversity exists among this indigenous population, as well as among any other "cultural unit" or "cultural site." Except for the shared language and cultural tradition, themselves subject to intense flux and change, the diversity of Chamorro experiences and memories of World War II—and indeed loyalties—helps scholars to understand that notions of cultural homogeneity, biological identity, and gendered sexuality are *also* socially constructed.

These interpretations of cultural change and continuity allow scholars to view colonialism as a network of relationships through which the colonizer and the colonized seek power and legitimization. My second goal in this book has been to demonstrate that colonialism operates as an ambivalent process of control and resistance, as well as adaptation and mutation. The Chamorro political elites of Guam and Saipan, for example, used the rhetoric of loyalty to try to acquire what they perceived as increased political autonomy and perhaps recognition as "American" or "Japanese" "national subjects." Given the imperialist, militarist, and racist nature of American and Japanese colonialisms, the cultivation of indigenous loyalties in the time before the war did not include full incorporation into the American or Japanese nation-states respectively.

The politics of colonialism and indigenous cultural agency sometimes ensured that Chamorros acquired varying levels of authority and autonomy, but never detracted from the violent circumstances and conditions that American and Japanese colonialisms imposed on this indigenous population. Although I have examined colonialism as an ambivalent process of control, by no means do I wish to suggest that American and Japanese colonialisms were benevolent acts of introducing Asian and Western forms of "modernity" to the Pacific. In the war's aftermath, the politics of colonialism changed, as did indigenous bids for authority and sovereignty. The emergence of postwar rehabilitation projects in the wider Cold War era ushered in new conditions in the American colonial governance of Guam and what would later be called the Commonwealth of the Northern Mariana Islands. The rise of World War II commemorations in the Mariana Islands has provided important and innovative sites for the study of the politics of colonialism and indigenous cultural agency. American National Historic Landmarks, Japanese bone-collecting missions and peace pilgrimages, and Liberation Day festivities all illustrate the various forms of war remembrance and commemoration that have emerged since the end of the war in 1945. Indigenous and colonial memories of the war, as reflected in these commemorations, are informed by the politics of the past and by the politics of the present.

By drawing scholarly attention to these histories of commemorative activity in this project, I urge everyone to move beyond what historian John Dower called "triumphant" and "tragic" narratives of the war—narratives that continue to dominate scholarly and popular remembrances of the war in the United States and Japan (1995, 1126). Here, I have demonstrated that no single narrative of the war has dominated the meaning and direction of Liberation Day, the now pivotal war commemoration in the Mariana Islands. The concepts of loyalty and liberation have undergone constant reflection, scrutiny, and change; moreover, they are concepts that continue to mediate Chamorro memories of and social relations with a war past they have never really left behind.

That Chamorros annually commemorate Liberation Day does not necessarily connote an interest in the American narrative of wartime triumph, the economic value of tourism, the Japanese narrative of postwar victimization, or even indigenous memories of the war. Rather, Chamorros continue to commemorate Liberation Day because of its ability to make real and relevant the idea called "history." The stories of the lives and deaths of Father Dueñas, Nettie Durham, George Tweed, Churima, Joaquin Dueñas, and Mariquita Perez Howard, among others, give profound shape and meaning to the historical production of knowledge in the Mariana Islands because they are stories that matter. As evidenced in activities commemorating the war, Chamorros are coming to terms with the power of the past to affect those in the present. And it is precisely through these engagements that they are starting to appreciate the significance of interpreting histories in local and global, colonial and indigenous, and even transnational terms (Sturken 1997, 259).

Thus, my third objective in this book has been to demonstrate that Chamorros, along with Americans and Japanese, actively and consciously make "history," as much as "history" makes them. History is not only about fashioning empirical or postcolonial studies of the past. It is not solely about creating linear or cyclical narratives. Histories of colonization and decolonization warrant scholarly attention, too, though they need not be the only focus of discussion (L Smith 1999, 29). In the Pacific Islands, the making of history is a vibrant process of contestation and celebration, as revealed in the commemorative activities of the war in the Mariana Islands since 1945. My hope is that Chamorros will continue to commemorate the war, as they have done in the past, in ways that foster more mutual grounds for understanding between themselves and others (Trouillot 1995, 150). It is a difficult and sometimes violent task to interpret the past with a common and compassionate view, but it is a view urgently needed in a Pacific Island setting of twenty-first century American colonialism.

Notes

Introduction

1. Increasing numbers of Pacific Islander writers choose literature as their medium of expression over other disciplinary forms. See, eg, DeLoughrey 2007; Najita 2006; Lyons 2006; Sharrad 2003.

2. The shorthand 9/11 refers to the attacks, on 11 September 2001, on the World Trade Center in New York, and on the Pentagon in Washington, DC, as well as the plane crash in a field in Pennsylvania the same day.

3. Numerous subtopics of war exist, and so do a wide array of interpretations on these subtopics. This book only focuses on a few studies of war, especially as they pertain to discussions of World War II in the Pacific. For more on the philosophical, anthropological, and scientific origins and repercussions of war, see Dawson 1996; Nelson and Olin 1980; Pruitt and Snyder 1969.

4. For more on militarism, see Gillis 1989.

5. Understandably, the terms "World War II" and the "Pacific War" oversimplify the plurality of experiences and views about the war. For the purpose of this book, these terms are used interchangeably, as are any general reference to "war" to connote the war's impact in the Pacific Islands.

6. These studies discuss the contexts and consequences of World War II in the Pacific as perceived especially by US and Japanese government officials and policy makers. For studies on Japanese expansion into the Pacific, see Blakeslee 1922. On US interest in the Pacific, see Pomeroy 1948.

7. On oral histories of World War II in Melanesia, see White and Laracy 1988; White, Gegeo, Akin, and Watson-Gegeo 1988.

8. For an introduction to the postwar Maasina Rule movement in the Solomons, see Laracy 1971; Laracy 1983. On the issue of war and race, see Inglis 1969.

9. Recent developments in multimedia ethnography illustrate the growing scope and reach of interdisciplinary studies in the Pacific. For a sampling of these approaches, see K Teaiwa 2004.

10. For overviews on the theory and historiography of memory studies, see Jeffrey and Edwall 1994; Radstone 2000.

11. For problems in the study of memory and history, see Confino 1997; Gedi and Elam 1996.

12. In the Hebrew language, *shoah* means "great disaster." For a fuller treatment of the critical distinctions in terms used to describe the German persecution of Jews in World War II, see Bartov 1998.

13. John W Dower stated that the United States has repeatedly constructed narratives of heroism and value, giving shape to a discourse he called "triumphalism." With regard to Japan, Dower argued that *higaisha ishiki* (victim consciousness) has developed among Japanese since the American atomic bombing of Hiroshima on 6 August 1945. Yet he reminded readers that Japan was not solely responsible for presenting itself as a nation of victims. As he indicated, the "soft-pedaling of Japan's war responsibility was an American policy, and not merely a peculiarly Japanese manifestation of nationalistic forgetfulness. Downplaying prewar Japanese militarism, sanitizing Japanese atrocities, minimizing the horror of war in general— including the horror of Hiroshima and Nagasaki—was a bilateral agenda" (Dower 1996, 68).

14. For more on the multiple interpretations, commemorative activities, and operations associated with Pearl Harbor, see White 2001.

15. The Smithsonian Institution exhibition of the *Enola Gay*, the B-29 Superfortress known for dropping an atomic bomb on Hiroshima, culminated in intense debates between US government officials, museum curators, historians, war veterans, and peace activists as to how to represent the role of the atom bomb in ending World War II. For more on this exhibit, which eventually resulted in portraying a celebratory and triumphal view of the *Enola Gay*, see Nobile 1995; Hogan 1999; Linenthal and Engelhardt 1996.

16. Few if any Japanese military records exist that document the conscription of "comfort women" in the Pacific. For assessments of gender issues in the Pacific, see Ralston 1992; Jolly and Macintyre 1989.

17. Revisions to Japanese textbooks on World War II, legal demands for formal apologies and wartime reparations, American anti-nuclear protests, and organized peace meetings for war veterans all illustrate critical spaces through which activists and scholars attempt to understand marginal memories of the war in Asia and the Pacific. For more on these issues as they pertain to the Asian region, see Figal 2001; Hammond 1995.

18. Homi K Bhabha has described the ambivalence associated with colonialism in terms of "mimicry" and "mockery," whereby the power of colonialism is both reinforced and disavowed by the colonial subjects' efforts to imitate and mock colonial authority (1994).

19. For a brief overview of imperialism, see Mommsen 1982.

20. For centuries, the Refaluwasch navigated to the Mariana Islands, as did others, interacting and trading with the Chamorros. The imposition of Spanish colonialism in the 1600s severed most of these relations. From 1815 to the mid 1800s, the Refaluwasch migrated, once again, to the Mariana Islands. Their purpose was to seek shelter from typhoons and earthquakes that had devastated their atolls, and to acquire new resources and partnerships with the Spanish colonial government. Seeing interest in using Refaluwasch methods of navigation to travel throughout the Mariana archipelago, the Spanish government granted permission to the Refaluwasch to settle in Saipan, Tinian, and Guam. Today, the Commonwealth of the Northern Mariana Islands legally recognizes both the Refaluwasch and Chamorros as "indigenous people." In the American territory of Guam, the Refaluwasch receive no comparable form of political identity and sovereignty; instead, their rights are premised more closely to US federal, constitutional, and local governmental laws than to indigenous notions of political representation and authority. The various

issues and implications of Refaluwasch migration and settlement in the Mariana Islands beg closer study. However, a cross-cultural analysis of Chamorro and Refaluwasch relations is beyond the scope of this project. For a cinematic overview of Refaluwasch history in the Mariana Islands, see the film *Lieweila: A Micronesian Story* (Strong and Kaipat 1998). See also Olopai 2005; Alkire 1984.

Chapter 1: Loyalty and Liberation

1. See *Oxford English Dictionary,* second edition, under "liberation."
2. The politics of conversion—Christian, Islamic, or otherwise—are particularly fraught with varying degrees of local and global appropriation, resistance, and acculturation. For a compelling ethnography on the subject of conversion, see Comaroff and Comaroff 1991.
3. As early as the late 1800s, debates emerged in Japan about the significance of *hokushin* (northern expansion) into Asia and *nanshin* (southern expansion) into the Pacific. Similarly, politicians and legal analysts debated the issue of American expansionism beyond California at the turn of the twentieth century. For more on these debates, see Peattie 1988, 34–40; Lawson and Seidman 2004.
4. The US Navy assumed control of Guam, the southernmost island, while Germany ruled the northern islands, from Rota to Farallon de Pajaros. In this chapter I focus solely on American and Japanese colonial rule in the Marianas, as extensive comments on the German colonial period are beyond the scope of this project. On the political separation of the Mariana Islands in the early twentieth century, see Farrell 1994. He argued that the United States did not acquire the entire Mariana Islands partly because it did not see any immediate economic or military benefit in pursuing such an endeavor.
5. A closer discussion of American views of Chamorros in Guam is provided in K Camacho 1998. For a fuller account on images of "savagery" in the Pacific, see Kjellgren 1993.
6. For more on Japanese expansion, see Iriye 1972; Lebra 1975.
7. Copra production, trade, tuna fishing, and other economic enterprises succeeded in part because the Japanese monopolized the region's limited resources. The economic infrastructure left behind by the Germans (ie, mining buildings and equipment) also contributed greatly to the development of these Japanese economies. See Purcell 1976.
8. Wakako Higuchi clarified the shared and divergent meanings associated with such terms and phrases as "assimilation" *(doka),* "Japanization" *(nihonka),* and "being something like Japanese" *(nihonteki narumono);* see Higuchi 2001a.
9. Although many Islanders devoted their loyalties to Japan (a complicated issue worth closer examination from one island society to another), not every Islander succumbed to Japan's patriotic zeal. For instance, the Palauan anti-Japanese movement, Modekngei, challenged Japanese authority in the early 1900s. However, Modekngei's members failed to increase in number and to mature in political strength due to the efforts of pro-Japanese indigenous factions that helped to identify, find, and arrest the key leaders of the movement. Donald Shuster wrote briefly about the significance of this movement in his essay on Shinto in Micronesia (1982).

10. The gendered dynamics of these relations (the number of Japanese men married to Chamorro women, motivations for marriage, etc) are not yet known and demand further study.

11. Kayoko Kushima, a researcher and graduate of the master's program in Micronesian studies at the University of Guam, found the petition in Ajia 1992, 128–129. I thank Kushima for alerting me to this document. Her translation of the text from Japanese to English is also greatly appreciated.

12. Chamorro-Japanese families (nisei) in Guam were an exception. Prior to World War II, a few Japanese entrepreneurs migrated to Guam and formed a small Japanese community. Many of the Japanese migrants owned stores, learned the Chamorro language and customs, and, overall, maintained amicable relations with the American colonial administration. In 1940, Laura Thompson estimated that approximately thirty-nine Japanese nationals lived in Guam. In her book, *Guam and Its People: A Study of Culture Change and Colonial Education,* Thompson stated that these nisei families raised about 211 Chamorro-Japanese children, all of whom were classified as "natives" by the American naval government (1941, 30). The topic of Chamorro-Japanese social, religious, and sexual intercultural relations, as framed within the context of "marriage," lies beyond the scope of this book, yet warrants scholarly attention.

Chapter 2: World War II in the Mariana Islands

1. Father Eric Forbes, himself a scholar of Chamorro culture and history, serves various Catholic parishes in Guam.

2. Duties assigned to the Insular Patrol, a token police unit composed of only Chamorro men, included assisting naval operations and guarding naval facilities on the island. Their tokenism became evident during the Japanese invasion of Guam, when it was found that none of them knew how to operate firearms. The US Naval Government had previously trained the men of the Insular Force Guard using only fake, wooden rifles in their mock-fighting drills.

3. Fewer than fifty men, consisting of US Marines and Chamorros of the Insular Force Guard, defended the naval governor's headquarters in Hagåtña. Small in number and lacking sufficient weaponry, the men quickly surrendered to the Japanese military forces.

4. Chamorro-Japanese families (nisei) in Guam proved an exception.

5. George R Tweed survived the war because of the generosity of several Chamorro families. During the war, many Chamorros viewed Tweed as a figure symbolic of the United States and held him in high regard because of that belief.

6. Limited documentary materials exist on the subject of sex and sexual relations during World War II in the Pacific. In *Senso Daughters* (1990), however, filmmaker Noriko Sekiguchi offered a critical examination of Japan's establishment of "comfort stations" in Papua New Guinea. The film provides much insight into the role of prostitution and sexual slavery during Japan's war campaigns in the Pacific and East and Southeast Asian regions.

7. The figure of Uncle Sam first appeared in the *Troy Post* (New York) on 7 September 1813. Although initially conceived as an antiwar symbol, it now represents the federal government.

8. The exact wording of this song varies slightly from one version to another. For the sake of clarity, I have referred to two accounts (P Sanchez 1979, 160; Josephy 1946, 79).

9. For a review of the US invasion of Guam, see Lodge 1954.

10. The island of Tinian housed mostly Japanese, Korean, and Okinawan laborers of the sugar industry. Chamorro families, many of whom had previously worked in Yap under the Japanese mandate, did not reside there until the end of the war in 1945.

11. Considerable debate still occurs as to when Japan decided to militarize the mandated islands of Micronesia. For more on the political and military implications of this debate, see Peattie 1988, 230–256.

12. A small number of Chamorro women served as nurses and medical assistants for the Japanese government. No documentation can be found, at least in English translation, that accurately quantifies the number of Chamorro men and women employed by the Japanese government before the war. A substantial amount of material was lost during the war as a result of the US bombings of Saipan.

13. The exact number of these deaths is not known. Haruko Taya Cook estimated that about one thousand civilians died as a result of *gyokusai* (2001).

14. The US military secured Saipan on 9 July 1944 and Tinian on 1 August 1944. Don Farrell stated that a total of sixty thousand Japanese (many of whom were actually Okinawans) and five thousand Americans lost their lives in the battle for the Marianas, though it is unknown exactly how many Chamorros and Refaluwasch died (1991a, 383).

15. The island of Pagan held a very small population of Chamorros and Refaluwasch. Aguiguan and Anatahan hosted an even smaller number of Japanese and Okinawan civilians and soldiers. The US forces ignored these islands, seeing them as nonthreatening to their larger war effort in the Pacific. In the late 1940s, the peoples of these islands received food and aid from the United States.

16. The story of shifting loyalties, as expressed in the life of Solomon Islander George Bogese, is one example. For more on this subject, see Laracy 1991.

Chapter 3: The War's Aftermath

1. For a brief overview of America's rise as a global power, see Lundestad 1991, 145.

2. For more on Allied reconstruction efforts in Asia and Southeast Asia, see Thompson 2001.

3. C.B.S. The Columbia Broadcasting System to [Agueda I. Johnston], 3 July 1945, 6. Agueda Iglesias Johnston's Papers, Box 4, Correspondence Folder, MARC Manuscript Collection, University of Guam.

4. After the war, intermarriages between Chamorros and stateside peoples increased. This issue is briefly discussed in L Souder 1992.

5. Press release number 238-46, 23 July 1946. RG 313, National Archives.

6. The Japanese garrison in Rota surrendered a year later, in September 1945.

7. *Navy Military Government Bulletin*, 30 April 1945, 1. RG 313, National Archives.

8. *Navy Military Government Bulletin*, 30 April 1945, 1.

9. Henry L Larsen to Commander in Chief, US Pacific Fleet and Pacific Ocean Areas, 25 February 1945. RG 313, National Archives.

10. Review Civil Affairs Administration: Forward Area-Central Pacific, September 1944. RG 313, National Archives.

11. *Navy Military Government Bulletin,* 30 April 1945, 9.

12. F J Horne to Judge Advocate General, 5 December 1944. RG 313, National Archives.

13. Henry L Larsen to Commander in Chief, US Pacific Fleet and Pacific Ocean Areas, 25 February 1945, 1.

14. Scout platoons, composed of armed Chamorro men and sometimes Marines, were set up around the island immediately after the war. Their mission was to capture Japanese stragglers. Robert Rogers estimated that, in the late 1940s, 114 Japanese surrendered and an unknown number were killed (1995, 194). The last known straggler, Sergeant Shoichi Yokoi, evaded capture until 1972 when hunters Manuel de Garcia and Jesus M Dueñas found him in the village of Talo'fo'fo. He immediately became a celebrity in Japan for surviving in the jungles of Guam for almost thirty years. For more on the subject of Japanese stragglers, see Rogers 1995, 194, 245–246.

15. The lack of access to maintenance facilities, and the high salt content of Guam's air, contributed to the rust, malfunction, and use of obsolete guns and grenades. Many eventually resorted to homemade knives and spears for self-defense and hunting purposes.

16. Tutuhan is also called Agaña Heights.

17. Review Civil Affairs Administration: Forward Area-Central Pacific, September 1944, 1. RG 313, National Archives.

18. Peter R Onedera is a Chamorro language teacher at the University of Guam. He is also an established poet, playwright, and social activist.

19. John W Vandercook to Frank Mason, 10 August 1942, 2. RG 313, National Archives.

20. Believing that the war still raged on between Japan and the United States, a small group of Japanese civilians lived on Anatahan until they finally surrendered on 30 June 1951.

21. Yet these policies did not prevent interethnic relationships from occurring among Chamorros and non-Chamorros; for example, some Chamorros married Koreans and Japanese, and some Americans also formed new relationships with both the indigenous and Asian populations.

22. In response to these land conflicts in the late 1940s, Chamorros filed property claims with the Land and Claims Commission. "Some 5,935 property claims totaling $10,427,404 had been processed by the Land and Claims Commission" (P Souder 1971, 196). These claims illustrate that numerous Chamorros were clearly upset with the land problems on the island. But because many title records, landmarks, and boundaries had been destroyed during the war, land problems were not easily resolved. As a result, the "land title situation on Guam was in extraordinary confusion" (P Souder 1971, 196).

23. With the establishment of the Marianas Public Land Corporation in 1976, Chamorros and Refaluwasch were finally able to receive new (or return to traditionally managed) lands for their individual and family use.

24. For a discussion of the Chamorro settlement in Tinian, see Spoehr 1951. Regarding Chamorro migration to Yap and Palau, from the late 1800s to the 1940s, see Hezel 1995, which briefly discusses the histories of Chamorro travel to these islands under Spanish, German, and Japanese colonial rule.

25. For more on the issue of military deterrence, see Kenny 1985.

Chapter 4: From Processions to Parades

1. For instance, Guam's main thoroughfare in Hagåtña was named "Marine Drive" after the 1st Provisional Marine Brigade and the 3rd Marine Division. (It was redesignated "Marine Corps Drive" on Liberation Day, 21 July 2004.)

2. Agueda I Johnston to Margaret and Tommy, 15 October 1944. Agueda Iglesias Johnston's Papers, Box 4, Correspondence Folder, 2 of 2, MARC Manuscript Collection, University of Guam.

3. These notions were not unique to Liberation Day, as they have defined commemorative activities elsewhere. For example, the theme of sacrifice played an important role in the popular remembrance of the American Civil War. In *Remaking America,* John Bodnar wrote, the idea of sacrifice related "to the grief and sorrow people felt over the loss of friends and ancestors. . . . It could also stand as an act of loyalty or a contribution to the salvation of the nation itself" (1992, 28).

4. Iris Weehorn Dodd to Agueda I Johnston, 18 May 1945. Copy in Johnston's Papers, Box 4, Correspondence Folder, 2 of 6, MARC Manuscript Collection, University of Guam.

5. In *Sites of Memory, Sites of Mourning* (1995), Jay Winter suggested that, despite their different national affiliations, communities across Britain, France, and Germany collectively grieved and memorialized the loss of lives in the Great War. As in the case of expatriate Americans offering consolation for lives lost in Guam, mourners can sometimes transcend the political, cultural, and geographical boundaries that separate them.

6. On 1 August 1950, President Harry Truman signed bill HR 7273 into law as the Organic Act. "The Organic Act, passed by Congress without a vote on it by the people of Guam, made Guamanians U.S. citizens, established civilian government, and remains the basic law of the island until the local people approve a constitution of their own" (Rogers 1995, 222). Debates about the constitutional validity and political implications of the Organic Act have arisen since its passage. See Dames 2000 and Leibowitz 1989 for differing views on the passage of the Organic Act in particular and on the question of US citizenship in general. For an ethnographic assessment of these issues, see Stade 1998.

7. For a literary examination of tourism in Guam, see K Camacho 1998.

8. This policy was officially titled "The Guam Island Defensive Area and the Guam Island Naval Airspace Reservation." For more on this issue, see McHenry 1975.

9. Japanese Buddhist and Shinto priests conducted bone-collecting missions as early as 1953, about a decade before Japan nationally endorsed the memorialization of its war dead. See *Guam Daily News* 1953b.

10. Documents on the American South and Central Pacific Society held by the

University of Guam's Micronesian Area Research Center can be accessed at the center's vertical files, under the heading "Memorials."

11. On 22 July 1996, another memorial was added to the War in the Pacific National Historic Park. It was called the Memorial Wall of Names, the first federal commemoration of Chamorros who experienced the war. Guam's Congressman Robert Underwood was instrumental in seeing this memorial through to completion.

12. In 1940, approximately 20,000 Chamorros, 800 whites, and 1,300 primarily Filipino and Asian residents lived on the island. By 1980, the number of people had increased to 100,000, with Chamorros making up almost half of the population. See Bettis 1996, 102–118.

13. Literally, *dinaña* means "a mixture," but Bordallo intended it to mean cooperating with different ethnic groups.

14. For a discussion of Chamorro political activism in Guam, see M Perez 2001.

15. The word *maga'låhi* translates into English as leader, governor, chief, or boss. Also, the United Chamorro Chelus for Independence Association was later renamed Nasion Chamoru, or Chamoru Nation. Members of the organization argued that Nasion Chamoru better represented their goal of decolonizing the island.

16. At the time of my interview with Eddie Benavente (2002), he was the *maga'låhi* of Nasion Chamoru. He also taught the Chamorro language at John F Kennedy High School in Tomhom.

Chapter 5: The Land without Heroes

1. Island Commander to Commander Marianas, 8 July 1947, 3. RG 313, National Archives.

2. Civil Administrator to High Commissioner, 25 May 1951, 2–3. RG 313, National Archives.

3. Civil Administrator to High Commissioner, 25 May 1951, 5.

4. Del Rosario is an archivist at the Pacific Collection, Northern Marianas College, Saipan, and an avid researcher of oral history.

5. The United Nations presents three political status options for colonized countries: (1) independence from the colonial power; (2) integration into the colonial power; and (3) free association with the colonial power. For more on political status debates in the Mariana Islands, see Monnig 2005; Willens and Siemer 2002; M Perez 2001.

6. Petition from the House of Council and the House of Commissioners, Saipan, Concerning the Pacific Islands, 17 April 1950. Records of the Military Government/ Civil Affairs Branch of the Office of the Commander of Naval Operations, Subseries R, Operational Archives Branch, Naval Historical Center, Washington, DC.

7. I thank Mark A Ombrello for clarifying the origins and purpose of Rota Kai. He is presently a PhD candidate in the History Department at the University of Hawai'i at Mānoa.

8. US military statisticians often homogenized all Asian subjects and citizens of wartime Japan as "Japanese."

9. Tokuichi Kuribayashi to Neiman N Craley Jr, 4 May 1971, 1. Japanese Memorials in Saipan, microfilm reel 0047:0076, NMCPC.

10. Tokuichi Kuribayashi to Office of High Commissioner, 13 October 1969, 1. Japanese Memorials in Saipan, microfilm reel 0047:0076, NMCPC.

11. District Administrator to Deputy District Administrator, 24 May 1973, 10. Documents Regarding (collection of bones of Japanese war dead) Japan Grave (bones) Mission to the Trust Territory of the Pacific Islands, 1973–1976, microfilm reel 0796:0164, NMCPC.

12. *Latte* are limestone pillars once used to raise houses above land. Today, Chamorros view the *latte* sites with respect, believing that ancient spirits still dwell there.

13. Francisco C Ada to High Commissioner, 7 December 1971, 4. Correspondence, Dispatches and Documents Regarding Bone Collections of Japanese War Dead (WWII), Also to Construct Memorial Monuments. Microfilm reel 0170:0000, NMCPC.

14. District Administrator to District Management Officer, 3 September 1974, 1. Japanese Memorials in Saipan. Microfilm reel 0047:0076, NMCPC.

15. Wyman X Zachary to Tokuichi Kuribayashi, 4 August 1971, 1. Japanese Memorials in Saipan. Microfilm reel 0047:0076, NMCPC.

16. Francisco C Ada to the Honorable Chobiyo Yara, 1 August 1973, 3. Japanese Memorials in Saipan. Microfilm reel 0047:0076, NMCPC.

17. Francisco C Ada to the Honorable Chobiyo Yara, 1 August 1973, 1.

18. District Administrator to Deputy District Administrator, 5 June 1973, 3. Documents Regarding (collection of bones of Japanese war dead) Japan Grave (bones) Mission to the Trust Territory of the Pacific Islands, 1973–1976. Microfilm reel 0796:0164, NMCPC.

19. Samuel McPhetres has worked in various capacities as an educator and archivist at the Northern Marianas College, Saipan. He presently teaches courses in United States government and history there.

20. Three organizations—the Wives of the Trust Territory Administration, the 73rd United States Air Corps bomb wing, and the United States Park Service—separately financed the construction of these memorials.

21. For more on the Northern Marianas' quest for incorporation into the United States, see Leibowitz 1989; Willens and Siemer 2002.

22. Public Law 94-241 designated 133 acres of land in Garapan to serve as an American Memorial Park for the American and Marianas war dead.

23. At the time of this interview, Chuck Sayon was the site manager and unit leader for the American Memorial Park.

24. The political and economic stakes for commemorating the war in terms of American loyalty and liberation are great. Like Guam and Hawai'i, the CNMI tourism industry often promotes the image of a stable and productive American island society in order to attract tourists from Japan and elsewhere in East Asia. By commemorating American Memorial Park and Liberation Day in ways that celebrate the American presence in the Northern Marianas, planners for these commemorations perpetuate this stereotypical and romanticized image of the archipelago and its peoples. For an economic analysis of CNMI tourism, see Osman 1995.

25. Some estimated that the entire project would cost $18 million, a substantial increase from the initial projections of $13 million in the late 1970s. At the time of the fiftieth anniversary of the war, the park needed only $3 million to complete the essential parts of the project, such as the memorial wall, visitors' center, and

museum. The most recent addition is a memorial dedicated to the Chamorros and Refaluwasch who died during the war.

26. Diary of Vern Norman Steyer's Trip to Iwo Jima, [1994?], 7. Microfilm reel 6359:0215, NMCPC.

27. On 31 January 2001, sixty-four Chamorro and Refaluwasch men acquired official recognition by the US Marine Corps. Marine officials swore in and discharged these men, honoring them for their service to the military during World War II. See Wright and Knight 2001.

Chapter 6: On the Margins of Memory and History

1. For an examination of the Japanese colonial police in Korea, see Lee 1999.

2. A Copy of Japanese Records, translated by William S Reyes [1975?], 9. Copy in Mark Peattie's Nan'yō Papers, Box 2, Folder 3, MARC Manuscript Collection, University of Guam.

3. A Copy of Japanese Records [1975?], 17. It is quite possible that some Chamorros (and maybe Refaluwasch) were arrested for making *agi* (local whiskey) as well.

4. I thank Dominica Tolentino for interviewing her mother, Tan Concepcion M Tolentino, about the roles of "comfort women" in wartime Guam.

5. I appreciate Masami Tsujita's translation from Japanese into English of Higuchi's research findings on the comfort women of Guam.

6. Carmen O Herrero to E R J Ojida, 12 October 1944. RG 313, National Archives.

7. *Dinga* translates into English as "twins."

8. Jesus L G Cruz to Joseph L G Cruz, 25 September 1944, 1. RG 313, National Archives.

9. The topic of war crime trials in Guam is beyond the scope of this book, as it requires further investigation and analysis of the political, social, and legal implications of "war crimes."

Chapter 7: On the Life and Death of Father Dueñas

1. The Kaikuntai was an agricultural unit established in Guam to provide food for the island's military force.

2. The first Chamorro ordained as a priest was Father Jose Bernardo Y Torres, in 1859.

3. I thank Vicente M Diaz for sharing the transcripts of his interview with Father Calvo.

4. History of the Death of Father Dueñas, 1945, 1. Father Dueñas File, Government Collection, Nieves Flores Memorial Library, Hagåtña, Guam.

5. Diary of Father Jesus Baza Dueñas [1942?]. Father Dueñas File, Government Collection, Nieves Flores Memorial Library, Hagåtña, Guam.

6. Dueñas also used the term *mestizu*, a label of Spanish origin indicating the "mixture" of Amerindian and Iberian peoples. In the Marianas context, this term

has come to signify the "upper class" of Chamorros, also called the *manakhilo*. For more on this issue, see Monnig 2005.

7. George R Tweed to *Pacific Daily News,* 7 June 1977. Copy in Agueda Iglesias Johnston's Papers, Box 14, Folder 8, 1 of 1, MARC Manuscript Collection, University of Guam.

8. J C to J [George R Tweed to Agueda I Johnston], 31 August 1943. Copy in Johnston's Papers, Box 14, Folder 8, 1 of 1, MARC Manuscript Collection, University of Guam.

9. History of the Death of Father Dueñas, 1945, 1.

10. I thank Margot A Henriksen for making this important observation.

References

Adams, Jim
  1996   World War II Battlefields and National Parks in the Pacific. *Creative Resources Management* 19 (3): 57–61.

Aguon, Julian
  2006   *Just Left of the Setting Sun: Essays for a Decolonizing Island.* Guam: Blue Ocean Press; Tokyo: Aoishima Research Institute.

Aguon, Katherine B
  [1971?]   A Proposal to Commemorate the Birth of the Organic Act of Guam. Agueda Iglesias Johnston's Papers, Subject File, Box 1, Folder 6, Richard F Taitano Micronesia Area Research Center (MARC) Manuscript Collection, University of Guam.

Ajia Minshū Hōtei Junbi Kai (Asian People's Tribunal Preparatory Group)
  1992   *Shashin Zusetsu: Nippon no Shinryaku.* Tokyo: Ōtsuki Shoten.

Alkire, William H
  1984   The Carolinians of Saipan and the Commonwealth of the Northern Mariana Islands. *Pacific Affairs* 57 (2): 270–283.

Anderberg, Roy
  1966   Guam Matriarch—Agueda I. Johnston. *Territorial Sun,* 16 October, 14.

Apple, Russell A, and Jerry L Rogers
  1976   Historical Integrity and Local Significance in the Pacific Island Context. *Guam Recorder* 6 (1): 33–36.

Arroyo, Rafael H
  1992   Inclusion of Park Funding in FY '93 Budget Uncertain. *Marianas Variety News and Views,* 11 June, 11.

  1993   US Support for Park Urged. *Marianas Variety News and Views,* 8 December, 1.

  1995   Borja Asks US: Allow Tinian Rites. *Marianas Variety News and Views,* 21 June, 3.

Ashplant, T G, Graham Dawson, and Michael Roper
  2000   The Politics of War Memory and Commemoration: Contexts, Structures and Dynamics. In *The Politics of War Memory and Commemoration,* edited by T G Ashplant, Graham Dawson, and Michael Roper, 3–85. London: Routledge.

Babauta, Antonio "Min" C
 2002   Interview by author. Tape recording. Agat, Guam, 5 March.
Ballendorf, Dirk Anthony
 1997   Guam Military Action in World War II. In *Guam History: Perspectives,* edited by Lee D Carter, William L Wuerch, and Rosa Roberto Carter, 1:219–238. Mangilao: Micronesia Area Research Center.
Barker, Joanne
 2005   For Whom Sovereignty Matters. In *Sovereignty Matters: Locations of Contestation and Possibility in Indigenous Struggles for Self-Determination,* edited by Joanne Barker, 1–31. Lincoln: University of Nebraska Press.
Bartov, Omer
 1998   Antisemitism, the Holocaust, and Reinterpretations of National Socialism. In *The Holocaust and History: The Known, the Unknown, the Disputed, and the Reexamined,* edited by Michael Berenbaum and Abraham J Peck, 75–98. Bloomington: Indiana University Press.
Bassler, Paul
 1991   Liberation Is Great, but Time Does Move On. *Pacific Daily News,* advertising supplement, 21 July, 16.
Benavente, Eddie L G
 2002   Interview by author. Tape recording. Mangilao, Guam, 12 March.
Bettis, Leland
 1996   Colonial Immigration in Guam. In *Kinalamten Pulitikåt: Siñenten I Chamorro (Issues in Guam's Political Development: The Chamorro Perspective),* 102–118. Agaña: PSECC.
Bhabha, Homi K
 1994   *The Location of Culture.* London: Routledge.
Blakeslee, George H
 1922   The Mandates of the Pacific. *Foreign Affairs: An American Quarterly Review* 1 (1): 98–115.
Blaz, Ben
 1998   *Bisita Guam: A Special Place in the Sun.* Fairfax Station, VA: Evers Press.
Bodnar, John
 1992   *Remaking America: Public Memory, Commemoration, and Patriotism in the Twentieth Century.* Princeton: Princeton University Press.
Bordallo, Ricardo J
 1977   Opening Remarks—July 1st. Papers of Governor Ricardo J Bordallo, Box 59, Speeches, Etc (First Adm), MARC Manuscript Collection, University of Guam.
Borja, Paul
 1980   GVB Had Roots Planted in 1952. *Pacific Daily News,* 1 May, 8.
Bosse, Paul C
 1945   Polling Civilian Japanese on Saipan. *Public Opinion Quarterly* 9 (2): 176–182.
Bowers, Neal M
 2001   *Problems of Resettlement on Saipan, Tinian and Rota, Mariana Islands.* Garapan: CNMI Division of Historic Preservation.

Braley, Tricia J
  1994 We Are Not Celebrating the Past but the Present. *Pacific Daily News*, Liberation Day supplement, 21 July, 16.
Brook, Timothy
  2005 *Collaboration: Japanese Agents and Local Elites in Wartime China.* Cambridge, MA: Harvard University Press.
Brooks, Donovan
  1994 Guam Liberation Veterans Honored. *Pacific Stars and Stripes*, 21 July, 6.
Brown, George Mark
  1966 George Tweed—The Ghost of Guam. *Guam Daily News*, 22 July, 19.
Butterbaugh, Wayne A
  1967 Catholics-Buddhists Join Forces to Emphasize Need for Peace. *Guam Daily News*, 19 January, 11, 24.
Cabrera, Genevieve
  2001 Rediscovering Liberation: Celebrating Freedom. In *Liberation Day 2001*, 2–3. Garapan: 2001 Liberation Day Committee.
Calvo, Oscar Lujan
  1994 Interview by Vicente M Diaz. Mangilao, Guam, 24 May. Transcript in author's files.
Camacho, Gloria F
  1952 Liberation Day—It Brings Back Memories of Joy and Sorrow. *Guam Daily News*, 21 July, 34.
Camacho, Juan C
  2004 Interview by author. Tape recording. Yigo, Guam, 30 March.
Camacho, Keith Lujan
  1998 Enframing I Taotao Tano': Colonialism, Militarism, and Tourism in Twentieth-Century Guam. MA thesis, University of Hawai'i, Mānoa.
Camacho, Vicente T
  1992 The Japanese Blood Shed in Saipan Is Still With Us. Interview by Yoshiaki Kamisawa. *Journal of the Pacific Society* 14 (4): 17–38.
Carano, Paul
  1973 Liberation Day: Prelude to Freedom, Lean Liberty is Better than Fat Slavery. *Guam Recorder* 3 (2–3): 3–8.
Castro, Daniel T
  1971 The Crave for Apples? *Micronesian Star*, 30 July, 5.
Castro, Rick
  2004 Interview by author. Tape recording. Mangilao, Guam, 10 January.
Celes, Manuel
  2002 Interview by author. Tape recording. Garapan, Saipan, 6 February.
Chappell, David A
  1995 Active Agents versus Passive Victims: Decolonized Historiography or Problematic Paradigm? *The Contemporary Pacific* 7:303–326.
Chen, Ching-chih
  1984 Police and Community Control Systems in the Empire. In *The Japanese Colonial Empire, 1895–1945,* edited by Ramon H Myers and Mark R Peattie, 213–239. Princeton: Princeton University Press.

Ching, Leo T S
   2001   *Becoming "Japanese": Colonial Taiwan and the Politics of Identity Formation.*
           Berkeley: University of California Press.
Christian Science Monitor [Daily, Boston]
   1946   Pacific Islands Still Bear Scars of Warfare. 4 December, 139.
Chung, Chin-Sung
   1997   The Origin and Development of the Military Sexual Slavery Problem in
           Imperial Japan. *Positions* 5 (1): 219–253.
Comaroff, Jean, and John L Comaroff
   1991   *Of Revelation and Revolution,* Volume 1: *Christianity, Colonialism, and Con-
           sciousness in South Africa.* Chicago: University of Chicago Press.
Commonwealth Examiner [Daily, Saipan]
   1979a   Bone Collectors' Mission a Hard One. 27 July, 8.
   1979b   In Old Japan the Warrior Always Carried Two Swords. 29 June, 5.
   1979c   35 Years Ago: Sgt. Engle Saved Three Saipan Families. 29 June, 3.
Commonwealth Newsletter [Monthly, Saipan]
   1979   An American War Memorial Park. November, 9.
   1980   July 4, 1980 Liberation Day. September, 1.
   1981   Increased Japan/NMI Air Service Essential for NMI Economy. March, 3.
Confino, Alon
   1997   Collective Memory and Cultural History: Problems of Method. *American
           Historical Review* 102 (5): 1386–1403.
Cook, Haruko Taya
   2001   The Myth of the Saipan Suicides. In *No End Save Victory: Perspectives
           on World War II,* edited by Robert Cowley, 583–597. New York: Berkley
           Books.
Cook, Scott B
   1996   *Colonial Encounters in the Age of High Imperialism.* New York: Harper Collins.
Coontz, Virginia
   1946a   American Welcome after Tragic Years. *Oakland Tribune,* 19 December, 3.
   1946b   Saipan Transformed from Field of Battle into U.S. Showplace. *Oakland
           Tribune,* 29 December, 16A.
Crisostomo, Marikita Palacios
   2002   The Interpreter's Wife. In Petty 2002, 82–85.
Crumrine, N Ross
   1982   Praying and Feasting: Modern Guamanian Fiestas. *Anthropos* 77:89–112.
Cruz, Jose Q
   2002   Interview by author. Tape recording. Mangilao, Guam, 6 March.
Cummings, Bruce
   1993   Japan's Position in the World System. In *Postwar Japan as History,* edited by
           Andrew Gordon, 35–64. Berkeley: University of California Press.
Cunningham, Lawrence J
   1992   *Ancient Chamorro Society.* Honolulu: Bess Press.
Curti, Merle
   1946   *The Roots of American Loyalty.* New York: Columbia University Press.
Dames, Vivian Loyola
   2000   Rethinking the Circle of Belonging: American Citizenship and the Cha-
           morros of Guam. PhD dissertation, University of Michigan.

Dawson, Doyne
  1996   The Origins of War: Biological and Anthropological Theories. *History and Theory* 35 (1): 1–28.
dé Ishtar, Zohl
  1994   *Daughters of the Pacific*. North Melbourne: Spinifex Press.
de la Torre, Ferdie
  1995   Lib-Day '95: A CNMI Celebration of Freedom. *Marianas Variety News and Views*, 5 July, 1.
De Leon Guerrero, Antonio R
  1984   Japanese Military Government Ordered Workers from Saipan and Rota (to Guam). 8 February. Available in World War II Virtual Museum, American Memorial Park, Saipan, Northern Mariana Islands: http://www.nps.gov/amme/wwii_museum/chamorros_and_carolinians_wwii/nmi_natives_in_guam_wwii_01.html.
  1993   Served 23 Years as Saipan's Vice-Mayor. Interview by Yoshiaki Kamisawa. *Journal of the Pacific Society* 15 (4): 29–42.
DeLisle, Christine Taitano
  2001   Delivering the Body: Narratives of Family, Childbirth, and Prewar *Pattera*. MA thesis, University of Guam.
DeLoughrey, Elizabeth M
  2007   *Routes and Roots: Navigating Caribbean and Pacific Island Literatures*. Honolulu: University of Hawai'i Press.
Del Rosario, Hebert S
  2002   Interview by author. Tape recording. Fakpis, Saipan, 14 February.
Denfeld, D Colt
  1984   Korean Laborers in Micronesia during World War II. *Korea Observer* 15 (1): 3–15.
Diaz, Vicente M
  1992   Repositioning the Missionary: The Beatification of Blessed Diego De Luis SanVitores and Chamorro Cultural and Political History in Guam. PhD dissertation, University of California, Santa Cruz.
  1994   Simply Chamorro: Telling Tales of Demise and Survival in Guam. *The Contemporary Pacific* 6:29–58.
  1995   Grounding Flux in Guam's Cultural History. In *Work in Flux*, edited by Emma Greenwood, Klaus Neumann, and Andrew Sartori, 159–171. Parkville: University of Melbourne History Department.
  2001   Deliberating "Liberation Day": Identity, History, Memory, and War in Guam. In Fujitani, White, and Yoneyama [eds] 2001, 155–180.
  2004   "To 'P' or Not to 'P'?" Marking the Territory between Pacific Islander and Asian American Studies. *Journal of American Asian Studies* 7 (3): 183–208.
Diaz, Vicente M, and J Kēhaulani Kauanui
  2001   Native Pacific Cultural Studies on the Edge. *The Contemporary Pacific* 13:315–342.
Dickhudt, Jane L
  1980   Saipan's Liberation Day. *New Pacific Magazine* 5 (5): 32.
Dirks, Nicholas B
  1992   Introduction: Colonialism and Culture. In *Colonialism and Culture*, edited by Nicholas B Dirks, 1–25. Ann Arbor: University of Michigan Press.

Dirlik, Arif
  1999   The Past as Legacy and Project: Postcolonial Criticism in the Perspective of Indigenous Historicism. In *Contemporary Native American Political Issues,* edited by Troy R Johnson, 73–97. Walnut Creek, CA: Altamira Press.
District Panorama [Weekly, Saipan]
  1966   Twenty Years Ago. 8 July, 5.
Dower, John W
  1986   *War Without Mercy: Race and Power in the Pacific War.* New York: Pantheon Books.
  1995   Triumphal and Tragic Narratives of the War in Asia. *Journal of American History* 82 (3): 1124–1135.
  1996   Three Narratives of Our Humanity. In *History Wars: The* Enola Gay *and Other Battles for the American Past,* edited by Edward T Linenthal and Tom Engelhardt, 63–96. New York: Henry Holt.
  1999   *Embracing Defeat: Japan in the Wake of World War II.* New York: W W Norton.
Duchen, Claire, and Irene Bandhauer-Schöffmann
  2000   Introduction. In *When the War Was Over: Women, War and Peace in Europe, 1940–1956,* edited by Claire Duchen and Irene Bandhauer-Schöffmann, 1–9. London: Leicester University Press.
Dudley, Uncle
  1947   Our Pacific Outposts. *Boston Globe,* 10 January, 18.
Dueñas, Jesus Baza
  var   File, Government Collection, Nieves Flores Memorial Library, Hagåtña, Guam.
Dueñas, Lucia Aldan
  1994   Interview by Herbert S Del Rosario. Saipan, 20 January. Translated by Nominanda L Kosaka and Herbert S Del Rosario. Finiho Yan Estoria Ginen I CNMI Archives Kolehon San Kattan Na Islas Marianas (CNMI Oral History Project, Northern Marianas College).
Dumat-Ol, Gaynor
  1995a   Defense Decision Draws Fire from CNMI. *Pacific Daily News,* 14 June, 3.
  1995b   Tinian Aims at Balanced View of Atomic History. *Pacific Daily News,* 27 March, 4.
  1995c   Tinian Won't Get Military Support for Ceremonies. *Pacific Daily News,* 9 June, 3.
Eclavea, Gina
  1994   Departing Liberators Pledge Political Support. *Pacific Daily News,* 23 July, 3.
Embree, John F
  1946   Military Government in Saipan and Tinian. *Applied Anthropology* 5 (1): 1–39.
Enloe, Cynthia H
  1987   Feminist Thinking about War, Militarism, and Peace. In *Analyzing Gender: A Handbook of Social Science Research,* edited by Beth B Hess and Myra Marx Ferree, 526–547. Newbury Park, CA: Sage Publications.
Erai, Michelle
  2004   Exile, Maori and Lesbian. In *Queer in Aotearoa New Zealand,* edited by Lynne Alice and Lynne Star, 35–46. Palmerston North, NZ: Dunmore Press.

Estrada, Jose S
  1968   Message. In *Liberation Day 1968*, 4. Agaña: Guam Junior Chamber of Commerce.

Falgout, Suzanne, Lin Poyer, and Laurence M Carucci
  2008   *Memories of War: Micronesians in the Pacific War.* Honolulu: University of Hawai'i Press.

Farrell, Don A
  1989   *Tinian: A Brief History.* Saipan: Micronesian Productions, CNMI.
  1991a   *The History of the Northern Mariana Islands.* Saipan: CNMI Public School System.
  1991b   *The Pictorial History of Guam: The Sacrifice, 1919–1943.* San Jose, Tinian: Micronesian Productions.
  1994   The Partition of the Marianas: A Diplomatic History, 1898–1919. *Isla: A Journal of Micronesian Studies* 2 (2): 273–301.

Fichter, Cherie
  1977a   A Matter of Survival. *Islander (Pacific Sunday News)*, 25 September, 3.
  1977b   Tweed and the Schoolmarm. *Islander (Pacific Sunday News)*, 11 September, 2.

Figal, Gerald
  2001   Waging Peace on Okinawa. *Critical Asian Studies* 33 (1): 37–69.

Findley, L G
  1947   To the Native People of Saipan. *Pregonero*, 2 May, 2.

Firth, Stewart
  1997   The War in the Pacific. In *The Cambridge History of Pacific Islanders*, edited by Donald Denoon, Stewart Firth, Jocelyn Linnekin, Malama Meleisea, and Karen Nero, 291–323. Cambridge, UK: Cambridge University Press.

Fletcher, George P
  1993   *Loyalty: An Essay on the Morality of Relationships.* New York: Oxford University Press.

Flinn, Juliana
  1990   Catholicism and Pulapese Identity. In *Christianity in Oceania,* edited by John Barker, 221–235. Lanham, MD: University Press of America.

Flores, Evelyn Rose
  2002   Rewriting Paradise: Countering Desire, Denial, and the Exotic in American Literary Representations of the Pacific. PhD dissertation, University of Michigan.

Forbes, Eric
  1997   The Origins of Protestantism in Guam. In *Guam History: Perspectives*, edited by Lee D Carter, William Wuerch, and Rosa Roberto Carter, 1:123–140. Mangilao: Micronesia Area Research Center.
  2002   Interview by author. Tape recording. Hagåtña, Guam, 10 March.

Free Press [Daily, Saipan]
  1974   Wake Up Marianas. 11 October, 11.

Friedländer, Saul
  1998   Afterword: The Shoah between Memory and History. In *Breaking Crystal: Writing and Memory after Auschwitz,* edited by Efraim Sicher, 345–357. Urbana: University of Illinois Press.

Friedman, Hal M
  1995   The Limitations of Collective Security: The United States and the Micro-
          nesian Trusteeship, 1945–1947. *Isla: A Journal of Micronesian Studies* 3 (2):
          339–370.
  2001   *Creating an American Lake: United States Imperialism and Strategic Security in
          the Pacific Basin, 1945–1947.* Westport, CT: Greenwood Press.
Fujitani, T
  2001   Go for Broke, the Movie: Japanese American Soldiers in U.S. National,
          Military, and Racial Discourses. In Fujitani, White, and Yoneyama [eds]
          2001, 239–266.
Fujitani, T, Geoffrey M White, and Lisa Yoneyama
  2001   Introduction. In Fujitani, White, and Yoneyama [eds] 2001, 1–29.
Fujitani, T, Geoffrey M White, and Lisa Yoneyama, editors
  2001   *Perilous Memories: The Asia-Pacific War(s).* Durham, NC: Duke University Press.
Gaddis, John Lewis
  1972   *The United States and the Origins of the Cold War, 1941–1947.* New York:
          Columbia University Press.
Gedi, Noa, and Yigal Elam
  1996   Collective Memory—What is It? *History and Memory* 8 (1): 30–50.
Gegeo, David Welchman
  1988   The Big Death: What Pacific Islanders Can Teach Us about World War II.
          'O'O: A Journal of Solomon Islands Studies (4): 7–16.
Gillis, John R
  1989   *The Militarization of the Western World.* New Brunswick, NJ: Rutgers Univer-
          sity Press.
  1994   Memory and Identity: The History of a Relationship. In *Commemorations:
          The Politics of National Identity,* edited by John R Gillis, 3–24. Princeton:
          Princeton University Press.
Goodwin, Janet
  1967   War Memorial Again. *Guam Daily News,* 25 July, 14.
Gordon, Milton M
  1964   *Assimilation in American Life: The Role of Race, Religion, and National Origins.*
          New York: Oxford University Press.
Graves, Howard
  1994   Code Talkers Start Drive to Return to Islands. *Pacific Daily News,* 11 July, 3.
Grosfoguel, Ramón
  2003   *Colonial Subjects: Puerto Ricans in a Global Perspective.* Berkeley: University of
          California Press.
Gross, Jan Thomas
  1991   Collaboration and Cooperation. In *World War II, Crucible of the Contem-
          porary World: Commentary and Readings,* edited by Loyd E Lee, 70–86.
          Armonk, NY: M E Sharpe.
Guam Code Annotated
  1996   Section 1011. Title 1. Agaña: Government of Guam.
Guam Daily News [Hagåtña]
  1953a   Coronation Ball at 8 Tonight Climaxes 2-Day Celebration. 21 July, 1.
  1953b   The Enemy Came Seeking His Dead. 21 July, 16.
  1953c   Messages from Governor, Military. 21 July, 2.

1954   Salute to Builders. 21 July, 2.

1955   Stress Economic Liberation—Calvo: Lawmaker Calls for Development of Independent Economy. 22 July, 2.

1960   Because of Tweed: In They Came Again . . . and Back He Went. 21 July, 8.

1962   Prices of Victory and Freedom. 21 July, 6.

1966a   A Chance to Pause and Reflect about War. 21 July, 4.

1966b   Why Are Japanese Building Memorial? 13 May, 1.

1967a   Calls Government of Guam "Prejudicial": Congress Gets Resolution to Block Japanese War Memorial. 10 July, 1.

1967b   "This Infuriates Me": Asks U.S. Congress to Oppose War Memorial. 11 February, 1.

1967c   "War in Pacific" Park OK. 6 May, 1.

Guam News [later became *Guam Daily News*]

1948   "Little Mother of Guam" Grows Up: Dolores Mesa Recalls Painful Memories of Japanese Occupation. 1 February, 1.

Guam Recorder [Monthly, US Naval Government, Guam]

1927   The Fourth of July. *Guam Recorder* 4 (4): 85.

1934   Flag Day: Guam's Greatest Patriotic Celebration. *Guam Recorder* 10 (12): 213.

Guerrero, Consolacion C

1994   Interview by Herbert S Del Rosario. Saipan, 25 April. Written and Translated by Nominanda L Kosaka and Herbert S Del Rosario. Finiho Yan Estoria Ginen I CNMI Archives Kolehon San Kattan Na Islas Marianas (CNMI Oral History Project, Northern Marianas College).

Haberman, Clyde

1984   40 Years after Pacific D-Day, No Crowds and No Parades. *New York Times*, 16 June 1984, 1.

Hall, James V

1976   Bulwark of the Pacific. *Marianas Review* 24 (6): 47–52.

Hammond, Ellen H

1995   Politics of the War and Public History: Japan's Own Museum Controversy. *Bulletin of Concerned Asian Scholars* 27 (2): 56–59.

Hanlon, David

1994   Patterns of Colonial Rule in Micronesia. In *Tides of History: The Pacific Islands in the Twentieth Century*, edited by K R Howe, Robert C Kiste, and Brij V Lal, 93–118. Honolulu: University of Hawai'i Press.

1998   *Remaking Micronesia: Discourses over Development in a Pacific Territory, 1944–1982.* Honolulu: University of Hawai'i Press.

Hattori, Anne Perez

1995   Righting Civil Wrongs: The Guam Congress Walkout of 1949. *Isla: A Journal of Micronesian Studies* 3 (1): 1–27.

2001   Guardians of Our Soil: Indigenous Responses to Post-World War II Military Land Appropriation on Guam. In *Farms, Firms, and Runways: Perspectives on U.S. Military Bases in the Western Pacific*, edited by L Eve Armentrout Ma, 186–202. Chicago: Imprint Publications.

2004   *Colonial Dis-Ease: US Navy Health Policies and the Chamorros of Guam, 1898–1941.* Pacific Islands Monograph Series 19. Honolulu: University of Hawai'i Center for Pacific Islands Studies and University of Hawai'i Press.

2005 Church, State, and Chamorro Culture: The Struggle for Power in Pre-War Guam. Paper presented at the University of Guam's College of Liberal Arts and Social Sciences Conference, March. Unpublished manuscript in author's possession.

Hein, Laura, and Mark Selde
1997 Commemoration and Silence: Fifty Years of Remembering the Bomb in America and Japan. In *Living with the Bomb: American and Japanese Cultural Conflicts in the Nuclear Age*, edited by Laura Hein and Mark Selden, 3–34. Armonk, NY: M E Sharpe.

Henriksen, Margot A
1997 *Dr. Strangelove's America: Society and Culture in the Atomic Age*. Berkeley: University of California Press.

Henson, Maria Rosa
1999 *Comfort Woman: A Filipina's Story of Prostitution and Slavery under the Japanese Military*. Lanham, MD: Rowman & Littlefield.

Hereniko, Vilsoni
1995 *Woven Gods: Female Clowns and Power in Rotuma*. Pacific Islands Monograph Series 12. Honolulu: University of Hawai'i Center for Pacific Islands Studies and University of Hawai'i Press.

Hewlett, Frank
1969 Over 2,500 Acres Complete Master Plan for Pacific War Park. *Guam Daily News*, 9 December, 1.

Hezel, Francis X
1982 From Conversion to Conquest: The Early Spanish Mission in the Marianas. *Journal of Pacific History* 17 (3): 115–137.
1995 *Strangers in Their Own Land: A Century of Colonial Rule in the Caroline and Marshall Islands*. Pacific Islands Monograph Series 13. Honolulu: University of Hawai'i Center for Pacific Islands Studies and University of Hawai'i Press.

Hicks, George
1996 The "Comfort Women." In *The Japanese Wartime Empire, 1931–1945*, edited by Peter Duus, Ramon H Meyers, and Mark R Peattie, 305–323. Princeton: Princeton University Press.

Higonnet, Margaret Randolph, and Patrice L R Higgonet
1987 The Double Helix. In *Behind the Lines: Gender and the Two World Wars*, edited by Margaret Randolph Higonnet, Jane Jenson, Sonya Michel, and Margaret Collins Weitz, 31–47. New Haven, CT: Yale University Press.

Higonnet, Margaret Randolph, Jane Jenson, Sonya Michel, and Margaret Collins Weitz
1987 Introduction. In *Behind the Lines: Gender and the Two World Wars*, edited by Margaret Randolph Higonnet, Jane Jenson, Sonya Michel, and Margaret Collins Weitz, 1–17. New Haven, CT: Yale University Press.

Higuchi, Wakako
1999 *A Report on Ian-fu and Ian-jyo on Guam during the Japanese Occupation Period*. Mangilao: Micronesia Area Research Center.
2001a The Japanization Policy for the Chamorros of Guam, 1941–1944. *Journal of Pacific History* 36 (1): 19–35.
2001b *Remembering the War Years on Guam: A Japanese Perspective*, submitted to War

in the Pacific National Historical Park Service, United States Department of Interior.

Hobsbawm, Eric
1997   Introduction: Inventing Traditions. In *The Invention of Tradition,* edited by Eric Hobsbawm and Terence Ranger, 1–14. Cambridge, UK: Cambridge University Press.

Hofschneider, Penelope Bordallo
2001   *A Campaign for Political Rights on the Island of Guam, 1899 to 1950.* Saipan: CNMI Division of Historic Preservation.

Hogan, Michael J, editor
1999   *Hiroshima in History and Memory.* Cambridge, UK: Cambridge University Press.

Hook, Anita
1983   Sam Weintraub: Search. *Mid-South: The Commercial Appeal Magazine* [weekly, Memphis], 14 August, 4–10.

hooks, bell
1995   Feminism and Militarism: A Comment. *Women's Studies Quarterly* 23 (3/4): 58–64.

Howard, Chris Perez
1986   *Mariquita: A Tragedy of Guam.* Suva: Institute of Pacific Studies, University of the South Pacific.

Howard, Michael C
1989   Ethnicity and the State in the Pacific. In *Ethnicity and Nation-building in the Pacific,* edited by Michael C Howard, 1–49. Tokyo: United Nations University.

Hutton, Patrick H
1988   Collective Memory and Collective Mentalities: The Halbwachs-Ariès Connection. *Historical Reflections/Reflexions Historiques* 15 (2): 311–322.

Imada, Adria L
2004   Hawaiians on Tour: Hula Circuits through the American Empire. *American Quarterly* 56 (1): 111–149.

Inglis, K S
1969   War, Race and Loyalty in New Guinea, 1939–1945. In *The History of Melanesia,* 503–509. Canberra: Research School of Pacific Studies, Australian National University; Port Moresby: University of Papua and New Guinea.

Inos, Joseph S
1991   Be Ready to Guard Our Freedom Anytime—Inos. *Marianas Review* [weekly, Saipan], 5 July, 4.

Inos, Vicente Atalig
1981   Interview by Ted Oxborrow and associates. The War Years on Saipan: Transcripts of Interviews with Residents, Micronesia Area Research Center, Mangilao.

Iriye, Akira
1972   *Pacific Estrangement: Japanese and American Expansion, 1897–1911.* Cambridge, MA: Harvard University Press.

Iyechad, Lilli Perez
2001   *An Historical Perspective of Helping Practices Associated with Birth, Marriage and Death among Chamorros in Guam.* Lewiston, NY: Edwin Mellen Press.

Jeffrey, Jaclyn, and Glenace Edwall, editors
  1994   *Memory and History: Essays on Recalling and Interpreting Experience.* Lanham, MD: University Press of America.
Johnson, Chalmers
  2004   *The Sorrows of Empire: Militarism, Secrecy, and the End of the Republic.* New York: Henry Holt.
Johnston, Agueda I
  var   Papers. MARC Manuscript Collection, University of Guam.
Johnston, Agueda I, and Clyde M Cramlet
  [1965?]   Chamorrita. Manuscript. Copy in Agueda I Johnston's Papers, Box 7, Folder 42, 1 of 3, MARC Manuscript Collection, University of Guam.
Jolly, Margaret, and Martha Macintyre, editors
  1989   *Family and Gender in the Pacific: Domestic Contradictions and the Colonial Impact.* New York: Cambridge University Press.
Jorgensen, Marilyn Anne
  1984   *Guam's Patroness: Santa Marian Kamalen.* Austin: University of Texas.
Joseph, Alice, and Veronica F Murray
  1951   *Chamorros and Carolinians of Saipan.* Cambridge, MA: Harvard University Press.
Josephy, Alvin M, Jr
  1946   *The Long and the Short and the Tall: The Story of a Marine Combat Unit in the Pacific.* New York: Alfred A Knopf.
Kame'eleihiwa, Lilikalā
  1992   *Native Land and Foreign Desires: Pehea Lā E Pono Ai?* Honolulu: Bishop Museum Press.
Kaplan, Amy
  1993   "Left Alone with America": The Absence of Empire in the Study of American Culture. In *Cultures of United States Imperialism,* edited by Amy Kaplan and Donald E Pease, 3–21. Durham, NC: Duke University Press.
  2004   Violent Belongings and the Question of Empire Today: Presidential Address to the American Studies Association, October 17, 2003. *American Quarterly* 56 (1): 1–18.
Kauanui, J Kēhaulani
  2007   Diasporic Deracination and "Off-Island" Hawaiians. *The Contemporary Pacific* 19:138–160.
Kelly, Liz
  2000   Wars against Women: Sexual Violence, Sexual Politics and the Militarized State. In *States of Conflict: Gender, Violence and Resistance,* edited by Susie Jacobs, Ruth Jacobson, and Jen Marchbank, 45–65. London: Zed Books.
Kenny, Anthony
  1985   *The Logic of Deterrence.* Chicago: University of Chicago Press.
Kiener, Robert
  1978   A Bulwark of the Pacific. *Glimpses of Micronesia and the Western Pacific* 18 (1): 33–38.
Kim, Hyun Sook
  1997   History and Memory: The "Comfort Women" Controversy. *Positions: East Asia Cultures Critique* 5 (1): 73–106.

Kim, Kyon Shik

1972   Message. In *1972 July 21st, 28th Anniversary of Guam's Liberation Day, 1944–1972: Peace through Brotherhood of Man*, 7. Agaña: Guam Jaycees.

Kjellgren, Eric P

1993   Rousseau and Hobbes in the Pacific: Western Literary Visions of Polynesia and Melanesia. *Mana: A South Pacific Journal of Language and Literature* 10 (1): 95–111.

Kramer, Paul A

2006   *The Blood of Government: Race, Empire, the United States, and the Philippines.* Chapel Hill: University of North Carolina Press.

Kurashige, Lon

2002   *Japanese American Celebration and Conflict: A History of Ethnic Identity and Festival in Los Angeles, 1934–1990.* Berkeley: University of California Press.

LaCapra, Dominick

1998   *History and Memory after Auschwitz.* Ithaca, NY: Cornell University Press.

Lamont-Brown, Raymond

1998   *Kempetai: Japan's Dreaded Military Police.* Stroud, UK: Sutton Publishing.

Laracy, Hugh M

1971   Marching Rule and Missions. *Journal of Pacific History* 6:96–114.

1983   *Pacific Protest: The Maasina Rule Movement, Solomon Islands, 1944–1952.* Suva: Institute of Pacific Studies, University of the South Pacific.

1991   George Bogese: "Just a Bloody Traitor"? In White [ed] 1991, 59–75.

Lawson, Gary, and Guy Seidman

2004   *The Constitution of Empire: Territorial Expansion and American Legal History.* New Haven, CT: Yale University Press.

Lebra, Joyce C, editor

1975   *Japan's Greater East Asia Co-Prosperity Sphere in World War II: Selected Readings and Documents.* Kuala Lumpur: Oxford University Press.

Lee, Chulwoo

1999   Modernity, Legality, and Power in Korea under Japanese Rule. In *Colonial Modernity in Korea*, edited by Gi-Wook Shin and Michael Robinson, 21–51. Cambridge, MA: Harvard University Asia Center and Harvard University Press.

Leeke, Jim

1977   Antonio Artero: A Modest Guam Hero. *Islander, Pacific Sunday News,* 9 October, 2–3.

Le Goff, Jacque

1992   *History and Memory.* Translated by Steven Rendall and Elizabeth Claman. New York: Columbia University Press.

Leibowitz, Arnold H

1989   *Defining Status: A Comprehensive Analysis of United States Territorial Relations.* Dordrecht, Netherlands: Martinus Nijhoff.

Leon Guerrero, Anthony

1996   The Economic Development of Guam. In *Kinalamten Pulitikåt: Siñenten I Chamorro (Issues in Guam's Political Development: The Chamorro Perspective),* 83–101. Agaña: PSECC.

Levi, Werner
    1948   American Attitudes toward Pacific Islands, 1914–1919. *Pacific Historical Review* 17 (1): 55–64.
Limtiaco, Joaquin
    1960   The Last Days of Fr. Duenas. *Guam Daily News,* 21 July, 8.
Limtiaco, Steve
    1994   Chamoru Nation Calls Off Liberation Day Protests. *Pacific Daily News,* 20 July, 3.
Lindstrom, Lamont, and Geoffrey M White
    1989   War Stories. In *The Pacific Theater: Island Representations of World War II,* edited by Geoffrey M White and Lamont Lindstrom, 3–40. Pacific Islands Monograph Series 8. Honolulu: University of Hawai'i Center for Pacific Islands Studies and University of Hawai'i Press.
    1993   Singing History: Island Songs from the Pacific War. In *Artistic Heritage in a Changing Pacific,* edited by Philip J C Dark and Roger G Rose, 185–196. Honolulu: University of Hawai'i Press.
Linenthal, Edward Tabor
    1993   *Sacred Ground: Americans and Their Battlefields.* Urbana: University of Illinois Press.
Linenthal, Edward T, and Tom Engelhardt, editors
    1996   *History Wars: The* Enola Gay *and Other Battles for the American Past.* New York: Henry Holt.
Linnekin, Jocelyn
    1990   The Politics of Culture in the Pacific. In *Cultural Identity and Ethnicity in the Pacific,* edited by Jocelyn Linnekin and Lin Poyer, 149–173. Honolulu: University of Hawai'i Press.
    1992   On the Theory and Politics of Cultural Construction in the Pacific. *Oceania* 62 (4): 249–263.
Lipsitz, George
    2001   "Frantic to Join . . . the Japanese Army": Black Soldiers and Civilians Confront the Asia-Pacific War. In Fujitani, White, and Yoneyama [eds] 2001, 347–377.
LiPuma, Edward
    1995   The Formation of Nation-States and National Cultures in Oceania. In *Nation Making: Emergent Identities in Postcolonial Melanesia,* edited by Robert J Foster, 33–68. Ann Arbor: University of Michigan Press.
Lodge, O R
    1954   *The Recapture of Guam.* Washington, DC: US Government Printing Office.
Los Angeles Examiner [Daily]
    1955   Guam Heroine Here to Aid Liberation Fete. 22 July, 1.
Lowenthal, David
    1997   *The Past Is a Foreign Country.* Cambridge, UK: Cambridge University Press.
Lujan, Francisco G, and Joaquin Aflague Limtiaco
    1965   Political Martyr: Last Hours of Father Dueñas. *Pacific Profile,* July, 10.
Lundestad, Geir
    1991   Empire by Invitation? The United States and Western Europe, 1945–1952. In *The Cold War in Europe,* edited by Charles S Maier, 143–165. New York: Markus Wiener Publishing.

Lyons, Paul
 2006   *American Pacificism: Oceania in the U.S. Imagination.* New York: Rout-
          ledge.
Macpherson, Cluny
 1996   Pacific Islands Identity and Community. In *Nga Patai: Racism and Ethnic
          Relations in Aotearoa/New Zealand,* edited by Paul Spoonley, David Pear-
          son, and Cluny Macpherson, 124–143. Palmerston North, NZ: Dunmore
          Press.
Maga, Timothy P
 1985   Democracy and Defense: The Case of Guam, U.S.A., 1898–1941. *Journal of
          Pacific History* 3 (4): 156–172.
 2001   "Away from Tokyo": The Pacific Islands War Crime Trials, 1945–1949. *Jour-
          nal of Pacific History* 36 (1): 37–50.
Mangloña, Benjamin T
 2001   Remarks of Rota Mayor Benjamin T. Mangloña on the Occasion of the
          Visit to Rota of the Rota Kai Group. June. Unpublished manuscript in
          author's possession.
Mangloña, Concepcion
 1986   Beautiful Tinian Can Still Be Improved. *Marianas Variety News and Views,*
          13 June, 16.
Manibusan, Rose S N
 1993   The Mariana Home Front: Dealing with Adversity—Chamorro Life dur-
          ing the Pacific War. *Islander, Pacific Sunday News,* 11 April, 10.
Marianas Variety News and Views [Daily, Saipan]
 1973   Liberation Day with a New Attitude. 13 July, 2.
 1976   Saipan's Liberation Day Festivities. 7 July, A.
 1980   Ranger Has No Use for Skis in Saipan. 29 May, 9.
 1983   Landscaping for Memorial Due. 15 July, 17.
 1986a Absence of Monuments Shocks Veteran. 24 January, 5.
 1986b Finally, a Local Monument for US Marines. 6 June, 11.
 1986c 123 Attend Tower of Okinawa Rites. 13 June, 27.
 1992   Lack of Funds for Local Park Disappoints Babauta. 10 September, 5.
 1993a Babauta Pushes Park Project. 6 May, 2.
 1993b Public Urged to Support Memorial Park Project. 1 June, 5.
 1994a Tenorio, Babbit Sign Park Accord. 3 March, 6.
 1994b National Rites Remembering the Marianas Campaign Set. 17 June, 3.
Marsh, Selina Tusitala
 1998   Migrating Feminisms: Maligned Overstayer or Model Citizen? *Women's
          Studies International Forum* 21 (6): 665–680.
Mathews, Shailer
 1918   *Patriotism and Religion.* New York: Macmillan.
McClintock, Anne
 1995   *Imperial Leather: Race, Gender, and Sexuality in the Colonial Conquest.* New
          York: Routledge.
McCormick, Thomas J
 1991   America's Half Century: United States Foreign Policy in the Cold War.
          In *The Cold War in Europe,* edited by Charles S Maier, 21–50. New York:
          Markus Wiener Publishing.

McHenry, Donald F
   1975   *Micronesia, Trust Betrayed: Altruism vs. Self Interest in American Foreign Policy.* New York: Carnegie Endowment for International Peace.
McManus, Larry
   1944   Pacific Liberation. *YANK* [Saipan, weekly], 1 September, 11.
McPhetres, Samuel F
   1993   The History of Land Issues in the Commonwealth of the Northern Marianas. *Umanidát: A Journal of the Humanities* 1 (1): 14–19.
   2002   Interview by author. Tape recording. Garapan, Saipan, 1 February.
Meller, Norman
   1999   *Saipan's Camp Susupe.* CPIS Occasional Paper 42. Honolulu: Center for Pacific Islands Studies, University of Hawai'i, Mānoa.
Micronesian Star [Daily, Saipan]
   1971   American Affiliation Will Give Equal Chance to All Says Borja. 24 April, 14.
Minow, Martha
   1998   *Between Vengeance and Forgiveness: Facing History after Genocide and Mass Violence.* Boston: Beacon Press.
Mittelman, James H, and Christine B N Chin
   2005   Conceptualizing Resistance to Globalization. In *The Global Resistance Reader,* edited by Louise Amoore, 17–27. London: Routledge.
Miyoshi, Masao
   1991   *Off Center: Power and Culture Relations between Japan and the United States.* Cambridge, MA: Harvard University Press.
Mommsen, Wolfgang J
   1982   *Theories of Imperialism.* Translated by P S Falla. Chicago: University of Chicago Press.
Monnig, Laurel
   2005   "Proving Chamorro": Indigenous Narratives of Race, Identity and Decolonization in Guam. PhD dissertation, University of Illinois, Urbana-Champaign.
Muña, Nicolas Q
   1995   Interview by Herbert S Del Rosario. Saipan, 1 December. Written and Translated by Nominanda L Kosaka and Herbert S Del Rosario. Finiho Yan Estoria Ginen I CNMI Archives Kolehon San Kattan Na Islas Marianas (CNMI Oral History Project, Northern Marianas College).
Murdock, George P
   1948   How Shall We Administer Our Pacific Trust Territory? Paper presented at Society for Applied Anthropology, Philadelphia, 29 May. Record Group 313: Records of the Naval Operating Forces. National Archives, Washington, DC.
Murphy, Joe
   1983   Agueda Johnston: Spirit of Liberation. *Pacific Daily News,* 21 July, 4A.
Najita, Susan Y
   2006   *Decolonizing Cultures in the Pacific: Reading History and Trauma in Contemporary Fiction.* New York: Routledge.
Narangoa, Li, and Robert Cribb
   2003   Japan and the Transformation of National Identities in Asia in the Impe-

rial Era. In *Imperial Japan and National Identities in Asia, 1895–1945*, edited by Li Narangoa and Robert Cribb, 1–22. London: Routledge Curzon.

Narokobi, Bernard

1983   *The Melanesian Way.* Boroko: Institute of Papua New Guinea Studies; Suva: Institute of Pacific Studies, University of the South Pacific.

National Archives

var   Naval Bases and Naval Operating Bases. Record Group 313: Records of the Naval Operating Forces. National Archives, Washington, DC.

Navy News [Daily, US Naval Government Guam]

1947   Festivities Herald Liberation Day: Parade, Parties Highlight Date of Deliverance. 22 July, 1.

Nelson, Keith L, and Spencer C Olin, Jr

1980   *Why War? Ideology, Theory, and History.* Berkeley: University of California Press.

New York Times [Daily]

1945   Koreans on Tinian Island, Grateful to U.S. for Liberation, Give $666 to War Effort. 5 February, 4.

NMCPC, Northern Marianas College Pacific Collection

var   Microfilm correspondence and diaries. Pacific Collection, Northern Marianas College, Saipan.

Nobile, Philip, editor

1995   *Judgment at the Smithsonian.* New York: Marlowe.

Nora, Pierre

1989   Between Memory and History: Les Lieux de Mémoire. In *Memory and Counter-Memory,* edited by Natalie Zemon Davis and Randolph Starn. Special issue of *Representations* 26 (Spring): 7–25.

NPS, National Park Service, US Department of the Interior

1969   *Master Plan, Proposed War in the Pacific National Historic Park, Guam.* Washington, DC: US Government Printing Office.

1989   *General Management Plan: American Memorial Park, Saipan.* Washington, DC: NPS.

2001   *Special Study, North Field Historic District: Tinian, Commonwealth of the Northern Mariana Islands.* Washington, DC: NPS.

Oh, Bonnie B C

2001   The Japanese Imperial System and the Korean "Comfort Women" of World War II. In *Legacies of the Comfort Women of World War II,* edited by Margaret Stetz and Bonnie B C Oh, 3–25. Armonk, NY: M E Sharpe.

Ohnuki-Tierney, Emiko

2002   *Kamikaze, Cherry Blossoms, and Nationalisms: The Militarization of Aesthetics in Japanese History.* Chicago: University of Chicago Press.

Okihiro, Gary Y

2006   Toward a Black Pacific. In *AfroAsian Encounters: Culture, History, Politics,* edited by Heike Raphael-Hernandez and Shannon Steen, 313–330. New York: New York University Press.

Olopai, Lino M

2005   *The Rope of Tradition: Reflections of a Saipan Carolinian.* Saipan: Northern Mariana Islands Council for the Humanities.

Ombrello, Mark A
  2003   Interview by author. Tape recording. Honolulu, Hawai'i, 4 November.
Omi, Michael, and Howard Winant
  1994   *Racial Formation in the United States: From the 1960s to the 1990s.* New York: Routledge.
Onedera, Peter R
  2002   Interview by author. Tape recording. Mangilao, Guam, 8 January.
Orr, James J
  2001   *The Victim as Hero: Ideologies of Peace and National Identity in Postwar Japan.* Honolulu: University of Hawai'i Press.
Osman, Wali M
  1995   *Commonwealth of the Northern Mariana Islands Economic Report.* Honolulu: Bank of Hawaii.
Owings, Kathleen R W, editor
  1981   *The War Years on Guam: Narratives of the Chamorro Experience.* Volume 1. Mangilao: Micronesia Area Research Center.
Oyen, Frale
  1990   Longtime Asan Resident Remembers: Joaquin Cruz Describes Some Childhood Events. *Pacific Daily News,* 21 July, 17A.
Pacific Daily News [Hagåtña]
  1970   Who was Father Duenas? 9 July, 24.
  1973   "Quick, Like a Spark": Again, the Story of a Priest Who Died. 21 July, 38A.
  1990   Survivors Recall Joy of Liberation. 21 July, 2A.
Palomo, Tony
  1959   Thousands See Floats on Parade. *Guam Daily News,* 20 July, 1.
  1984   *An Island in Agony.* Agaña: Tony Palomo.
  1991   Island in Agony: The War in Guam. In White [ed] 1991, 133–144.
Pangelinan, Henry S
  2002   The Interpreter. In Petty 2002, 79–82.
Paxton, Robert O
  1972   *Vichy France: Old Guard and New Order, 1940–1944.* New York: Alfred A Knopf.
Peattie, Mark R
  1984a   Introduction. In *The Japanese Colonial Empire, 1895–1945,* edited by Ramon H Myers and Mark R Peattie, 3–52. Princeton: Princeton University Press.
  1984b   The Nan'yō: Japan in the South Pacific, 1885–1945. In *The Japanese Colonial Empire, 1895–1945,* edited by Ramon H Myers and Mark R Peattie, 172–210. Princeton: Princeton University Press.
  1988   *Nan'yō: The Rise and Fall of the Japanese in Micronesia, 1885–1945.* Pacific Islands Monograph Series 4. Honolulu: University of Hawai'i Center for Pacific Islands Studies and University of Hawai'i Press.
  var   Nan'yō Papers. MARC Manuscript Collection, University of Guam.
Peck, W M
  1983   Rota's Ginalagan Cliff Unchallenged. Copy in Mark Peattie's Nan'yō Papers, Box 2, Folder 3, MARC Manuscript Collection, University of Guam.
Perez, Cecilia T
  1996   A Chamorro Re-Telling of "Liberation." In *Kinalamten Pulitikåt: Siñenten I Chamorro (Issues in Guam's Political Development: The Chamorro Perspective),* 70–77. Agaña: PSECC.

Perez, Michael P
   2001   Contested Sites: Pacific Resistance in Guam to U.S. Empire. *Amerasia Journal* 27 (1): 97–115.
   2005   Colonialism, Americanization, and Indigenous Identity: A Research Note on Chamorro Identity in Guam. *Sociological Spectrum* 25 (5): 571–591.
Perez, Vicente L G
   [1970?]   *Guam Historical Monuments.* Mangilao: Micronesia Area Research Center.
Petty, Bruce, editor
   2002   *Saipan: Oral Histories of the Pacific War.* Jefferson, NC: McFarland.
Phillips, Ken
   1984   Saipan Translator: We Had No Choice. *Pacific Daily News,* 21 July, 16.
Phillips, Michael F
   1996   Land. In *Kinalamten Pulitikåt: Siñenten I Chamorro (Issues in Guam's Political Development: The Chamorro Perspective),* 2–16. Agaña: PSECC.
Pike, David Wingeate
   2001   Foreword. In *The Closing of the Second War: Twilight of a Totalitarianism,* edited by David Wingeate Pike, xi–lxvi. New York: Peter Lang.
Pomeroy, Earl S
   1948   American Policy Respecting the Marshalls, Carolines, and the Marianas, 1898–1941. *Pacific Historical Review* 17 (1): 43–53.
Pownall, C A
   1947   Governor's Memorial Day Address: Stresses Debt of Gratitude We Owe Our War Dead. *Navy News,* 1 June, 3.
Poyer, Lin
   1991   Micronesian Experiences of the War in the Pacific. In White [ed] 1991, 79–89.
   1997   *Ethnography and Ethnohistory of Taroa Island, Republic of the Marshall Islands.* San Francisco: Micronesian Endowment for Historic Preservation, Republic of the Marshall Islands, and US National Park Service.
Poyer, Lin, Suzanne Falgout, and Laurence Marshall Carucci
   2001   *The Typhoon of War: Micronesian Experiences of the Pacific War.* Honolulu: University of Hawai'i Press.
   2004   The Impact of the Pacific War on Modern Micronesian Identity. In *Globalization and Culture Change in the Pacific Islands,* edited by Victoria S Lockwood, 307–323. Upper Saddle River, NJ: Pearson Prentice Hall.
Pregonero [Daily, Saipan]
   1947   July 4th Official Holiday for Saipan-Liberation Day. 8 April, 2.
Price, Willard
   1944   Springboards to Tokyo. *National Geographic,* October, 385–407.
Pruitt, Dean G, and Richard C Snyder, editors
   1969   *Theory and Research on the Causes of War.* Englewood Cliffs, NJ: Prentice Hall.
PSECC, Political Status Education Coordinating Commission
   1993   *Hinasso': Tinige' Put Chamorro/Insights: The Chamorro Identity.* Agaña: PSECC.
   1995   *I Manfåyi: Who's Who in Chamorro History.* Volume 1. Agaña: PSECC.
Purcell, David C, Jr
   1976   The Economics of Exploitation: The Japanese in the Mariana, Caroline and Marshall Islands, 1915–1940. *Journal of Pacific History* 11 (3/4): 189–211.

Puyo, Ann Maria
    1964   The Acceptance of Americanization by the Chamorros and Carolinians of
            Saipan. MA thesis, Saint Louis University.
Rachlis, Eugene
    1946   Navy Rule in the Pacific. *New Republic*, 9 December, 756.
Radstone, Susannah, editor
    2000   *Memory and Methodology.* Oxford: Berg.
Ralston, Caroline
    1992   The Study of Women in the Pacific. *The Contemporary Pacific* 4:162–175.
Ramirez, Anthony J
    1984   South Pacific Memorial Park: A Symbol of Eternal Peace, Yigu, Guam. In
            46th Anniversary "Freedom to Be": The Liberation of Guam, 56–58. Tamuning,
            Guam: Pacific Color Press.
    2004   Interview by author. Tape recording. Hagåtña, Guam, 13 August.
Ray, Barbara
    1994a   The Invasion Begins: Memories of Battle for Guam Deeply Etched. *Pacific
            Daily News,* Liberation Day supplement, 21 July, 41, 60.
    1994b   Land Taking: A Liberation Irony. *Pacific Daily News,* 21 July, 54.
Rebusio, Janet R
    1992 $18M Needed for Park Dev't. *Marianas Review,* 28 January, 7.
Reyes, Rafael J M
    1991   Terror in the Waning Days of Occupation. *Pacific Sunday News,* 21 July, 10.
Reynolds, Quentin
    1945   These Are Americans. *Collier's* [weekly], 19 May, 5.
Richard, Dorothy E
    1957   *United States Naval Administration of the Trust Territory of the Pacific Islands.* 3
            volumes. Washington, DC: US Government Printing Office.
Rivera, Catherine Okada
    1984   Chamorro/Japanese: The Okada Family. In *46th Anniversary "Freedom
            to Be": The Liberation of Guam,* 82–83. Tamuning, Guam: Pacific Color
            Press.
Rogers, Robert F
    1995   *Destiny's Landfall: A History of Guam.* Honolulu: University of Hawai'i Press.
Rosenberg, Emily S
    2003   *A Date Which Will Live: Pearl Harbor in American Memory.* Durham, NC:
            Duke University Press.
Roxas, Mario S, Jr
    1989   WWII Veteran Recalls Liberation of Saipan. *Marianas Review,* 30 June, 10.
Runquist, Pam
    1994   Santos Appeals to Chamoru Nation. *Pacific Daily News,* 14 July, 5.
Russell, Scott
    1983   Camp Susupe: Postwar Internment on Saipan. *Pacific Magazine* (May/
            June): 21–23.
    2002   Interview by author. Tape recording. Chalan Kanoa, Saipan, 7 February.
Sablan, Benigno
    1981   Interview by Ted Oxborrow and associates. The War Years on Saipan:
            Transcripts of Interviews with Residents, Micronesia Area Research Cen-
            ter, Mangilao.

Sablan, David
  2002   Arrested by the Kempeitai. In Petty 2002, 40–45.
Sablan, Ignacio M
  1981   Interview by Ted Oxborrow and associates. The War Years on Saipan:
          Transcripts of Interviews with Residents, Micronesia Area Research Center, Mangilao.
Sablan, Joaquin Flores
  1957   To My Guamanian People. In *13th Anniversary of Liberation of Guam,* 7.
          Agaña: Liberation Day Committee.
  1990   *My Mental Odyssey: Memoirs of the First Guamanian Protestant Minister.* Poplar
          Bluff, MO: Stinson Press.
Sablan, Manuel T
  2002   Messenger Boy for the Japanese Police. In Petty 2002, 34–38.
Said, Edward W
  1978   *Orientalism.* New York: Vintage Books.
Saito, Natsu Taylor
  2007   *From Chinese Exclusion to Guantánamo Bay: Plenary Power and the Prerogative
          State.* Boulder: University Press of Colorado.
Sakamoto, Larry
  1971   27 Years Ago on Saipan. *Micronesian Star,* 26 June, 13.
Salesa, Damon
  2007   Samoa's Half-Castes and Some Frontiers of Comparison. In *Haunted by
          Empire: Geographies of Intimacy in North American History,* edited by Ann
          Laura Stoler, 71–93. Durham, NC: Duke University Press.
Salii, Lazarus E
  1972   Liberation and Conquest in Micronesia. *Pacific Islands Monthly* 43 (6): 37,
          39, 41, 123.
Sanchez, Adrian C
  1990   *The Chamorro Brown Steward.* Tamuning, Guam: Star Press.
Sanchez, Pedro C
  1979   *Uncle Sam, Please Come Back to Guam.* Tamuning, Guam: Pacific Island Publishing Company; Agaña: Star Press.
  1989   *Guahan Guam: The History of Our Island.* Agaña: Sanchez Publishing House.
Sandler, Stanley
  2001   Introduction. In W*orld War II in the Pacific: An Encyclopedia,* edited by Stanley Sandler, vii–x. New York: Garland Publishing.
Santos, Angel
  1991   U.S. Return Was Reoccupation, Not Liberation. *Pacific Daily News,* 21
          July, 20.
Sato, Tatsu
  1985   *A Record of the Japanese Pioneers' Achievements Obliterated by the War: Photographic Collections of Saipan, Tinian, Rota.* Tokyo: South Sea Islands Album
          Publication Committee.
Sayon, Chuck
  2002   Interview by author. Tape recording. Garapan, Saipan, 16 February.
Scanlan, John E
  1994a   Fallen Comrades, Former Enemies Honored. *Pacific Daily News,* 17 June, 2.
  1994b   Fallen Comrades Remembered on Saipan. *Pacific Daily News,* 16 June, 4.

1994c   Governor Offers Gratitude of Commonwealth. *Pacific Daily News*, 16 June, 4.

1994d   Saipan Bids Farewell to 70 WWII Heroes. *Pacific Daily News*. 18 June, 3.

Schmidt, David Andrew

2000   *Ianfu—The Comfort Women of the Japanese Imperial Army of the Pacific War.* Lewiston, NY: Edwin Mellen Press.

Schoonover, Thomas

2003   *Uncle Sam's War of 1898 and the Origins of Globalization.* Lexington: University Press of Kentucky.

Scott, James C

1985   *Weapons of the Weak: Everyday Forms of Peasant Resistance.* New Haven, CT: Yale University Press.

Sekiguchi, Noriko

1990   *Senso Daughters.* Documentary. 54 min. New York: First Run/Icarus Films.

Sharrad, Paul

2003   *Albert Wendt and Pacific Literature: Circling the Void.* Auckland: Auckland University Press.

Sheeks, Robert B

1945   Civilians on Saipan. *Far Eastern Survey* 14 (9): 109–113.

Shigematsu, Setsu, and Keith L Camacho, editors

2010   *Militarized Currents: Toward a Decolonized Future in Asia and the Pacific.* Minneapolis: University of Minnesota Press.

Shogakukan Progressive Japanese-English Dictionary

1986   Tokyo: Shogakukan.

Shuster, Donald R

1982   State Shinto in Micronesia during Japanese Rule, 1914–1945. *Pacific Studies* 5 (2): 20–43.

Shy, John

1993   The Cultural Approach to the History of War. *Journal of Military History* 57 (5): 13–26.

Silva, Noenoe K

2004   *Aloha Betrayed: Native Hawaiian Resistance to American Colonialism.* Durham, NC: Duke University Press.

Smith, Joseph

1994   *The Spanish-American War: Conflict in the Caribbean and the Pacific, 1895–1902.* London: Longman.

Smith, Linda Tuhiwai

1999   *Decolonizing Methodologies: Research and Indigenous People.* London: Zed Books; Dunedin, NZ: University of Otago Press.

Somerville, John

1981   Patriotism and War. *Ethics* 91 (4): 568–578.

Souder, Laura Marie Torres

1991   Psyche under Siege: Uncle Sam, Look What You've Done to Us. In *Uncle Sam in Micronesia: Social Benefits, Social Costs,* edited by Donald H Rubinstein and Virginia L Dames, 120–124. Papers from the Ninth Annual Social Work Conference, March 1989, Guam. Mangilao: Micronesia Area Research Center. Reprinted in *Sustainable Development or Malignant Growth? Perspectives of Pacific Island Women,* edited by 'Atu Emberson-Bain, 193–198. Suva: Marama Publications (1994).

1992   *Daughters of the Island: Contemporary Chamorro Women Organizers on Guam.*
        Lanham, MD: University Press of America; Mangilao: Micronesia Area
        Research Center.

Souder, Paul B
1971   Guam: Land Tenure in a Fortress. In *Land Tenure in the Pacific,* edited by
        Ron Crocombe, 192–205. Melbourne: Oxford University Press.

Spickard, Paul, Joanne L Rondilla, and Debbie Hippolite Wright, editors
2002   *Pacific Diaspora: Island Peoples in the United States and Across the Pacific.*
        Honolulu: University of Hawai'i Press.

Spoehr, Alexander
1951   The Tinian Chamorros. *Human Organization* 10 (4): 16–20.
2000   *Saipan: The Ethnology of a War-Devastated Island.* Saipan: CNMI Division of
        Historic Preservation.

Stade, Ronald
1998   *Pacific Passages: World Culture and Local Politics in Guam.* Stockholm Studies
        in Social Anthropology 42. Stockholm: Almquist and Wiksell International.

Steinberg, David Joel
1967   *Philippine Collaboration in World War II.* Ann Arbor: University of Michigan
        Press.

Stoler, Ann Laura
2007   Tense and Tender Ties: The Politics of Comparison in North American
        History and (Post) Colonial Studies. In *Haunted by Empire: Geographies of
        Intimacy in North American History,* edited by Ann Laura Stoler, 23–67. Dur-
        ham, NC: Duke University Press.

Strong, Beret E, and Cinta Matagolai Kaipat
1998   *Lieweila: A Micronesian Story.* Documentary. 57 min. New York: First Run/
        Icarus Films.

Sturken, Marita
1997   *Tangled Memories: The Vietnam War, the AIDS Epidemic, and the Politics of
        Remembering.* Berkeley: University of California Press.
2007   *Tourists of History: Memory, Kitsch, and Consumerism from Oklahoma City to
        Ground Zero.* Durham, NC: Duke University Press.

Sudo, Naoto
2004   Colonial Mirror Images of Micronesia and Japan: Beyond the Tug of War
        between "Americanization" and "Japanization." *Postcolonial Text* [online]
        1 (1) (30 July). Available from http://www.pkp.ubc.ca/pocol/viewarticle
        .php?id=19.

Sullivan, Julius
1957   *The Phoenix Rises: A Mission History of Guam.* New York: Seraphic Mass
        Association.

Syjuco, Ma Felisa A
1988   *The Kempei Tai in the Philippines: 1941–1945.* Quezon City: New Day Publishers.

Sylvester, Eugene A
1983   The Real Battle Has Just Begun. *Marianas Variety News and Views,* 17 June, 12.

Taitano, John M
1981   Interview by Ted Oxborrow and associates. The War Years on Saipan:
        Transcripts of Interviews with Residents, Micronesia Area Research Cen-
        ter, Mangilao.

Takashima, Eiichi
  1981   The Memorable Island of Rota. *I Isla* [weekly, Rota], 5 August, 2.
Tanaka, Yuki
  1996   *Hidden Horrors: Japanese War Crimes in World War II.* Boulder, CO: Westview
          Press.
  2002   *Japan's Comfort Women: Sexual Slavery and Prostitution during World War II
          and the US Occupation.* London: Routledge.
Tarling, Nicholas
  2001   *A Sudden Rampage: The Japanese Occupation of Southeast Asia, 1941–1945.*
          Honolulu: University of Hawai'i Press.
Teaiwa, Katerina Martina
  2004   Multi-sited Methodologies: "Homework" in Australia, Fiji, and Kiribati. In
          Anthropologists in the Field: Cases in Participant Observation, edited by Lynn
          Huwe and Jane Mulcock, 216–233. New York: Columbia University Press.
Teaiwa, Teresia K
  1999   Reading Paul Gauguin's *Noa Noa* with Epeli Hau'ofa's *Kisses in the Neder-
          ends:* Militourism, Feminism, and the "Polynesian" Body. In *Inside Out:
          Literature, Cultural Politics, and Identity in the New Pacific,* edited by Vilsoni
          Hereniko and Rob Wilson, 249–263. Lanham, MD: Rowman & Littlefield.
  2005   Native Thoughts: A Pacific Studies Take on Cultural Studies and Dias-
          pora. In *Indigenous Diasporas and Dislocations,* edited by Graham Harvey
          and Charles D Thompson Jr, 15–35. Aldershot, UK: Ashgate.
Tenorio, Froilan C
  1994   Proclamation: Observance of the 50th Anniversary of World War II in the
          Northern Mariana Islands, 15 June. Microfilm reel 6319:0149, Northern
          Marianas College, Pacific Collection.
Thelen, David
  1989   Memory and American History. *Journal of American History* 75 (4):
          1117–1129.
Thomas, Nicholas
  1994   *Colonialism's Culture: Anthropology, Travel, and Government.* Princeton:
          Princeton University Press.
Thompson, Laura
  1941   *Guam and Its People: A Study of Culture Change and Colonial Education.* San
          Francisco: American Council Institute of Pacific Relations.
Thompson, Roger C
  2001   *The Pacific Basin since 1945.* Second edition. Harlow, UK: Longman.
Tipton, Elise K
  1990   *The Japanese Police State: Tokkō in Interwar Japan.* Honolulu: University of
          Hawai'i Press.
Tolentino, Concepcion M
  2005   Interview by Dominica Tolentino, Maite, Guam, 10 October. Transcript in
          author's files.
Tolentino, Dominica M
  1999   Images of History, Commemoration and Cultural Identity: The Santa
          Marian Kamalen Tradition on Guam. December. Unpublished manu-
          script in author's possession.

Trouillot, Michel-Rolph
    1995   *Silencing the Past: Power and the Production of History.* Boston: Beacon Press.
Turner, James West, and Suzanne Falgout
    2002   Time Traces: Cultural Memory and World War II in Pohnpei. *The Contemporary Pacific* 14:101–131.
Tweed, George Ray
    1944   31 Months Behind the Jap Lines. *American Magazine,* December, 18–21, 98, 101–116.
    1994   *Robinson Crusoe, U.S.N.: The Adventures of George R. Tweed, Rm1 on Japanese-held Guam.* Barrigada: Pacific Research Institute.
Umatuna Si Yu'us [Weekly newsletter, Catholic Diocese of Agana]
    1954a   Ten Years Afterward. 11 July, 5.
    1954b   Tenth Anniversary of Liberation of Guam to Be Celebrated Wednesday. 18 July, 1–5.
    1959   Liberation Day 1959. 19 July, 4.
Underwood, Robert
    1977   Red, Whitewash and Blue: Painting over the Chamorro Experience. *Islander, Pacific Sunday News,* 17 July.
    1997   Teaching Guam History in Guam High Schools. In *Guam History: Perspectives,* edited by Lee D Carter, William L Wuerch, and Rosa Roberto Carter, 1:1–10. Mangilao: Micronesia Area Research Center.
USDN, United States Department of the Navy
    1944   *Civil Affairs Handbook: Mandated Mariana Islands.* Navy Department: Office of the Chief of Naval Operations.
    1946   Naval Government of Guam Monthly Report, 31 August. Record Group 313: Records of the Naval Operating Forces. National Archives, Washington, DC.
    1951   *U.S. Navy Report on Guam, 1899–1950.* Washington, DC: US Government Printing Office.
Useem, John
    1945   The American Pattern of Military Government in Micronesia. *American Journal of Sociology* 51 (2): 93–102.
USTTPI, United States Trust Territory of the Pacific Islands
    [1947?] *Civil Administration Unit, Saipan District; Quarterly Report Number 1–48.* Saipan: Trust Territory of the Pacific Islands.
Votaw, John F
    1979   An Approach to the Study of Military History. In *A Guide to the Study and Use of Military History,* edited by John E Jessup Jr and Robert W Coakley, 41–46. Washington, DC: US Government Printing Office.
Waller, Michael, and Andrew Linklater
    2003   Introduction: Loyalty and the Post-national State. In *Political Loyalty and the Nation-State,* edited by Michael Waller and Andrew Linklater, 1–14. London: Routledge.
Wang Gungwu
    2000   Memories of War: World War II in Asia. In *War and Memory in Malaysia and Singapore,* edited by P Lim Pui Huen and Diana Wong, 11–22. Singapore: Institute of Southeast Asian Studies.

Ward, Alan, John Connell, and Michael Spencer
    1988   Introduction: The Coq and the Cagou. In *New Caledonia: Essays in Nation-alism and Dependency*, edited by Michael Spencer, Alan Ward, and John Connell, 1–21. St Lucia: University of Queensland Press.
Warren, Karen J, and Duane L Cady
    1994   Feminism and Peace: Seeing Connections. *Hypatia* [University of Washington] 9 (2): 4–20.
White, Geoffrey M
    1991   Preface. In White [ed] 1991, v–xii.
    1995   Remembering Guadalcanal: National Identity and Transnational Memory-Making. *Public Culture* 7:529–555.
    2001   Moving History: The Pearl Harbor Films. In Fujitani, White, and Yoneyama [eds] 2001, 267–295.
White, Geoffrey M, editor
    1991   *Remembering the Pacific War.* CPIS Occasional Paper 36. Honolulu: Center for Pacific Islands Studies, University of Hawai'i, Mānoa.
White, Geoffrey M, David W Gegeo, David Akin, and Karen Watson-Gegeo, editors
    1988   *The Big Death: Solomon Islanders Remember World War II.* Honiara: Solomon Islands College of Higher Education; Suva: University of the South Pacific.
White, Geoffrey, and Hugh Laracy, editors
    1988   *Taem Blong Faet: World War II in Melanesia.* Special Issue of *'O'O: A Journal of Solomon Islands Studies* 4.
Willens, Howard P, and Deanne C Siemer
    2002   *An Honorable Accord: The Covenant between the Northern Mariana Islands and the United States.* Pacific Islands Monograph Series 18. Honolulu: University of Hawai'i Center for Pacific Islands Studies and University of Hawai'i Press.
Williams, Raymond
    1977   *Marxism and Literature.* Oxford: Oxford University Press.
Williams, Walter L
    1988   American Imperialism and the Indians. In *Indians in American History: An Introduction,* edited by Frederick E Hoxie, 231–249. Wheeling, IL: Harlan Davidson.
Winter, Jay
    1995   *Sites of Memory, Sites of Mourning: The Great War in European Cultural History.* Cambridge, UK: Cambridge University Press.
Wiseman, Paul
    1984   The Survivors: Woman Lives to Tell about Grisly Execution. *Pacific Daily News,* 21 July, 19.
Wright, Michael D, and Lynn Knight
    2001   *Now for Then: The Marianas Marine Scouts.* Garapan: Office of the CNMI Resident Representative of the United States.
Yoneyama, Lisa
    1999   *Hiroshima Traces: Time, Space, and the Dialectics of Memory.* Berkeley: University of California Press.

Index

Page numbers in boldface type refer to illustrations.

About the Author

Keith L Camacho is a Chamorro scholar from the Mariana Islands. He received an MA in Pacific Islands studies and a PhD in history from the University of Hawai'i at Mānoa. Keith is presently an assistant professor in the Department of Asian American Studies at the University of California, Los Angeles. With Setsu Shigematsu, he coedited *Militarized Currents: Toward a Decolonized Future in Asia and the Pacific* (University of Minnesota Press, 2010).

Production Notes for Camacho/CULTURES OF COMMEMORATION

Designed by UH Press Design & Production Department
with text in New Baskerville and display in Palatino

Composition by Lucille C. Aono

Printing and binding by Edwards Brothers, Inc.

Printed on 60 lb. Arbor, 444 ppi